MISSED

OPPORTUNITIES

FOR PEACE

U.S. MIDDLE EAST POLICY 1981-1986

By Ronald J. Young

A report prepared for the

AMERICAN FRIENDS SERVICE COMMITTEE

Published in the United States by The American Friends Service Committee,
1501 Cherry Street, Philadelphia, PA 19102
Cover designed by H. Booth Collins, Inc.
First Printing May, 1987

Library of Congress Cataloging-in-Publication Data
Young, Ronald J.
Missed opportunities for peace.
"A report prepared for the American Friends Service Committee."
Bibliography: p.
1. Middle East—relations—United States. 2. United States—Foreign
relations—Middle East. 3. Jewish-Arab relations—1973-.
I. American Friends Service Committee. II. Title.
DS63.2.U5Y68   1987   327.56073   87-7014972

ISBN 0-910082-11-1

Maps reproduced with permission of Mobilization for Survival. Taken from *Middle East Peace Alternatives*, designed by Rick Bickhart.

Missed Opportunities for Peace

U.S. Middle East Policy: 1981-1986

Contents

American Friends Service Committee
Middle East Peace Education Program
A Commitment to Justice, Human Rights, Peace and Reconciliation

Beginning in 1975, the American Friends Service Committee (AFSC) has developed a nationwide network of peace education programs focused on issues concerning the Middle East. AFSC has sought to bring about greater understanding of the Arab-Israeli-Palestinian conflict and U.S. policy toward that conflict. AFSC, through its national office in Philadelphia, its Washington, DC office and its nine regional offices, also cooperates with other civic, religious and peace organizations on programs of Middle East peace education and action.

Issues of concern in Middle East peace education include: working for a lasting resolution to the Arab-Israeli-Palestinian conflict based on mutual recognition among Israel, the Arab States and the Palestine Liberation Organization (PLO); campaigning for an international conference to negotiate a comprehensive peace agreement under the auspices of the United Nations Security Council; and challenging domestic bigotry toward both Jews and Arabs.

AFSC publishes a wide range of informational and educational materials on Middle East issues. Both of AFSC's major book-length studies on the Arab-Israeli-Palestinian conflict, *Search for Peace in The Middle East* (1970) and *A Compassionate Peace: A Future for the Middle East* (1982), suggest steps for achieving peace and justice in the region.

Realizing that those in the Middle East can speak with the greatest authority, AFSC arranges speaking tours for Palestinians and Israelis, including Israeli-Palestinian teams. One such team was featured in a documentary produced by PBS' *Frontline* series.

Additional Middle East programming includes action campaigns, media briefings, local speakers, conferences and occasional study tours of the Middle East.

Foreword

T he study that follows was written by Ronald J. Young, at the request of the American Friends Service Committee (AFSC) Middle East Peace Education Program, after he and Carol Jensen, his wife, had spent three years in the Middle East, as Middle East representatives for the AFSC. He and Carol Jensen followed others in that role and represented a continuation of AFSC's concern for the Middle East—a concern which evolved out of service to Jewish refugees in and from Europe in the 1930s and 1940s and assistance to Palestinian refugees in Gaza immediately after the creation of Israel and the 1948 war.

The Middle East representatives, like AFSC international affairs representatives in other settings, are stationed in a region of conflict or potential conflict where the United States has or has expressed a national interest. They visited widely in the assigned region, seeking generally to meet with governmental, political, and sometimes military leaders; with professionals and academics; with journalists for both national and international media; with representatives of various ethnic groups and factions; and with students, workers, farmers, and "ordinary people." The role is shaped to a degree by the context of the area served and the specific skills and experience of the person involved.

The value of the representatives' work hinges on development of a deep knowledge of, and non-partisan sympathy for, the situation of the area's people. In particular, their work requires understanding of the roots and features of differences and conflict. The representatives seek insights that may be possible to an impartial observer and may share these insights with others on all sides. They will also often be asked for their own views; and, though non-partisan, will have perceptions and principles from which to speak.

In the course of this quiet role in international affairs, a representative may bring together groups for dialogue on themes or common concerns identified in the course of discussions with individuals. Groups may consist of a few people or two to three dozen; meetings may be for a few hours or a few days. The goal is to increase mutual understanding and to help build the personal and intellectual bases for eventual conflict reduction or resolution. When face-to-face meetings are not possible, representatives may serve as useful channels for confidential communication among differing parties. Representatives may write articles for publication and regular reports for a constituency in the United States and elsewhere, providing analyses not otherwise generally available to those concerned with constructive policy development. Much of the information shared with AFSC headquarters will help to shape future programs.

Measurements of the representatives' achievements are difficult and depend, to a large degree, upon faith in people's capacity and desire to search for solutions to conflict, solutions that ideally are not violent and are achieved at the least possible human cost. Faith is also required that what is done in one year or one epoch may positively affect what happens in another. But while much depends on faith, there are also evidences of appreciation for the representatives' role among those visited and for their occasional direct participation in moves toward peace. Frequently, the work is most effective and acceptable when it is one of several AFSC modes of service in a region—when it is parallel to relief, development, educational, and other more tangible undertakings.

During Ronald Young's tenure in the Middle East, the AFSC was also supporting an extensive program of pre-school education in the Gaza Strip, providing staff and funds to the Middle East Council of Churches for relief and development work in Beirut and southern Lebanon, operating a legal aid and information center in East Jerusalem, and supporting the Van Leer Institute's work in Israel to develop curriculum materials countering Israeli Jews' and Israeli Arabs' stereotypes of each other.

Ronald Young writes out of his work experience in the Middle East as well as his extensive experience as a peace educator in the United

States. But to preserve the confidentiality of that work, he draws almost entirely on published sources for the text of *Missed Opportunities for Peace*. From interviews he conducted as AFSC's Middle East representative, he uses only material which the parties involved understood could be shared publicly. It will be clear to the reader, however, that his work in the Middle Est has contributed greatly to this book—to its range, its tone, its sensitivity to the issues, its caring for the people—and probably also to the disappointment it expresses with failures and missed opportunities of U.S. Middle East policy.

Ronald Young's recounting and interpretation of this aspect of the history of the Middle East warrant a careful reading, not only for what they tell us of the past but also for the directions they may show for more successful approaches in the future.

Philadelphia, January 1987

Corinne B. Johnson
Secretary of the International Division
American Friends Service Committee

Preface

*F*rom 1982 to 1985 my wife, Carol Jensen, and I served as Middle East representatives for the American Friends Service Committee. Our assignment was to live and travel in the region, meeting regularly with Arabs and Israelis of many different viewpoints to explore what are the requirements for peace, what are the obstacles, and what the United States can do to encourage prospects for peace. To my knowledge, the AFSC, which also supports war relief efforts as well as community service and development projects in the region, is unique in sponsoring a program since 1967 focused directly on understanding the different viewpoints in the Arab-Israeli conflict and on seeking ways to promote a peaceful settlement.

During the three years my family lived in the Middle East, from our residence in Jordan we made more than twenty-five visits to Israel, the West Bank and Gaza, twelve to Egypt and Syria and three to Lebanon. My wife and I conducted several hundred interviews with more than three hundred persons, including senior officials in the governments of all the countries we visited and in the Palestinian Liberation Organization (PLO).

Most of the documentation in this study is from readily available sources, primarily major daily U.S. newspapers. But the perspective and theme for the book are drawn directly from my experience in the Middle East. Since the interviews we conducted, for the most part, were ''off-the-record,'' I have included quotations from these interviews only in cases when the persons have stated the same views publicly or when it was understood that the persons were willing to be quoted.

The book assumes some knowledge of Middle East affairs and is heavily footnoted, but it makes no pretense to be a scholar's definitive analysis. Rather it is a recording of impressions of apparent patterns in U.S. policy, documented by the press, which I experienced during three years of living in the midst of what was happening in the Middle East. I rely for documentation on major U.S. newspapers (even though my wife and I regularly read English translations of Arabic and Hebrew press) not only to check my firsthand impressions of what was happening against what was being reported in the United States, but also to demonstrate that there is ample evidence in readily available sources for critical discussion of U.S. Middle East policy.

This work identifies failures in U.S. policy and indicates how a different approach might have contributed to better outcomes. This does not, however, suggest at all that wise and constructive U.S. policies are the only hope for peace. Indeed, the American Friends Service Committee (AFSC) and I believe that every party in the Arab-Israeli conflict could do more for peace and that lasting peace is more likely if it is the product of several nations cooperating rather than one superpower trying to bring it off alone. It is in the context of this basic belief that it seems important to understand the failure of U.S. policy.

The study certainly does not attempt to make a thorough analysis of why U.S. policy is what it is or to offer a blueprint for what the United States should do in the Middle East. It does discuss several underlying problems in U.S. foreign policy that have negative consequences in the Middle East, as they do in other areas of the world, and suggests some alternatives to policies pursued in recent years. The revelations about U.S. arms deals with Iran make public discussion of U.S. policy in the Middle East—what it is and what it should be—even more urgent and timely. If this study makes a small contribution to public debate, I will be more than satisfied.

I wish to thank the American Friends Service Committee for providing me the extraordinary opportunity of serving in this assignment and for supporting my work on this study. The opportunity to meet and get to know many people, including high officials in Israel, the West Bank and Gaza, Egypt, Syria, Lebanon, Jordan and the PLO was a rare privilege. My experience helps me to be able to feel something of the fears and the hopes of many Israelis and Arabs, although to suggest that I have "stood in their shoes" would be an arrogant and false claim. I am deeply grateful for the interest and insights offered so generously and patiently by so many people we met in the Middle East.

How I have understood and interpreted this experience—including ways which some of the people we met will likely view as mistaken—clearly is not their responsibility but mine.

I wish especially to thank Everett Mendelsohn for his challenging and very helpful comments on many substantive issues in the study and John Sullivan for his considerable editorial work, making the final text much more coherent and readable than earlier drafts. Obviously, I am responsible for the study's arguments and for its errors.

I am grateful to Gail Pressberg, director of Middle East Programs for the American Friends Service Committee, not only for her support of this project but even more for the consistent example she has offered since the mid-1970s of a uniquely well-informed and sensitive commitment to work for peace in the Middle East.

My thanks go also to AFSC staff who have shepherded this work to final publication, including especially Joe Volk, secretary of the Peace Education Division, Norma Corey Tower, who coordinated the production of the book, Gerry Henry, for her work in designing the book and Mary Morrell for her patient proof-reading.

Finally, I wish to thank my wife, Carol Jensen, and my sons, Jonah and Jamie, for their patience and support during the time I have been working on this book.

Ronald J. Young
December, 1986

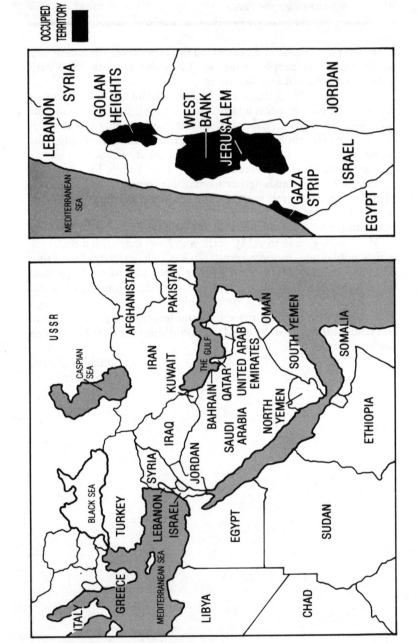

OCCUPIED TERRITORY

Chapter One

Arab-Israeli Peace and the United States

*F*or forty years, there has been bitter conflict between Israel and its Arab neighbors. At the core of this conflict is the struggle, dating back at least a hundred years, between the Palestinian Arabs and the Jews, two peoples with competing claims to the same land. The conflict is compounded by the deep emotional attachment Jews, Christians and Muslims feel for Jerusalem and other sites in the area based on their religious and historical significance. Viewed in this light, it is not surprising that many people despair that the Arab-Israeli conflict will ever be resolved.

But a closer look reveals growing reason for a more hopeful view. From 1947 to 1967 most Israelis accepted the U.N. proposal of partition of Palestine into two states, the Jewish state of Israel and a Palestinian Arab state. During these years Arabs almost universally rejected the idea of partition on the ground that the founding of Israel represented a grave injustice against Arab claims of sovereignty in all of Palestine.

Following the 1967 war, in a rare example of unanimity, the United Nations Security Council adopted Resolution 242, formally ending the war and providing an important foundation for future peace negotiations. Resolution 242 affirmed two principles as essential to ''the establishment of a just and lasting peace in the Middle East'':

(1) Withdrawal of Israeli armed forces from territories oc-

cupied in the recent conflict;

(2) Termination of all claims or states of belligerency and respect for and acknowledgement of the sovereignty, territorial integrity and political independence of all states in the area and their right to live in peace within secure and recognized boundaries free from threats or acts of force. [1]

Israel, Egypt and Jordan all accepted Resolution 242 at the time; Syria accepted it later on the conditions that the rights of the Palestinians were protected and the need for an international peace conference was recognized. This began a trend among leaders of most Arab states toward recognition of Israel in the context of a negotiated peace. This trend has also been evident in the Palestinian nationalist movement; while insisting on the Palestinian people's right of self- determination, major Palestinian leaders since 1974 have publicly shown willingness to accept a state in part of Palestine, i.e., in the West Bank and Gaza, which have been occupied by Israel since the 1967 war.

Israel's decisive victory in the 1967 war fostered a growing movement to establish Israeli sovereignty in all of Eretz Israel,[2] at least from the Jordan River to the Mediterranean. But, although occupying this area for the last twenty years, many, perhaps most, Israelis remain willing to have Israel withdraw from some or all of the West Bank and Gaza in exchange for peace. In April 1982 Israel completed its withdrawal from the Sinai in exchange for peace with Egypt.

The historic 1979 Camp David peace treaty between Egypt and Israel, based on the principle of exchange of occupied territory for peace, may not be permanently irreversible, but it has been maintained despite bitterness and frustration on both sides over the failure of the peace process to develop in ways each side had hoped for.

My interviews of political leaders and a wide variety of persons in Israel, Egypt, Lebanon, Syria, Jordan and among the Palestinians, including leaders of the Palestine Liberation Organization (PLO), over a period of three years from 1982 to 1985, provided new understandings of the depth of this decades-old conflict but also encouraging indications that a negotiated settlement of the conflict is possible. Of course, this is complicated by the differing interests and positions of different Arab parties, as well as by internal divisions within Israel. Getting negotiations started is a tremendous challenge in itself; once negotiations begin, they will be very complex and difficult. But peace in the Middle East is possible.

Every party in the conflict faces real dangers if the conflict continues and every party has real interests in achieving a peace settlement. At the same time leaders of every party operate within real political constraints on how much flexibility they can demonstrate and what steps—especially unilateral steps—they feel they can take for peace. Many leaders express a sense of urgency, which they have felt for a long time, that if there is no progress toward negotiated peace soon, the growing extremism, including religious fundamentalism, on both sides will make the conflict much more difficult to resolve and will make another, even more dangerous, Arab-Israeli war almost inevitable.

Looking to the United States

There are important Israeli and Arab, including Palestinian, leaders who believe that peace is possible. Many of these also believe that outside parties, particularly the United States, will play an important and, perhaps, decisive role in determining whether a negotiated peace settlement can happen. There is little support for the idea that the United States can or should impose a settlement in the Middle East, but there is widespread agreement that a peace settlement is extremely unlikely without direct U.S. encouragement and support. While both Arab and Israeli leaders at times turn to the United States for help as a way to avoid taking the difficult steps toward peace which they must take, nevertheless, U.S. policy is a very important factor in the search for peace in the Middle East. U.S. influence in the region is such that whatever the United States does or does not do in relation to the conflict has significant effects on prospects for peace.

As long as Arab and Israeli leaders urged directly contradictory advice on the United States, or on other outside parties, as they did during most years of the conflict, the chances of developing a successful peace process were remote. However, in recent years the advice which at least some important Arab and Israeli political leaders have given to the United States has been less contradictory and at times remarkably compatible. Indeed, my working definition of an opportunity for peace is a period of time when significant Arab and Israeli political leadership believes movement toward negotiated peace is possible and when the advice they offer for a constructive U.S. role is relatively compatible.

When I refer to "Arab and Israeli leaders" I mean current leaders in their respective governments, in the PLO, and, in the case of Israel, major leaders of the opposition who could become—and, indeed, did become during the years this study covers—leaders of their government. While there are a number of individual Israelis, Palestinians and other Arabs who have made important contributions to hopes for peace, this study is concerned primarily with opportunities as perceived by government leaders and by leaders in the PLO.

My thesis is that between 1981 and 1986 there were several periods when major Israeli and Arab leaders saw opportunities for peace, appealed for U.S. help, and did not get it. While the PLO, various Arab governments and the government of Israel all can be faulted for not doing enough themselves, the United States contributed significantly to the failure to achieve progress toward peace during these years. In the last twenty years, the United States has on several occasions played an important and constructive role in achieving agreements between Israel and various Arab states. Following the 1967 and 1973 wars the United States successfully helped to negotiate ceasefire and disengagement agreements between Israel and Egypt, Israel and Jordan, and Israel and Syria. The United States played an important role in gaining agreement on the two U.N. Security Council Resolutions, 242 and 338,[3] which continue to be viewed by Israel and Arab governments as essential foundation blocks for building a negotiated peace. (The Palestinians and Arab governments to varying degrees believe the Palestinians' right of self-determination is also an essential principle for any lasting peace settlement.) The Camp David peace process and the peace treaty between Israel and Egypt, despite its failure effectively to address the Palestinian issue, represented an historic breakthrough in the Arab-Israeli conflict and certainly would not have been possible were it not for the high-level commitment of the United States, including the personal involvement of President Jimmy Carter.

In the period the book examines, 1981-86, the United States and, more specifically, Special U.S. Ambassador Philip Habib played the key role in mediating the 1981 Israeli-PLO ceasefire in southern Lebanon and the 1982 Beirut agreement between Israel and the PLO. Furthermore, the Reagan initiative of September 1982, while it did not succeed, evoked substantial positive interest among major political leaders in Israel and on the Arab side.

There are several important reasons why those Arab and Israeli leaders who actively seek peace look primarily to the United States for help in moving toward any possible agreements. First, as British influence waned after World War II, the United States became the predominant outside power in the Middle East. Even with the growth in power and influence of the Soviet Union as the second superpower, the United States has continued to dominate the region economically, politically and militarily.

The Soviet Union was actively involved with Egypt prior to 1974 and continues to be a major supporter of Syria, as well as having signficant influence in the Horn of Africa and in South Yemen. The Soviet

Union also has slowly been exploring relations with Kuwait and other Arab Gulf states. While a comprehensive peace settlement in the Middle East is unlikely without Soviet involvement, Soviet influence in the Arab-Israeli conflict is significantly less than U.S. influence, in part because the Soviet Union has had no diplomatic relations with Israel since 1967.

In earlier periods, Middle Eastern leaders, whether they wanted to or not, looked to whatever were the dominant powers—Turkey, France or Great Britain—to help resolve local or regional problems. So today Arab and Israeli leaders are forced by present power realities to look to the United States.

Second, the dependence of specific countries on U.S. economic and military aid increases this tendency. Israel is more dependent economically and militarily on the United States than any other country in the region, receiving approximately $4 billion in U.S. aid each year— the equivalent of more than $1,000 per Israeli citizen. In recent years Egypt, which faces huge economic and social problems, has also become heavily dependent on U.S. aid. Egypt is second to Israel in the total amount of U.S. aid it receives; with a population ten times as large, obviously the aid does not go as far. Jordan receives very little U.S. aid, but being a small, western-oriented state in a turbulent region, the Hashemite Kingdom has consistently tried to maintain close relations with the United States. Much of U.S. aid is military and in recent years at least seventy-five percent of U.S. military aid and arms sales went to the Middle East.[4]

Lebanon and Syria at this point are not dependent on the United States for aid, but each would welcome improved relations, including the possibility of economic aid. Lebanon is passing through an historic transition involving intense and violent civil war with unpredictable results; while having earlier ties with France, in the recent past Lebanese leaders, especially among the Maronite Christians, have looked to the United States for support in periods of crisis. Syria, which has the most negative relations with the United States of any of the countries mentioned and has turned to the Soviet Union as its superpower supporter, frequently has indicated its interest in improving relations with the United States and, at times, has specifically looked to the United States for help as an intermediary with Israel.

Frequently it is assumed that the degree of a country's economic and/or military dependence on the United States suggests the degree to which that country might be subject to U.S. influence to compromise in relation to possible moves toward peace. But Israel, each of the Arab states and the Palestinians all have very fundamental national and security interests at stake in the conflict and, therefore, there are definite limitations on how much any of the parties would be willing to compromise, no matter what degree of pressure might be exerted by the United States. In the case of Israel, there is significant counter-pressure exerted on the United States.

The unique relationship between Israel and the United States, reflecting complex moral, cultural and historical factors as well as certain common foreign policy interests, is a third reason why both Israeli and Arab leaders look to the United States hopefully and, at times, anxiously in relation to any possible moves toward peace.

So far, the reasons discussed for a special United States role in the Middle East can be described as pragmatic. A fourth set of reasons relates to perceptions among many Arabs and Israelis of principles such as fair play, peaceful resolution of conflict, protection of human rights, and self-determination for which the United States is considered to stand. The degree to which these "American principles" are a real factor is illustrated by how often Arabs and Israelis speak of them when discussing their hopes for a constructive U.S. role for peace. During recent years, in my own interviews and in published reports, there are indications that some Arabs and Israelis are worried by what they view as an increasing tendency for strategic considerations to have much more influence than moral concerns in the formation of U.S. policy. Many Arabs and Israelis believe that part of the reason President Carter engaged successfully in the negotiations process between Egypt and Israel was his deep moral commitment to peace.

Fears and Frustrations

Arabs and Israelis do have real fears and frustrations about the U.S. role in the region. While there are significant differences in their views, many Arabs and Israelis share a genuine and deep skepticism that they really can count on the United States.

Since its founding, Israel has had a sometimes troubled but fundamentally very close relationship with the United States. Most Israelis deeply appreciate U.S. support for Israel and hope the United States will help Israel achieve peace, but they also are profoundly distrustful of relying on the United States, or anyone else, to guarantee their security. What some observers have called the Israelis' abnormal concern for security is not really very hard to understand when one considers the abnormal history of the Jewish people and the experience of Israel in the Middle East since 1948; in several important respects, the contemporary experience seems to many Israelis to be a replay of that history, except that Israel is a nation-state and has the capacity to fight for its own survival.

Many Arabs continue to hope that the United States will develop a more even-handed policy, meaning by that term U.S. help in achieving a fair peace with Israel. Most Arab leaders do not expect the United States to abandon its special relation with Israel, but they are increasingly frustrated by what they view as the U.S. tendency always to take the side of Israel and in that context to be hostile to the Arabs. Furthermore, there is a much deeper and historical bitterness among Arabs, particularly among Muslim Arabs, dating from the Crusades, about western "Christian" domination. Thus, Arab skepticism about depending on the United States should also not be difficult to understand.

Despite the obvious differences in their experiences, many Arabs and Israelis, much more than is often recognized, share several common fears and frustrations in relation to U.S. policy in the Middle East. Leaders on both sides complain that U.S. policy often seems unclear or inconsistent. In part, this problem relates to frustration with the frequency of U.S. elections and the phenomenon of election year politics. This was the case during the first two years of the Reagan administration, 1981-82. Leaders on both sides complained that the United States did not appear to them to be committed to progress in the Camp David autonomy talks and appeared ambivalent toward the prospect of a new Israeli invasion of Lebanon. In fact, during this period many Arab and Israeli political leaders used identical words to describe the problem they saw, saying that "the United States does not have a Middle East policy."

Both Arabs and Israelis frequently expressed the view that U.S. political leaders lack adequate understanding of the peoples and the internal dynamics of the societies in the Middle East. Many Arabs and Israelis believe such shallowness impairs the U.S. ability to play a more constructive role. A particularly costly example is cited: the May 17, 1983 agreement negotiated by the United States between Israel and Lebanon, which made Israeli withdrawal from Lebanon conditional on Syrian withdrawal. Many knowledgeable people on both sides viewed the agreement as unworkable from the moment it was signed. In contrast to the demands of the Begin government in the negotiations, Israeli press reports at the time indicated that most Israelis would have supported Israeli withdrawal on the sole condition of security guarantees for their northern border. Reports to Washington from the U.S. Embassy in Damascus were among the many signs that Syria was very unlikely to accept the agreement as it stood. Despite this evidence, the United States pushed ahead to get the agreement signed. Lebanon and

Israel are still suffering the negative consequences.

At times in Israel and the Arab countries fears were expressed that U.S. pursuit of its strategic interests in the Middle East might conflict with the interests of Israel or of specific Arab countries. As an example, in 1981 Arab responses were almost all negative to the Reagan adminstration's idea of creating a strategic consensus of Middle Eastern countries against the Soviet Union because, in their view, the Soviet Union did not pose a significant threat to them. While Prime Minister Begin's government welcomed the strategic consensus idea, some Israeli Labor Party leaders criticized it at the time for placing Israel in "an unnecessarily antagonistic" posture toward the Soviet Union. A second example of this problem was in 1985 when Prime Minister Peres withdrew Israeli forces from most of Lebanon, while U.S. policymakers argued that U.S. strategic interests would have been better served by Israeli forces' staying in Lebanon to exert pressure on Syria.

Another important example of Arab and Israeli frustration with U.S. policy occurred in relation to the 1982 Reagan initiative. Important Egyptian, Jordanian and Palestinian leaders, as well as Israeli Labor Party leaders who welcomed the U.S. initiative, were frustrated by the lack of U.S. diplomatic effort on behalf of the initiative and were disappointed when it failed.

Even if the United States dealt wisely with the the Arab-Israeli conflict, it would be naive to suggest that peace can be achieved quickly or easily in the Middle East. It would be equally misleading to suggest that problems in U.S. policy, which are the focus of this study, are the only obstacles to peace. Frustrations with U.S. policy are often used by Arab and Israeli leaders as a way of absolving their own failures to take political risks necessary for peace. However, this does not lessen the need for more critical examination of the U.S. role in the lack of progress toward peace.

Constraints and Risks

The Arab-Israeli conflict has a long, bitter and complex history. Political dynamics and divisions within each country and in the Palestinian movement, as well as regional and international dynamics, are also complex, and impinge both positively and negatively on the prospects for peace.

Since the 1970s all of the parties directly involved in the conflict (Israel, Egypt, Jordan, Lebanon, Syria, and the PLO) have shown interest in a negotiated peace settlement. But each party has real constraints on how much it can eventually agree to for the sake of peace and what steps it can take, especially unilaterally, to pursue peace.

Moreover, pursuing peace presents real political risks to the leaders of each party. What has been relatively encouraging in recent years is that there are Israeli and Arab, including Palestinian, leaders with relatively strong support among their own people who apparently are convinced that the risks of continuing conflict are greater than the risks of pursuing peace. Many of these leaders believe the United States could help make peace more possible.

Yet, as we shall see in later chapters, Israeli and Arab leaders perceived several opportunites for movement toward peace during the years 1981 to 1986, but U.S. policy failed to respond to indirect and sometimes direct appeals from them for a more active and constructive U.S. role. A particularly ironic and sad fact about the failure of U.S. policy during these years is that on several occasions the advice from concerned Israeli and Arab leaders about what the United States should do was remarkably complementary.

Chapter Two

Israeli-PLO Ceasefire in Lebanon July 1981-May 1982

On July 24,1981, U.S. Special Envoy Philip C. Habib, with the help of third party intermediaries, succeeded in negotiating an unprecedented ceasefire between Israel and the PLO in southern Lebanon. While the PLO still did not recognize Israel and Israel claimed the agreement was between itself and the government of Lebanon, the ceasefire represented the first, even if indirect, negotiated agreement between Israel and the Palestinian national movement. There were important Israeli and Arab political leaders at the time who believed that the ceasefire represented an opportunity for movement toward negotiations to resolve the Palestinian issue; other leaders on both sides saw it only as an interlude in the ongoing war. What happened during the ceasefire? How did U.S. policy contribute to or frustrate hopes for peace?

Background to the Ceasefire Agreement

During the 1970s the PLO concentrated its military buildup in Lebanon after King Hussein expelled it from Jordan. Like Jordan, Lebanon shared a border with Israel. More than three hundred thousand Palestinian refugees living in Lebanon provided a base of popular support for the PLO. Palestinian forces came to play an important role in the 1975-76 civil war in Lebanon, tipping the internal balance in favor of the Muslims against the Maronite Christians. However, the PLO's primary interest in Lebanon always was the ongoing conflict with Israel. The PLO expanded its military and political organization in

Lebanon and provided substantial social and welfare services to Palestinians. By the late 1970s, it had built what amounted almost to a "state within a state" in southern Lebanon.[1]

The government of Lebanon, weakened by civil war and continuing internal struggles, did little to control the activities and buildup of the PLO. Many Lebanese were sympathetic with the Palestinian struggle, although there were increasing tensions with the PLO. This was especially true in southern Lebanon, where the PLO sometimes abused its power and where Lebanese suffered from Israeli-PLO war.[2]

Since the civil war in 1976, Syrian military forces had occupied a large area of eastern and northern Lebanon. The Syrian military presence in Lebanon was supported by an Arab League mandate and had been tacitly accepted by the United States and Israel as necessary to end the civil war. With both Israeli and Syrian military forces playing larger roles in Lebanon, the dangers of a confrontation leading to major war were recognized by both sides and by the two superpowers. While no formal agreement existed, following the 1978 Israeli invasion and withdrawal, there were understandings, referred to as "Red Lines," between Israel and Syria which were supposed to limit the nature and scope of each country's military activity in Lebanon.[3]

During the 1970s Israel's major concerns in relation to Lebanon were to limit the role of Syria, to support certain Maronite Christian forces and to stop PLO attacks from southern Lebanon against Israel.[4] At least from the mid-1970s, Israeli governments developed ties with and provided material support to elements in the Lebanese Phalange (the largest Maronite party). Prime Minister Begin's government increased this support on the basis that the Phalange forces were friendly to Israel and might eventually lead Lebanon to reach security agreements with Israel. PLO attacks on Israeli towns in the Galilee created a constant state of fear and generated intense internal pressure on the Israeli government to do whatever was necessary to prevent such attacks.

In the spring of 1981 several of the conflicts reached a new boiling point. In March Phalangist forces built a road near the predominantly Greek Orthodox Lebanese town of Zahle, in what Syrians feared was an attempt to link up with Israeli-backed Christian forces in southern Lebanon. Syrian forces responded with heavy shelling at Zahle. On April 25 Syrian helicopters attacked Maronite Christian Lebanese positions in the nearby Sannin Hills. Three days later Israeli jets shot down two Syrian helicopters in the same area as a warning that Israel would not allow the Syrians to defeat the Maronite forces. In response, Syria deployed antiaircraft missiles in the Bekaa Valley in eastern Lebanon, a move Israel charged was in violation of the "Red Lines" understanding. On April 30 Prime Minister Begin announced that bad weather had blocked implementation of his order for Israeli forces to destroy the Syrian missiles. On May 1 U.S. Secretary of State Alexander Haig urged Israeli restraint. On May 4, 1981, President Reagan also urged restraint and announced he was sending Philip C. Habib to the Middle East as a special envoy.[5]

The Habib Mission

On May 7 Philip Habib began his diplomatic shuttle among Israel, Lebanon, Syria and Saudi Arabia, the latter viewed by the United States as potentially a key moderating influence on Syria. During May Syrian missiles downed two unmanned Israeli reconnaissance aircraft over Lebanon and the Israeli government maintained its insistence that Syrian missiles be withdrawn from the Bekaa Valley. On May 28 Israel announced that its jets hit a complex of Libyan-supplied antiaircraft missiles guarding Palestinian guerrilla positions south of Beirut. Nevertheless, Ambassador Habib's efforts began to show some signs of easing the crisis. By the end of May when Habib flew home to brief President Reagan, Prime Minister Begin of Israel and President Assad of Syria were each saying publicly that his country would not be the first to escalate the confrontation. There also were some encouraging signs of progress in Egyptian-Israeli relations. During Habib's absence from the region the situation took a turn for the worse. Prime Minister Begin apparently believed that progress in diplomatic efforts with Egypt gave Israel more latitude to take military action on other fronts. Israeli forces carried out land and sea attacks on Palestinian bases in Lebanon and Israeli leaders reiterated a claim that attacks on PLO positions were outside the framework of the Habib mission. On June 7, just after President Sadat was in Israel for a summit meeting with Prime Minister Begin, in a move on another front Israeli jets bombed the Iraqi nuclear reactor near Baghdad. On June 9 Philip Habib returned to the Middle East with his mission under a cloud of doubt because of the Israeli raids.

In Israel, to the dismay of Israeli Labor Party leaders, the Israeli raids in Lebanon and Iraq seemed to strengthen the hand of Prime Minister Begin's ruling Likud coalition, which went on to win a one-seat majority in the national elections on June 30. While some Israelis believed the Likud still would have won the elections, others believed a stronger negative U.S. reaction would have made it more difficult for Begin to capitalize on the raids. On the Arab side, the Israeli raids contributed to strengthening the position of Syria and the PLO, both viewed as standing up to Israel in Lebanon.[6]

Despite the setbacks in June, there were indications by the beginning of July that the confrontation between Israel and Syria in Lebanon could be cooled. At the same time the confrontation between Israel and the Palestinians in Lebanon was becoming hotter. On July 10 Israeli planes struck Palestinian targets in southern Lebanon. Apparently in retaliation, Palestinian forces fired on the Israeli northern border town of Kiryat Shemona. On July 12 Israel bombed more Palestinian targets along the southern Lebanese coast, killing at least twenty-five people. On July 14-15 Israel shot down a Syrian plane over Lebanon and Palestinians fired dozens of rockets into Israeli towns, killing three people in Nahariya and wounding others in Kiryat Shemona. On July 16 Israeli jets destroyed bridges over the Zahrani and Litani Rivers, cutting major communication lines between Beirut and southern Lebanon. On July 17-18 Israeli jets struck Beirut. Lebanese authorities claimed that the air raids killed three hundred people and wounded eight hundred. Palestinian rocket attacks wounded six people in northern Israel. From the Israeli government viewpoint, its intensified attacks in Lebanon were meant not only to hurt the PLO but to generate Arab pressures to place restrictions on the PLO military buildup in southern Lebanon.

By late July 1981 the focus of Philip Habib's mission had shifted from Israel and Syria to Israel and the PLO. The Israeli government insisted that it would make no agreement with a "terrorist organization" and U.S. officials repeated that the United States would not talk with the PLO until the PLO agreed to recognize Israel and accept U.N. Resolution 242. During July Habib continued his shuttle diplomacy among Jerusalem, Beirut, Damascus and Riyadh. Increasingly, the focus of negotiations was on how to achieve a ceasefire on the Israeli-Lebanese border between Israel and the PLO. Negotiations were complicated because Lebanon would not negotiate directly with Israel and neither Israel nor the United States would talk with the PLO. Philip Habib and other U.S. officials served as intermediaries between Israel and Lebanon, while Lebanese leaders and U.N. representatives served as intermediaries between the United States and the Palestine Liberation Organization.

The escalation of hostilities in Lebanon during July, especially the air raids on Beirut, posed a serious challenge to the Habib mission. Angered by the Israeli raids, the Reagan administration announced a further postponement of delivery of F-16 jets to Israel, initially delayed after Israel bombed Iraq's nuclear reactor in June. Philip Habib made an urgent visit to Jerusalem where he obtained Israeli government support for talks about the framework for a ceasefire.

On July 21 the *Jerusalem Post* reported that pressures were building on the Israeli government to accept a ceasefire. Pressures included the pending U.S. decision about delivery of the F-16s, reports emanating from the U.N. that Yasser Arafat was actively considering a ceasefire, the presence in Israel of U.S. Special Envoy Habib and strong international reaction against the Israeli raids on Beirut. Domestic pressure on the Israeli government was also growing, both as a result of public criticism of Prime Minister Begin's handling of the crisis since April and the disruption of life in northern Israel caused by the increased hostilities.[7]

Within a week of the heavy air raids on Beirut a ceasefire was achieved. On July 24, after meeting with Prime Minister Begin, Ambassador Habib made a brief but dramatic announcement:

> I have today reported to President Reagan that as of 13:30 hours (1:30 p.m.) local time, July 24, 1981, all hostile military action between Lebanese and Israeli territory, in either direction, will cease.[8]

Israel and the PLO made separate announcements three hours apart that they had accepted the ceasefire. Israeli leaders said the agreement was negotiated by the United States with the government of Lebanon. PLO leaders said the agreement had been achieved through the offices of the United Nations. Several hours after the ceasefire was announced two salvos of rockets were fired into northern Israel by Palestinians in Lebanon, but the PLO quickly announced that it would take disciplinary action against the faction that fired the rockets. After this initial violation, the ceasefire agreement took hold and the Israeli-Lebanese border became quiet.

Debate in Israel

Debate among Israelis about their government's policies in Lebanon began in the spring of 1981 and continued long after the ceasefire. Criticism of government policies prefigured the large-scale public opposition to the Israeli invasion of Lebanon a year later.

The debate focused on several issues: the question of whether Israel had acted out of necessity or provocatively in the crisis with Syria in the spring of 1981; the nature and goals of Israel's relations with Maronite Christian forces in Lebanon; the relative gains and losses to Israel resulting from the escalation of hostilities with the Palestinians in Lebanon; the bombing of Beirut; the increase in tensions with the United States; and the meaning and value of the ceasefire announced on July 24.

Israeli public opinion divided basically along lines of the two major political groupings, i.e., the ruling Likud coalition versus the opposition Labor Alignment, with each side representing about one-third of the Israeli population. The remaining one-third sometimes supported one side and sometimes the other. From May to July 1981 the debate took place in the context of Israeli national elections, which doubtless caused arguments to be exaggerated. But the fact that the debate continued and even intensified after the elections on June 30 in part reflected the fact that the arguments in the debate represented fundamental differences in perception about Israeli short-term and long-term interests. It is significant that during this period, increasing U.S. pressure on Israel did not have the effect of uniting Israelis, as is commonly assumed would be the effect, but instead intensified the internal debate.

As early as May 1981 major Israeli Labor Party leaders, including Yitzhak Rabin and Haim BarLev, both former chiefs of staff of the Israeli Defense Forces, publicly challenged Prime Minister Begin's handling of the crisis in Lebanon. They accused the government of having fallen into a "Syrian trap," which would enhance President Assad's position in Lebanon and in the Arab world, reinforce the alliance between Syria and the Soviet Union and, in the long run, weaken the position of the Israeli-backed Christian forces in Lebanon.[9] On June 3 Yitzhak Rabin accused Begin of violating the unwritten "Red Lines" understanding with Syria, which limited each country's military role in Lebanon, and of dangerously escalating Israel's commitment to the Lebanese Phalange militia.[10]

Prime Minister Begin responded to the criticism in the Knesset and in a prepared article published June 12 in the *Jewish Press.* Begin confirmed that his government had expanded Israel's commitment to the Lebanese Christian forces and then, in the style for which he was famous, the prime minister compared Syrian attacks at Zahle to Nazi terror-bombings of civilians in Britain and asserted that Israeli action in shooting down Syrian helicopters had "rescued the Christians in Lebanon from a total collapse in morale which would have enabled the Syrians to take over all of North (sic) Lebanon and then start moving South."[11]

During June and July the debate in Israel did not diminish, but intensified. Public criticism reached a high point following the Israeli air raids on Beirut on July 17- 18 in which three hundred people were killed. On July 20 an editorial in the *Jerusalem Post*, reacting to the bombing of Beirut, predicted that

    . . .the present military strategy must lead either to an acceptance of the famous suggestion to "bomb 'em back to the Stone Age," made by a certain U.S. general. . .or to the physical occupation of the entire base area of terrorism.

Prefiguring public criticism a year later when Israel invaded and occupied a large area of Lebanon, the editorial called the first option "unthinkable" and the second option "unrealistic."[12]

For some Israelis the bombing of Beirut, the first direct Israeli attack on an Arab capital, raised profound moral issues. For example, Yosef Goel, a liberal but tough-minded political correspondent for the *Jerusalem Post*, wrote a column on July 24, entitled "Protecting Our Jewish Souls," in which he argued, "The bombing of innocent civilians must be condemned by all Israelis—even those who are subjected to PLO Katyusha attacks." The Peace Now movement in Israel organized demonstrations in response to the bombing.

Most Israeli criticism of the government's policy, however, focused on strategic or political issues. Labor Party leaders argued that Prime Minister Begin's policies created an unnecessary confrontation with Syria, that escalating hostilities with the Palestinians in Lebanon elevated the importance of the PLO and that the combination of these policies had generated negative tensions with the United States and with the United States' Jewish community. By July, the confrontation with Syria having cooled, most criticism focused on the negative consequences of the air raids in Lebanon and on the increasing tensions with the United States. On the eve of the ceasefire agreement, former Prime Minister Rabin declared that it was impossible to destroy the PLO by massive air attacks and that the only solution in the long run would be a political one.[13]

Israel's growing isolation in world opinion at the time and especially the tensions with the United States following the bombing of Beirut were disturbing to many Israelis. Israeli government officials publicly reacted angrily to U.S. pressures, including the announced postponement of delivery of the F-16s, but opposition leaders and important segments of the Israeli media charged that unwise Israeli policies were responsible for creating the crisis.[14] A *Jerusalem Post* editorial on July 22 stated the opposition's case in bold terms:

> To be sure, Israel has known outbursts of White House displeasure before, and it has survived them all. But never before has it known virtually the entire American political community to join in ganging up on this country. Even the organized American Jewish community has fallen nearly mute. For the first time, the voice unreservedly supporting

Israel is crying in the wilderness. This wilderness, however,
is of Israel's own creation. It is the product of an arrogant,
obtuse policy of "strength" which translates into a series
of self-inflicted blows.

While almost no one publicly attacked the ceasefire, supporters of
the Likud government's policies openly questioned the permanence and
even the value of the agreement. They warned that it was only a matter of time before the PLO would rebuild its forces and resume attacks
on Israeli towns, requiring Israel to go back into Lebanon to finish the
job it had started. Opposition leaders continued to attack the government's handling of the Lebanon crisis and argued that the ceasefire provided an opportunity to get the peace process started again.[15]

The public debate in Israel continued into the first five months of
1982; it is important to follow this debate up until Israel's invasion
of Lebanon in June 1982. But, meanwhile, it will be useful to look
at the parallel debate over the ceasefire within the PLO and at how
the ceasefire was viewed in the United States.

Debate Within the PLO

As in Israel, there was intense debate within the Palestinian movement about the meaning and value of the ceasefire. On one side, Yasser
Arafat and the majority of PLO leaders supported the ceasefire as providing at least a temporary respite from the suffering inflicted by Israeli
raids and as an opportunity to explore possible political strategies to
achieve the PLO goal of an independent Palestinian state. Interviewed
by western journalists in Beirut on July 25, Arafat insisted, however,
that "a ceasefire does not mean peace." He said, "To achieve peace
we must have a just solution. . .and. . .the PLO must be a part of any
attempt at finding a solution."[16]

In fact, both PLO leaders and Israeli critics of their government's
policies agreed that one effect of the recent hostilities and of the subsequent ceasefire agreement was to provide wider recognition of the central role of the PLO in the conflict and in its possible resolution. On
the other side, critics of the ceasefire, led by Ahmed Jebril of the small
Popular Front for the Liberation of Palestine-General Command (PFLP-
GC) faction, opposed the ceasefire on the ground that it constituted
de facto recognition of Israel; they argued that only by continued armed
struggle would the Palestinians achieve their aim to liberate Palestine.
Initially, the PFLP-GC refused to accept the ceasefire and apparently
it was this group which launched at least two rocket attacks on Israel
within hours after the ceasefire was announced. Arafat and other
mainstream leaders of the PLO denounced the violations and managed

to pressure the dissenting faction into line, so that by July 25 the ceasefire appeared to be working and the Lebanese-Israeli border was quiet.[17]

In the months which followed, while there were some indications of PLO interest in expanding the ceasefire with Israel to a general truce in exchange for Israeli acceptance of a PLO role in negotiations, the PLO leadership did little to press this idea publicly. From Arafat's viewpoint such an offer without the promise of some dramatic reciprocal move from the other side entailed serious internal political risks. There were no signs that Israel or the United States was interested in a quid pro quo.[18]

The U.S. Role

The United States welcomed the July 24 ceasefire for several reasons, not the least of which was that, at least temporarily, it eased growing tensions with Israel and with strategically important western-oriented Arab governments, such as Egypt and Saudi Arabia. Moreover, the United States viewed the ceasefire as critical for the continuing steps in the Egyptian-Israeli peace process. No knowledgeable observers of the Middle East believed the Israeli-PLO ceasefire in Lebanon would be permanent unless there were new initiatives to settle the internal problems in Lebanon and to move toward a negotiated settlement of the Palestinian issue and the wider Arab-Israeli conflict. Philip Habib and State Department officials emphasized this view in statements at the time Habib returned to Washington.

It was not at all clear that the Reagan administration was prepared to engage in new initiatives for peace in the Middle East. However, the administration did show readiness to engage in new military initiatives. The United States released the shipment of F-16s to Israel and moved ahead with plans to sell Airborne Warning and Control Systems (AWACS) to Saudi Arabia. Both steps were considered important "advances" in what clearly was the Reagan administration's priority at the time, i.e., developing a "strategic consensus" against the Soviet Union in the Middle East. The need for the Reagan administration to move quickly to clarify and develop the next steps in its Middle East policy was not only to preserve the precarious ceasefire but also to prepare for the visits of President Sadat and Prime Minister Begin to the United States in August and September.

If the United States decided to engage in a new effort for Middle East peace, there was encouraging evidence that it could count on broad public support. During the last week in July and first week in August several national U.S. newspapers and magazines, including the *New York Times, Los Angeles Times, Christian Science Monitor, Washington*

Post, Time and *Newsweek,* all carried editorials and/or commentaries focused on the need for new initiatives for peace and specifically urging the United States to press the Begin government for greater flexibility in the stalled Palestinian autonomy talks with Egypt.

On July 24 and again on July 26 the *Washington Post* called on the Reagan administration to rethink its policy of refusing to talk with the PLO. In the words of the July 26 editorial, "Everyone knows the PLO is ready for more war. The current calm provides an interval in which to probe whether, as some elements in it claim, the PLO is also ready for an honorable peace." [19]

A *Christian Science Monitor* editorial on July 26 identified two serious snags in expectations that the Reagan administration would engage in new Middle East peace initiatives.

> It is not yet clear that the President feels deeply enough
> about that issue to give it high priority. . . so far the Reagan
> policymakers have concentrated. . .on building up a
> "strategic consensus" in the Middle East to thwart Soviet
> ambitions in the region. [20]

President Reagan's view of the Middle East was very different from that of former President Carter, for whom peacemaking was a passionate priority.

Problems in the U.S. approach came clearly into focus in early August during the visit of President Anwar Sadat to Washington. In the public exchanges between President Sadat and President Reagan, the Egyptian leader expressed a sense of urgency and was quite specific about what he believed the United States needed to do to advance the cause of peace. Sadat spoke of "the willingness of the Palestinians to accept a ceasefire in Lebanon" as "a turning point that should not escape our notice" and a development which could help achieve "our goal for mutual and simultaneous recognition between the Israelis and the Palestinians." Sadat called on the United States to help the "process of reconciliation by holding a dialogue with the Palestinians through their representatives" as a way "to strengthen the forces of moderation among them." While making no reference to a Soviet threat in the region, he did speak about the danger of not pursuing peace. Appealing urgently for more U.S. help, Sadat warned that "The rising tension and violence. . .is living evidence of the urgent need for a comprehensive peace in the Middle East." [21]

In contrast to Sadat's sense of urgency and his specificity, President Reagan's public statements, for the most part, lacked urgency and remained on the level of generalities. Reagan spoke in warm praise of

President Sadat and of the Egyptian people, but made only slight reference to a possible connection between the achievement of the Israeli-PLO ceasefire in Lebanon and any next steps to achieve a comprehensive Middle East peace. In addressing the Egyptian leader, President Reagan emphasized what he called "our mutual concern for regional stability" and Egypt's role in combatting what he described as "external threats and foreign-inspired subversion." While he affirmed the U.S. commitment "to work closely with Egypt as full partners in our search for peace and stability in the Middle East," not once in any of his public statements did President Reagan even use the word "Palestinians."[22]

The next major test of U.S. priorities in relation to the Middle East came at the time of Israeli Prime Minister Begin's visit to Washington during the first week of September. In the weeks before the prime minister's visit three developments provided further encouragement for the view that an opportunity existed for a new peace intitiative by the United States. First, with each additional day it held, the ceasefire in southern Lebanon gained strength. Despite scattered violations, both Israeli and PLO leaders appeared for the time being to view the ceasefire as in their interests.[23]

Second, during early August, Crown Prince Fahd of Saudi Arabia proposed a new plan for peace. For the first time, Saudi Arabia, using the language of U.N. Resolutions 242 and 338, called for a comprehensive settlement which would provide security for "all states in the region," implying, though not explicitly stating, recognition of Israel.[24] The initiative was viewed at the time as both a reflection of Saudi interest in parlaying the southern Lebanon ceasefire, which it had helped to achieve, into a new effort toward comprehensive peace and also as the kind of positive move that would serve its interests in gaining U.S. approval for its purchase of AWACS. Reactions in the Arab world to Prince Fahd's proposal, on the whole, were positive, although Syria did not accept it at the time and the Arab summit could not agree on it. (It was essentially the Fahd plan that was approved a year later as the Arab Fez Declaration.) In an interview published in the *New York Times* on August 17, Yasser Arafat described Saudi Arabian support for the southern Lebanon ceasefire between Israel and the PLO as "a good beginning for a lasting peace in the Middle East." In Israel, reaction to the Fahd plan was negative or, at least, highly skeptical, but the Saudi initiative did tend to reinforce pressures on the Begin government to make progress in the autonomy talks with Egypt, stalled for almost a year since Israel had annexed East Jerusalem.

The third positive development, and one that surprised many people, was the agreement by Prime Minister Begin and President Sadat on August 24 in Alexandria to resume negotiations over autonomy for the West Bank and Gaza. In Israel, the ceasefire with the PLO in Lebanon created a new positive atmosphere. Moreover, many Israelis believed it was advantageous for Israel to seek an accord with Egypt on Palestinian autonomy while transfer of the Sinai, to be completed in April 1982, was still in progress. In addition, there was growing Israeli concern that the enhanced status of the PLO and the new Saudi Arabian initiative might cause the United States to explore an alternate peace process to the autonomy talks, which up to this point had produced no results.

Many Israelis believed—and some who favored peace publicly expressed hope—that the United States would now press hard for results in the autonomy talks: the thought was that the opportunity offered by the ceasefire with the PLO combined with U.S. dissatisfaction with Begin's policies in the previous several months would increase U.S. readiness to put pressure on Israel to help resolve the Palestinian issue.[25]

In the United States, also, many people believed the Reagan administration would and/or should now press the Israeli government on the autonomy negotiations. For example, Jacob Stein, White House liaison with the Jewish community, predicted to the *Jerusalem Post* that "Progress in the autonomy talks and trying to find a resolution to the Palestinian dilemma" would be the major issue in bilateral relations between Israel and the United States in the near future.[26] The *New York Times* and the *Washington Post* published editorials just before Prime Minister Begin's arrival calling on President Reagan to press Mr. Begin for greater flexibility in the autonomy talks, for Israel's sake and for the sake of U.S. interests in the Middle East.[27] However, to the Reagan administration, increasing U.S. military and strategic influence in the region was a much higher priority than advancing the peace process.

Based on an interview with Secretary of State Alexander M. Haig, Bernard Gwertzman reported in the *New York Times* on September 6 that the primary U.S. agenda for meetings with Prime Minister Begin would be strengthening U.S.-Israeli military links, including discussion of joint military exercises, logistics cooperation, increased sharing of intelligence information and the use of Israeli territory as "a forward facility" for the U.S. Rapid Deployment Force.[28] Reflecting an approach developed by Henry Kissinger in an earlier period, Reagan administration officials also hoped that enhancing Israel's "ally" status might soften Mr. Begin's public opposition to the proposed sale of the AWACS to Saudi Arabia. While both the southern Lebanon ceasefire and the autonomy talks with Egypt were also to be on the agenda, Gwertzman's report indicated that they were almost certain to take lower priority than the issues of strategic military cooperation and the AWACS sale.

On September 8, the day before Reagan and Begin were to hold their first meeting, the *Jewish Telegraphic Agency* quoted a senior U.S. official as saying that he did not expect "any great breakthroughs" on issues related to the autonomy talks.[29] When the official was asked about Israeli settlements in the West Bank, he said that the United States would stress that it considers them a "political problem," but there would be no discussion of their legality. This position was consistent with a 1980 campaign statement by Ronald Reagan that, in contrast to the official U.S. view since 1967, he did not view the settlements as illegal. As it turned out, the subject of the autonomy talks, reflecting the unfinished agenda of Camp David, never even was a focus for substantial discussion in the meetings involving President Reagan, but was relegated to a September 11 working breakfast between Mr. Begin and Mr. Haig.[30]

Claims by Reagan administration officials that the U.S.-Israeli summit had advanced prospects for Middle East peace left many questions unanswered. As the *Christian Science Monitor* asked in its editorial on September 14, "What good will it do to build an anti-Soviet strategic consensus in the Middle East without an equally vigorous effort to remove the political conflicts on which Soviet aggression feeds? And if such a parallel effort is indispensable, should not the United States be using its diplomatic leverage to push forward the peace process? There is no evidence it is doing so."[31]

Negative Arab reactions to U.S. "strategic collaboration" with Israel—which ranged from embarrassment to loud condemnation—came as no surprise to most observers, although some Reagan administration officials, including Secretary of State Haig, tried to interpret the results of the Reagan-Begin summit as in the interests of moderate Arab states as well as Israel. U.S. officials now argued with Arab leaders that increasing Israeli security would make Israel more flexible in peace talks, just as they had argued with Prime Minister Begin that strengthening Saudi Arabia by selling it AWACS would not only protect U.S. interests, but Israeli interests as well. To put it mildly, these arguments were never very convincing to Arabs or Israelis.

What may have been more of a surprise to some observers is that the "strategic cooperation" concept caused a significant debate in Israel, both within the Labor Alignment and between the Alignment and the Likud. Shimon Peres charged that Begin had "traded AWACS for the pact with the U.S."[32] Asher Maniv, then editor of the Labor Party monthly *Migvan*, raised more fundamental opposition to strategic cooperation with the United States, saying it showed "Israel straining to become a military outpost in the global conflict with the second superpower in the world."[33] Other Israelis argued that now was not the time to emphasize military power but to press more courageously for peace, especially in the autonomy talks with Egypt. Yossi Sarid, Labor Party member of the Knesset long known for his advocacy of peace, used the debate as an occasion to call on the Labor Party to launch a new initiative "whereby the Jewish nation would recognize the rights of the Arab Palestinian nation and that nation would recognize the Jewish nation's right to self-determination."[34] While Sarid's specific proposal gained little support, his belief that Israel should take advantage of the Israeli-PLO ceasefire in Lebanon to press for new initiatives toward a settlement with the Palestinians did reflect a view widely held in Israel.

To many Israelis who hoped for progress toward peace during this period, Begin's visit to Washington offered disturbing evidence that peace in the Middle East was not a high priority for the Reagan administration. To Egyptians, already discouraged by the lukewarm U.S response to the visit of President Sadat, the U.S. emphasis on increasing U.S.-Israeli military cooperation added to the frustration.

The Sadat Assassination

On October 6, 1981, President Sadat was assassinated by Islamic militants while he was reviewing a military parade at a stadium in Cairo. In the Arab countries Sadat's radical critics rejoiced. Tawfik Salah, a leading member of Syria's ruling Ba'th Party, told a large rally, "Traitor Sadat has met his inevitable fate. . . .let all the other traitors in the Arab world await that fate."[35] Adnan Abu Odeh, then minister of information of Jordan, reflected more moderate Arab opinion when he said that Sadat's death "confirms that any settlement for the Middle East crisis which ignores the Palestinian problem will never succeed."[36]

In Israel, the response to the assassination was shock and an emotional sense of loss, as well as uncertainty about the future of peace with Egypt. A few Israeli political leaders in the right wing Tehiya Party declared that Sadat's assassination vindicated their opposition to Camp David, but most Israeli leaders said they hoped the peace process with Egypt would continue. Prime Minister Begin said he believed this is what President Sadat "would wish with all his heart."[37] Some

Likud leaders, including Yitzhak Shamir, foreign minister, and Moshe Arens, chairman of the Knesset Foreign Affairs and Defense Committee, who had voted against Camp David, expressed a more cautious attitude toward continuation of the peace process. In contrast, Israel's President Yitzhak Navon declared that Israel was "duty bound" to continue the Camp David process.[38]

Echoing views expressed by several Egyptian supporters of Sadat, some Israeli political leaders charged that the U.S. failure to press for progress on resolving the Palestinian issue was a major factor leading to the assassinaton of President Sadat. Even former Prime Minister Yitzhak Rabin, known for his more hawkish views within the Labor Party leadership, openly chastised the Reagan administraton as having "contributed to the downfall of Sadat" because it "did not show interest in the implementation of several aspects of the (Camp David) agreements, including the autonomy talks."[39]

In the United States several political leaders responded to Sadat's assassination with a heightened sense of urgency that the administration become more actively involved in the search for peace. In a dramatic press conference on board their plane as they returned from Sadat's funeral, former Presidents Carter and Ford declared that the United States would eventually have to talk with the PLO. While arguing that the PLO had to take some steps toward recognition of Israel, Carter and Ford emphasized the centrality of the Palestinian issue, urged that people not look at Palestinians as "a single entity" or simply as "terrorists," and encouraged the Reagan administration to explore ways to bring the Palestinians into the peace process.[40] The advice offered by Carter and Ford echoed the views of many Arabs and Israelis, including the late President Sadat, who believed an opportunity for peace was being lost. As a *Washington Post* editorial on October 12 said, the two former Presidents had not offered a solution to the conflict, but they had "widened the political room open to Ronald Reagan, if he would but use it."[41]

Many other Democratic and Republican political leaders also stressed the urgency of continuing the peace process and at least a few suggested that the United States could do more than it was doing. On October 13 Senator John Glenn (D-Ohio), expressing support for the views of Carter and Ford on the necessity of talking with the PLO, said, "To say that we will not have any contact with one of the major parties to this settlement is not the way to go."[42] Two days later Senator Robert Byrd (R-Va) declared, "It is imperative that we get back on the track to peace in the Middle East." Openly critical of the Reagan administration's approach to problems in the region, Byrd said, "The Arab-Israeli dispute has been placed on the back burner by this administration. Yet the fundamental problems in the region stem from the continued unresolution of this dispute."[43]

The United States did take urgent action in response to the assassination of Sadat but the action was not focused on achieving progress in the peace process. In an interview from Cairo on *Meet the Press*, Secretary of State Haig announced that arms deliveries to Egypt and the Sudan would be speeded up and that U.S. military forces, possibly including B-52s, would participate in joint military exercises in Egypt in November. Haig also stressed the importance of congressional support for the sale of AWACS to Saudi Arabia. In relation to the Camp David process, while Haig said that the United States was "most anxious to get on with these autonomy talks and bring about a successful conclusion to them," he offered no indication of any new U.S. initiative for peace.[44]

Chapter Three

A Ceasefire in Lebanon is Not Enough

*B*y November 1981 the ceasefire in southern Lebanon was showing alarming signs of strain, reflecting the lack of any progress on basic issues in the Israel-Palestinian conflict. On November 23 *Newsweek* reported that both Israel and the PLO were reinforcing their positions in southern Lebanon: "Palestinians sent two armed battalions to the southern front (and) Israel moved additional artillery pieces across the border into the enclave controlled by Major Saad Haddad, their Lebanese Christian ally." A week earlier, Major Haddad, feeling pressure from PLO forces, declared, "For us the ceasefire no longer exists. The state of war has returned." The Reagan administration was sufficiently worried about the situation to announce that it planned to send Philip Habib back to the region, but there still appeared to be no plan for a new U.S. peace initiative and little urgency about the need for making progress on the fundamental issues.

During November the Reagan administration won congressional approval for the sale of AWACS to Saudi Arabia and on November 30 signed a memorandum of understanding on strategic cooperation with Israel. The AWACS sale provoked strong negative reactions from Israel while the U.S.-Israel strategic agreement provoked strong negative reactions from Arab leaders. Ironically, though the idea of strategic cooperation was intended in part to sooth Israeli nerves, many Israelis, especially in the opposition Labor Alignment, attacked the agreement as unnecessary and possibly harmful to Israeli interests. Repeating arguments of September, critics saw the agreement as tying Israel into the U.S. global confrontation with the Soviet Union without doing anything to enhance Israel's security in the region. Most Arabs viewed the U.S.-Israeli strategic cooperation agreement as additional reason to doubt the credibility of the United States as a mediator for resolving the Arab-Israeli conflict.In the third week of December Prime Minister Begin pushed a measure through his cabinet which applied Israeli law to the Golan Heights, interpreted by many as tantamount to annexation. The Reagan administration reacted angrily and suspended the strategic cooperation agreement. Prime Minister Begin called in U.S. Ambassador Samuel Lewis and gave him a severe "tongue lashing," charging that the United States was treating Israel like a "banana republic" and rejecting the idea that the United States had any right "to punish" Israel.[1]

Strains on the Ceasefire

By early January 1982 hopes for a breakthrough in the autonomy talks between Israel and Egypt had all but died. During January, once again, there were increased pressures from Israeli Labor Party leaders for greater Israeli flexibility in the talks. There was a brief shuttle effort by U.S. Secretary of State Haig. But by the end of January the *New York Times* reported that Haig saw "no chance of accord on Palestinian autonomy soon."[2]

During a visit to Washington in early February Egypt's new president, Hosni Mubarak, urged the U.S.—as Sadat had in August 1981—to open a dialogue with representatives of the Palestinians in order to keep the peace process alive. President Reagan repeated the U.S. commitment to the autonomy talks, but it was clear that the United States was no longer seeking a breakthough.

Whatever had been the chances of a breakthrough in the Egyptian-Israeli talks over the West Bank and Gaza—and some would argue that the talks were fatally flawed from the start by the failure to involve Palestinians—the fact that the United States did not give priority to the talks made the possibility of a breakthrough more remote. It is significant that Egyptian leaders Sadat, and then Mubarak, and many Israeli leaders from the Labor Alignment urgently wanted the United States to take a more active and forceful role in the talks; many of them believed more U.S. pressure could have made a difference.

In February 1982 public debate in Israel over the value of the ceasefire in southern Lebanon intensified. This time the debate was triggered by an incident in which five Palestinians apparently crossed the Jordan River into the Israeli-controlled West Bank in an aborted guerrilla raid.

On the night of the incident, Defense Minister Ariel Sharon and Chief of Staff Rafael Eitan held a televised press conference in which they presented the incident as if it had been a major military confrontation. Foreign Minister Shamir appeared on television the next night accusing the PLO of a "grave ceasefire violation," even though, as a *Jerusalem Post* editorial pointed out, the Begin government had consistently maintained that the ceasefire agreement was not with the PLO, but with the Lebanese government and, moreover, "all the evidence tended to show that the ceasefire had been strictly limited to the Lebanese frontier."[3]

The handling of this incident by Israeli officials, especially Defense Minister Sharon, was widely interpreted in Israel at the time as an attempt to justify possible new retaliatory raids against the PLO in Lebanon. The incident occurred only ten days after Prime Minister Begin had sent a letter to President Reagan reassuring him that Israel would not launch attacks in Lebanon unless there was a "clear provocation" by PLO or Syrian forces. What would be considered "clear provocation" remained ambiguous and subject to debate. This incident was not viewed by Begin at the time as clear enough. On February 9 David Shipler reported in the *New York Times* that Begin had rejected a proposal by Sharon to invade Lebanon in response to the aborted terrorist incident.[4]

For now, it appeared the Israeli-PLO ceasefire in southern Lebanon would hold, but speculation increased that Defense Minister Sharon planned a large-scale invasion and that probably the question was no longer whether Israel would invade Lebanon, but when. On February 25 Moshe Arens, the new Israeli ambassador to the United States, further fueled such speculation when he responded to a reporter's question about the possibility of Israel going back into Lebanon, by saying "I would almost say it's a matter of time."[5] During February and March the Likud government undertook a concerted campaign in the United States and elsewhere to present its case that there had been dozens of "ceasefire violations" by the PLO. In fact, U.S. and Israeli leaders acknowledged that the Israeli-Lebanon border had been quiet since late July 1981. Furthermore, Israeli officials, including Prime Minister Begin, indicated that there was not yet "clear enough provocation" by the PLO to justify an invasion. Nevertheless, the publicity campaign was effective in preparing Israeli and U.S. public opinion for the invasion.

One widely held view in Israel at the time was that the Israeli government would act before the completion of the withdrawal from Sinai at the end of April 1982, on the assumption that both Egyptian and

U.S. reaction to an invasion of Lebanon would be restrained so as not to derail this phase of Camp David. Consistent with this theory, U.S. criticism of Israeli policies from February through April was very restrained, apparently in part to avoid complicating Israeli withdrawal from Sinai. For the same reason, it was argued, the United States did not press harder for results in the autonomy talks.

Internal criticism of Israeli government policies greatly intensified during this period, based on the view held by many Israelis that the period before completion of the Sinai withdrawal was the most advantageous time to press for progress on resolving the Palestinian issue. While much attention was focused on the conflict over dismantling of Israeli settlements at Yamit in the Sinai, and the Begin government used the "trauma" of these events to emphasize what a sacrifice Israel was making, many other Israelis were worried that the withdrawal from Sinai would mark the end of the peace process. On March 27, 1982, there was a demonstration by thousands of Israelis in Tel Aviv, sponsored by Peace Now, protesting Israel's policies in the West Bank and Gaza, calling for greater flexibility in the autonomy talks with Egypt and warning against a possible Israeli invasion of Lebanon.

In contrast to the highly visible sense of urgency many Israelis felt during the spring of 1982, the United States made almost no public criticism of Israeli occupation policies, was resigned to making no progress in the autonomy talks and made no effort to counter the Israeli propaganda campaign alleging dozens of ceasefire violations by the PLO.Instead of identifying U.S. concerns with the views of Israeli political leaders who were speaking out about the urgent need for progress toward a wider peace, Secretary of State Haig at times was openly critical of such Israeli views. Interviewed on *Meet the Press* the last Sunday in March, Haig rejected the idea that any new U.S. initiative was needed in relation to the autonomy talks, either before or after the April 25 deadline for Israeli withdrawal from Sinai. Responding to the reporters' sense of impatience over the lack of more urgent U.S. pressures for peace, Haig said, "Clearly we have to recognize that excess impatience can bring about the very outcome we are seeking to avoid."[6]

Earlier in March former Israeli Foreign Minister Abba Eban had strongly criticized Israeli policies in the West Bank and Gaza after the Likud government removed several elected Palestinian mayors and municipal councils. Eban said, "I can't imagine anything more grotesque than a government which professes to aspire to full autonomy for Palestinians on a national scale cancelling the limited municipal autonomy that already exists." When asked by a reporter on *Meet the*

Press to comment on Eban's statement, Haig did not take the opportunity to identify U.S. concerns with this sentiment in Israel, but appeared to justify Israeli government policies and insisted that the U.S. should "maintain a level of objectivity on these very vexing issues."[7]

By early April, with no progress toward resolving the Palestinian issue, the prospects of the ceasefire holding in southern Lebanon were becoming even more shaky. There were leaders in Israel who continued to believe strongly in it. Even after the assassination in Paris on April 3 of an Israeli diplomat, Yacov Barsimantov, two former Israeli chiefs of staff, Haim Bar Lev and Mordecai Gur, publicly opposed Prime Minister Begin's attempt to get broad Knesset support for an Israeli retaliatory strike in Lebanon.[8] The United States also urged "utmost restraint" by all parties, but at the same time U.S. officials offered journalists a long list of reasons why Prime Minister Begin might find it to his government's advantage to act now. Reading the press accounts of these background interviews, it is difficult to tell where U.S. views differed significantly from what the officials explained were the views of the Begin government. Israeli Labor Party leaders, at some political risk in the face of public reaction to new terrorist attacks on Israeli civilians, publicly opposed the idea of military retaliation in Lebanon. At the same time the Reagan administration increasingly appeared to accept the inevitability of an Israeli invasion; some officials even began to sound as if they saw possible advantages of an invasion to U.S. goals in the region.

In the face of the growing threat of Israeli military action in Lebanon, debate within the PLO also intensified about the value of the ceasefire. Arafat and other major PLO leaders, however, apparently still believed in its value. On April 11, in an interview in Beirut with Flora Lewis of the *New York Times*, Yasser Arafat said that, although he expected an Israeli attack, the PLO would not be the first to break the ceasefire. Arafat denied the PLO had anything to do with the assassination of the Israeli diplomat in Paris. (It was believed at the time, among others by many Israeli experts on the PLO, that a Palestinian faction headed by Abu Nidal was responsible. This faction had also assassinated Arafat supporters within the PLO.)

Yasser Arafat reiterated his view that the ceasefire at the Lebanon-Israel border did not mean peace. "Peace is something completely different," he said. "We are looking for a comprehensive peace settlement through the U.N. resolution and international legality." According to Flora Lewis, Arafat clearly wanted "to convey a sense of moderation, a desire for a politically negotiated settlement."[9]

Later in the interview, Arafat offered his views about recent events in the West Bank and in Israel. Arafat described resistance activities by Palestinians in the West Bank and Gaza as a "referendum" supporting Palestinian nationalist aspirations. Arafat believed that the recent Israeli Peace Now demonstration in Tel Aviv was "most important" and that it was a "referendum among Israelis." Saying there were twenty thousand people in the demonstration (Peace Now leaders claimed fifty thousand), Arafat pointed out that many of them were reserve officers and said, "I respect this step."[10] While the PLO continued to refuse to recognize Israel unilaterally as a precondition for participation in negotiations, at the time of this interview, it did seem that Arafat still hoped that the Lebanon ceasefire could hold and, possibly, lead to other steps in the direction of a political solution.

On April 22, three days before the deadline for Israeli withdrawal from Sinai, Israeli jets bombed several Lebanese villages controlled by the PLO. The PLO did not retaliate. Acting against strong internal pressure, Arafat ordered Palestinian military forces to hold their fire, primarily, from his viewpoint, to avoid giving the Israeli government an excuse for all-out invasion.

The response by the United States to the raids was extremely cautious, reportedly out of fear that a stronger response might derail the final stage of Israeli withdrawal from Sinai. In fact, the United States concentrated almost all its diplomatic effort at the time on encouraging increased Arab pressure on the PLO to hold its fire. In Israel, the mild U.S. response to the Israeli bombing raid was interpreted as U.S. acceptance of the raid. Moreover, the U.S. response increased the perception among Israeli leaders that the United States would also probably accept an all-out invasion of Lebanon, if there were "clear provocation." To Defense Minister Sharon, the mild U.S. response was very encouraging. To Israeli leaders who hoped the ceasefire could be maintained, the U.S. response was disturbing.

The Invasion of Lebanon

On April 25 Israel completed its withdrawal from the Sinai as called for in the Camp David agreement. Egypt became the first Arab country to make peace with Israel and Israel returned a large territory it had captured in the 1967 war. Editorials in major U.S. newspapers praised this truly momentous achievement and the U.S. role in helping to bring it about. At the same time many of the editorials sounded warnings about the urgent need to get on with the the rest of the Camp David treaty, i.e., resolving the Palestinian issue and seeking a comprehensive peace settlement. The *New York Times*, which had strongly supported the Camp David process from the start, declared that so far the achievement of Camp David was "a separate peace in all but name—the kind that Anwar Sadat warned, in Jerusalem, would never last." Commenting on the large, and possibly growing, gap between the Egyptian and Israeli positions in the autonomy talks, and the need for the United States to play a more active and forceful role, the editorial said, "Only the United States can still hope to define a middle course." The editorial commented explicitly on how Israelis who opposed continued occupation of the West Bank and Gaza depended on the United States for support and how the Reagan administration was letting them down.

> This (Israeli) opposition still lives and it pants for U.S. support. . . .What this opposition urgently needs is America's help in clearing a path to the Palestinians. And this requires a dogged reaffirmation of the Camp David promise of "full autonomy."[21]

A *Washington Post* editorial, "Beyond Sinai," sounded some of the same themes in even stronger terms. Pointing out that Prime Minister Begin had signed up for "full autonomy" in the Camp David treaty, the editorial declared: "Let him deliver, with the United States defining what it means by the term and pushing him along. Since the administration accepts that settlements harm the peace process, let it say it expects settlements to end—at once." Then the editorial raised two questions and suggested what it believed to be the appropriate answers:

> Deal with the PLO, to bring it into direct negotiationswith Israel? Why must the U.S. be held to its pledge on not talking with the PLO when Mr. Begin falls away from his on "full autonomy?" Use aid as a lever? It's a question of tactics, not principles.[12]

It is important to understand that the basic message in this advice was that it was urgent for the United States to take a more active role in pressing for resolution of the Palestinian issue. This advice was neither new nor lacking in political support. Many prominent leaders in the United States and in the Middle East, including both Arabs and Israelis, had pleaded before for such a role by the United States. Now, following Israeli withdrawal from Sinai, these appeals were being made once again.

By late April 1982, many observers feared that it might be too late to save the Egyptian-Israeli autonomy talks. As one former official of the Carter administration put it, "The Arab world, the Soviets, our allies in Western Europe—all are ready to proclaim that Camp David is dead. If the (Reagan) administration is going to show that it's alive and breathing, it must start doing so right now. It no longer has the luxury of time."[13] Given the failure of the United States to respond to earlier appeals, it is reasonable to ask whether the administration, in fact, had a serious commitment to develop the wider peace process envisioned in the Camp David agreement.

Events during May 1982 tragically confirmed the view that it was too late for the autonomy talks. In the first week of May the ceasefire in southern Lebanon was again broken by Israeli air raids. This time, the PLO fired back with an attack across the border into northern Israel. There was a fierce, cross-border artillery duel between Palestinian and Israeli forces. After twenty-four hours the border was quiet again and both sides reaffirmed their commitment to the ceasefire. But these events and an ambivalent U.S. response appeared, finally, to set the stage for what would occur in early June. The PLO urgently reinforced its positions in southern Lebanon. The Israeli government confirmed reports that it had carried out a large build-up of its military forces at the border with Lebanon.

Interviewed in early May in *Yediot Aharonot* Israeli Chief of Staff Rafael Eitan said Israel should use massive force, not guerrilla tactics, to respond to the "terrorists" in Lebanon. Although by June most Labor Party leaders supported the forty kilometer phase of the invasion, claimed to be necessary for the security of Israel's northern border, during May many continued to oppose the concept of any Israeli invasion of Lebanon. Their opposition, however, was getting weaker. On May 14 Yitzhak Rabin, himself a former chief of staff and prime minister, said that an Israeli invasion, no matter what its size, could not destroy the PLO's military capacity in Lebanon, nor succeed in giving Christians control of most of Lebanon, nor expel the Syrian army from that country. In light of subsequent events, most Israelis would agree that Rabin's view was eminently wiser than the view of Sharon who believed an Israeli invasion of Lebanon could accomplish all Rabin spoke of and more.[14]

By mid-May 1982 the majority of Israelis viewed some form of Israeli military action in Lebanon as practically inevitable. Many Israelis felt desperate about continuing violent attacks, even though they were not violations of the ceasefire and the border with Lebanon remained quiet. Many Israelis were influenced by their government's campaign claiming that any attacks by Palestinians represented PLO violations of the ceasefire. Less understandably and more tragically, the United States also seemed increasingly to accept the "inevitability" of an Israel invasion of Lebanon.

On May 11 it was reported that Secretary of State Haig had asked Philip Habib to come to Washington for consultations about a new trip to the Middle East. According to Wolf Blitzer, the Washington correspondent for the *Jerusalem Post*, the United States was privately sending Israeli leaders negative messages regarding a possible invasion of Lebanon. Publicly, however, U.S. leaders were using very cautious language, according to Blitzer's view, to avoid "stirring up the hawks within the Israeli government."[15] Two other highly respected journalists, Ze'ev Shiff and Ehud Yaari, subsequently argued that the United States actually gave a green light to the Israeli invasion.

Many Israelis who opposed an invasion of Lebanon were highly critical of the U.S. role during this period. They believed that the failure of the United States forcefully and publicly to oppose the idea of an invasion undermined their own position in Israel and strengthed the hands of those Israeli leaders, most notably Defense Minister Sharon, who openly advocated the invasion.

During May Israeli government officials charged that the PLO had committed dozens of violations of the ceasefire, once again claiming that the July 1981 agreement applied to all hostile activities rather than only to hostilities across the Lebanese-Israeli border. Official U.S. responses to these claims were ambiguous. In an interview with *Wall Street Journal* editors and reporters published May 27, Defense Minister Sharon declared that maintaining the ceasefire depended on the PLO's understanding "that they must stop all terrorist activities." Sharon visited several U.S. media offices during this trip. According to reports at the time, he presented charts and maps to interpret the rationale for the Israeli invasion before it occurred.

Defense Minister Sharon repeatedly said "Israel does not want war," but practically everything else he said made the decision for massive military action in Lebanon sound as if it were a fait accompli. As an example of the kind of incident which could trigger Israeli action, Sharon cited a bomb blast at a school near Tel Aviv. The school children fortunately escaped injury but if they had not, Sharon said, "We would have been in Lebanon."[16] While press reports almost universally concluded that an Israeli invasion of Lebanon was imminent, the Reagan administration response to Sharon's visit was restrained and ambiguous. Israeli opposition to Sharon's views was much clearer and more visible, but not strong enough by itself to reverse the pull toward war. At the end of May the opposition tried to bring down the government, but Prime Minister Begin's Likud Coalition narrowly defeated a no-confidence vote in the Knesset.

On May 25 Israeli jet fighters shot down two Syrian fighter planes over Lebanon after a dogfight erupted during an Israeli reconnaissance mission. On June 2 Shlomo Argov, the Israeli ambassador in London, was seriously wounded in an assassination attempt, apparently by the same Palestinian faction which had killed the Israeli diplomat in Paris in April. On June 4 Israeli jets struck southern Lebanon and Beirut and Israeli-Palestinian artillery duels broke out across the Israeli-Lebanese border. On June 5 the intensity of fighting increased and a day later Israeli forces, including two hundred fifty tanks and thousands of ground troops, crossed into Lebanon.

In a dispatch to the *New York Times* datelined June 6 and head-lined, ''Why Israelis Invade Now,'' David Shipler reviewed several factors which appeared to ''line up'' in the view of Prime Minister Begin. One factor, the importance of which Shipler said was unclear, was that during the forty-eight hours after the attempted assassination of Ambassador Argov, no warning against invasion had come from the United States. A letter to Prime Minister Begin from President Reagan, who was attending a conference in Versailles, did arrive the morning Israeli forces crossed into Lebanon. However, in marked contrast to the response of President Carter to the Israeli invasion of Lebanon in 1978, President Reagan's letter weakly urged Israeli ''restraint.'' It is noteworthy that almost a year later when he recovered from his wounds, Ambassador Shlomo Argov voiced profound disagreement with his government's decision to invade Lebanon.

The U.S.-negotiated Israeli-PLO ceasefire in southern Lebanon was in shambles. The hopes for movement toward peace were shattered. For Israelis and Arabs who believed there had been an opportunity for peace, the U.S. role during the ceasefire was a bitter disappointment. At least for the time being, U.S. policy appeared to have strengthened the hands of those on both sides who argued that military power was the only way to resolve the Arab-Israeli conflict.

Chapter Four

The United States in Lebanon September 1982-April 1983

*T*he United States role in Lebanon, from the time of the massacres at Sabra and Shatila in September 1982 to the withdrawal of U.S. military forces and abrogation of the Israel-Lebanon agreement in February 1984, represented the biggest foreign policy failure during the first term of the Reagan administration. Yet at the beginning of September 1982 many people were cautiously optimistic that the United States could play a constructive role in Lebanon. What went wrong? What were the alternatives? What were the problems in U.S. policy and were there warnings which were ignored?

At the time of the Israeli invasion of Lebanon in June 1982 Philip Habib was on his way to the Middle East to try to preserve the ceasefire he had negotiated between Israel and the PLO in the summer of 1981. After diverting to the Versailles summit for consultation with President Reagan, Habib continued on to Jerusalem, once again to try to negotiate a ceasefire arrangement in Lebanon, but now with Israel occupying large areas of Lebanese territory.

Israeli forces did not stop after forty kilometers, but moved rapidly through southern Lebanon all the way to West Beirut, where for two months they surrounded and sporadically fought vastly outgunned, but desperate and well entrenched, Palestinian forces. Thousands of Palestinians and Lebanese were killed or wounded and there was considerable destruction in the southern and western predominantly Muslim areas of the city. Israeli casualties during the initial months of the invasion were relatively low, but the invasion became increasingly controversial in Israel nonetheless.

To Arabs the awful events in Lebanon during the summer of 1982 were a great shock and further evidence of Arab weakness. Almost all Arab leaders held the United States at least partially responsible for the Israeli invasion. However, given Israel's decided military superiority, Syrian forces agreed to an early ceasefire and several Arab states, including, prominently, Saudi Arabia, sought U.S. help in achieving a general ceasefire and the earliest possible withdrawal of Israeli forces from Lebanon. By July, with West Beirut under siege by Israeli forces in tacit alliance with Lebanese Phalangists, it was clear that significant Arab leaders, including Arafat and most of the PLO, had accepted the fact that PLO military withdrawal would be necessary to save Beirut. There were also indications by July that President Reagan was prepared to commit a small contingent of U.S. Marines to oversee the PLO withdrawal and help restore order in Beirut.[1]

The Multinational Force

As Ambassador Habib's mediation efforts progressed, it became clear that a U.S.-led multinational force would play a key role in implementing whatever agreeement was reached. On August 20, 1982 President Reagan announced the agreement negotiated by Philip Habib for the withdrawal of PLO forces and the end of the Israeli siege of West Beirut.

After offering high praise for the role of Ambassador Habib in carrying out the negotiations "in the most arduous circumstances," and emphasizing that success of the agreement would "require meticulous adherence to the ceasefire," the president explained the role of the U.S.-led multinational force:

> Our purpose will be to assist the Lebanese Armed Forces in carrying out their responsibility for insuring the departure of PLO leaders, offices and combatants in Beirut from Lebanese territory under safe and orderly conditions. The presence of U.S. forces also will facilitate the restoration of the sovereignty and authority of the Lebanese Government over the Beirut area. In no case will our troops stay longer than 30 days.[2]

In the published Schedule of Departures, the U.S. Department of State announced that the tentative plan was for the first purpose of the multinational force role to be accomplished during the days August 21-September 3, while the second purpose, i.e., helping "to insure good, and lasting security throughout the (Beirut) area," would be achieved in the seventeen day period September 4-21. The announced schedule called for the multinational force to leave Lebanon between September 21 and 26.

In fact, the U.S. Marines left Beirut on September 10, immediately after the PLO evacuation was complete and sixteen days before their mandate expired. On September 14 Bashir Gemayel, who had been elected president by the parliament amidst the crisis created by the Israeli invasion, was assassinated along with key aides in a large bomb explosion at the Phalange party headquarters in East Beirut. As the strong head of the Phalangist Lebanese forces, Bashir Gemayel was viewed by many Lebanese as Israel's proxy, although after his election tensions had developed between him and Israeli Likud leaders, especially Defense Minister Sharon.

In response to the assassination of Bashir Gemayel, Israeli forces moved into West Beirut and surrounded the Palestinian refugee camps, Sabra and Shatila, in clear violation of the ceasefire agreement worked out by Habib. A day later Lebanese Christian militias were observed with Israeli troops in Beirut's southern suburbs near the refugee camps. On September 18 reports circulated about massacres of Palestinian and Lebanese civilians in the two camps. On September 19 reporters who visited the camps confirmed that hundreds of civilians had been massacred at Sabra and Shatila.

During the complex and difficult negotiations leading to the Beirut agreement, Yasser Arafat and other PLO leaders had stressed their concern for the safety of Palestinian civilians, especially those in the camps, who would be left behind after the PLO military forces withdrew. A guarantee of the safety of Palestinian civilians was one of several conditions the PLO had sought to achieve as part of the negotiations. Other conditions put forward by the PLO related to the prospect that the Beirut agreement could become a step toward political negotiations to resolve the Palestinian-Israeli conflict.[3] This latter emphasis also had been reflected at the time in a Franco-Egyptian initiative in the U.N. Security Council to promote peace negotiations, an initiative rejected by the United States.

The Israeli government of Prime Minister Begin opposed making any concessions to the PLO in exchange for PLO military withdrawal from Lebanon. Indeed, Defense Minister Sharon continued to press Begin for permission to escalate military pressure on the PLO in Beirut, including all-out invasion of the city. Israeli public opinion, however, was increasingly divided over the invasion and even more so over the possibility of an assault on Beirut. A July 1 poll in Tel Aviv reported that one-third of the Israeli respondents had serious doubts about the rightness of the invasion once it went beyond the initial forty kilometer zone, viewed as essential for protecting northern Israel from rocket attacks. Forty-eight percent of the Israelis polled opposed an assault on Beirut.[4]

On June 26, only three weeks after the Israeli invasion began, twenty thousand Israelis participated in a demonstration in Tel Aviv called by the newly formed Committee Against the War in Lebanon. A week later more than fifty thousand Israelis joined a demonstration sponsored by the older and more mainstream Peace Now. As in the initial formation of the Peace Now movement after Sadat's historic visit to Jerusalem, Israeli soldiers and reservists played a key role in determining the tone and timing of Peace Now's response to events in Lebanon. For the first time during a war, there were public calls for Israeli soldiers to refuse to fight in Lebanon, and a new peace organization of soldiers, *Yesh Gevul* (There Is A Limit), was formed. Eventually, more than twenty-five hundred soldiers signed a statement saying they would refuse to go to Lebanon and most of these also said they would henceforth refuse to serve in occupied Gaza and the West Bank. Mothers and fathers of Israeli soldiers opposed to the war formed another new peace organization, calling it "Parents Against Silence."

Domestic opposition to the invasion of Lebanon served as a constraint on the Israeli government's policies and provided more opportunity for U.S. pressures in the negotiations during July and August. While the primary goal of Habib's efforts clearly had to be to avoid a bloody showdown in Beirut, many Israelis who opposed the invasion of Lebanon wished for stronger U.S. pressure on Israel to withdraw and some believed the United States could have positively used the crisis to achieve movement toward peace negotiations with the Palestinians. In contrast to these Israeli views, the Reagan administration seemed to share the view of Prime Minister Begin's government that the primary objective of the agreement was to get the PLO out of Lebanon.

In addition to guaranteeing the safety of the withdrawing PLO military forces, the United States did provide assurances for the safety of Palestinian civilians who remained behind. According to the section entitled "Safeguards" in the plan released by the State Department:

> Law-abiding Palestinian noncombatants left behind in
> Beirut, including the families of those who have departed,
> will be subject to Lebanese laws and regulations. The
> Governments of Lebanon and the United States will pro-

vide appropriate guarantees of safety in the following ways.
—The Lebanese government will provide its guarantees on
the basis of having secured assurances from armed groups
with which it has been in touch. —The United States will
provide its guarantees on the basis of assurances received
from the Government of Israel and from leadership of certain Lebanese groups with which it has been in touch.[5]

A letter from Ambassador Habib to Lebanon's Prime Minister Shafik
al Wazzan (and transmitted to Arafat) went even further in offering
U.S. guarantees based on Israeli assurances:

I would also like to assure you that the United States
government fully recognizes the importance of these
assurances from the government of Israel and that my
government will do its utmost to ensure that these assurances
are scrupulously observed.[6]

Given the weakness and the unreliability of Lebanon's government,
especially in relation to the Palestinians, it is understandable that the
PLO depended primarily on the U.S. guarantees to protect the large
numbers of Palestinians remaining in Beirut. Yasser Arafat, in turn,
assured PLO fighters, many of whom were leaving their own families
behind in the camps, that the United States had offered guarantees
for their safety. Understood in this context, it should not be surprising
that months after the massacres, Arafat still spoke with a deep sense
of bitterness about these events, declaring that "the United States lost
its honor at Sabra and Shatila."[7] Nor is it surprising that several of the
terrorist attacks since 1982 have been carried out by young Palestinians
whose families were massacred in Sabra or Shatila.

It is impossible to know for certain what would have happened in
Beirut if the U.S.-led multinational force had not been withdrawn early.
The decision to withdraw early was not a response to a Lebanese government request that it be withdrawn. In fact, Lebanese Prime Minister
Shafik al Wazzan privately and publicly pleaded that it not withdraw.
A number of Lebanese leaders, including the prime minister, expressed fears that there would be a new outbreak of violence if the multinational force left early, and they warned that more time was needed for
the new government to extend its authority over the Beirut area. The
early withdrawal reinforced the view that the Reagan administration
was primarily concerned with getting the PLO out of Lebanon.

Four days after the U.S. Marines pulled out on September 14—the
day I arrived for my first visit to Beirut—President Bashir Gemayel was
assassinated in a bomb explosion which could be heard throughout the

city. Most people seemed shocked and afraid of what might happen
next but the city remained calm. There were no outbreaks of fighting.
However, early on the morning of September 15, Israeli forces invaded
West Beirut. Planes dove at the city. Artillery, rocket and automatic
weapon fire could be heard. The statement released by the Israeli government claimed that the move into West Beirut was to control and prevent any further outbreak of violence, but reports from Beirut indicated
that there had not been any fighting after President Gemayel was
assassinated and before the Israeli forces moved.

The Israeli military action was a clear violation of the Beirut ceasefire
agreement negotiated by Ambassador Habib. U.S. reaction to the Israeli
military move into West Beirut, however, like U.S. response to the invasion of Lebanon in June, was ambiguous and weak, at best. President Reagan appeared to justify the Israeli move, saying that he
understood that the Israelis had acted ''in response to an attack by a
leftist militia.''[8] Even a day later when all reports from Beirut indicated
that there had been no attack on Israeli forces, senior State Department officials refused to criticize the movement of Israeli troops into
West Beirut. One U.S. official said, ''We're not sure yet how to play
it. It's hard to tell right now whether the Israeli presence is useful or
not—whether their being there (in West Beirut) for a few days will help
to keep the peace or whether it will aggravate tensions.''[9] This was the
same day that Israeli forces allowed Lebanese Phalange militia to enter
the Sabra and Shatila refugee camps and the massacres began.

When Defense Minister Sharon informed the Israeli cabinet that the
Phalangists were going into the camps, Deputy Prime Minister David
Levy raised a question about the danger of a massacre. Sharon or one
of the Israeli generals who was present reportedly responded that the
Phalangist commanders had been told firmly not to kill civilians.[10]
Rumors of massacres occurring in the camps began to spread in Beirut
on Thursday. U.S. officials in Washington reponded very slowly or not
at all to the rumors. Even when U.S. intelligence agencies intercepted
a cable on Thursday night from Israeli military headquarters in Beirut
to staff headquarters in Tel Aviv reporting that three hundred ''terrorists and civilians'' had been killed by Phalangist militia in the camps,
the United States failed to take any decisive action.[11] Three days later
when reporters visited the camps and confirmed that hundreds of people
had been massacred, everyone expressed shock.

Israeli popular reaction to the massacres at Sabra and Shatila was
spontaneous and strong. There were immediate calls in Israel for the
resignation of the government and widespread support for a thorough

independent investigation. A few days after the massacres became known, Israeli Energy Minister Yitzhak Berman of the Liberal Party resigned because Prime Minister Begin delayed authorizing an investigation. On September 25, four hundred thousand Israelis (approximately ten percent of the population of Israel) demonstrated in Tel Aviv to denounce the massacres and demand an investigation. Several speakers at the rally also denounced the invasion and called for the resignation of the government.

On Tuesday, September 28, Prime Minister Begin yielded to the heavy pressure and agreed to authorize a full-scale independent investigation. The Kahan Commission, named after Yitzhak Kahan, the chief justice of the Supreme Court who chaired the commission, issued its Final Report on February 8, 1983. The report detailed responsibility of major Israeli leaders, including Ariel Sharon, for the massacres committed by Lebanese Phalangists in Sabra and Shatila. Ariel Sharon, minister of defense, General Rafael Eitan, the Israeli chief of staff, and several other officials were forced to resign their posts, although Prime Minister Begin soon brought Sharon back into the government as minister of industry.

The Kahan Commission report, not suprisingly, was the focus of considerable attention and debate in Israel. According to a report in the *Jerusalem Post*, a majority of Israelis polled thought the Kahan Commission's conclusions were too harsh.[12] Many other Israelis criticized the investigation and the conclusions for not going far enough. Whatever judgment one makes about the Kahan Commission, a question people in the United States should ask is why there was almost no debate and no investigation about U.S. responsibility in events leading to the massacres at Sabra and Shatila. After all, it was on the basis of U.S. guarantees for the safety of Palestinian civilians that the PLO had agreed to withdraw its military forces from Beirut.

"Shatila and Sabra," a *Washington Post* editorial published several days after the massacres, raised several issues which deserved investigation and public debate in the United States. Why was the Reagan administration, as well as much of the U.S. media, so slow to respond to the dangers of the Israeli move into West Beirut? It was precisely in response to PLO fears of such a development that the United States had offered guarantees for the safety of Palestinian civilians remaining behind in the city. Why did President Reagan say the Israeli operation was in response to a leftist militia attack when none had been reported? Was it a mistake for the multinational force to be withdrawn early, before its mandated time had expired? Why didn't the multinational force stay to help restore order in Beirut as called for in its mandate and as as several Lebanese leaders, including Prime Minister Wazzan, pleaded for it to do? As the editorial concluded, these issues are "part of the somber picture that must be contemplated as the dead of Shatila and Sabra are mourned." [13] It was much easier for Americans to put all the blame on Israel, or on Israelis and Lebanese, than to face these hard questions about the responsibility of their own government.

Following events at Sabra and Shatila, the multinational force returned to Beirut. Before turning to this second phase of U.S. military involvement in Lebanon, however, it is useful to look at least briefly at an important question which received almost no attention in the United States.

Was There An Alternative?

The obvious alternative to the U.S.-led multinational force in Lebanon was a United Nations peacekeeping mission, operating under the authority of the U.N. Security Council. United Nations forces (UNIFIL) had been in southern Lebanon since 1978, with a mandate similar to that of the multinational force, i.e., to monitor the ceasefire and help restore Lebanese sovereignty. While the idea of sending a U.N. force to the Beirut area was raised on several occasions during the summer and again in the fall of 1982, it never got very far. The attitudes of most U.S. leaders toward a role for the United Nations ranged from apparent lack of interest to explicit opposition.

Even in the period after the massacres at Sabra and Shatila, when the United States was wary of returning the marines to Beirut, Senator Christopher J. Dodd of Connecticut was practically alone in suggesting that the United States try to arrange for the replacement of the marines by a United Nations peacekeeping force. There was considerable concern and debate in the U.S. Congress about possible dangers to the marines and implications for the War Powers Act if the U.S.-led multinational force were returned to Lebanon. Despite these concerns, there was no serious consideration among U.S. policymakers of actively pursuing the alternative of a U.N. force.

The dangers of a U.S.-led military force in Lebanon were clear to most knowledgeable observers. First, it was relatively easy to send the marines into Lebanon, but it would be more complicated and difficult to pull them out. Second, the ambiguity in the mission of the multinational force was a major cause of concern, to many U.S. military commanders among others. Third, the Soviet Union, as Syria's superpower supporter, was bound to view the presence of U.S. military forces as a challenge which it could not ignore. Fourth, the predominant role of the United States in the region and its partisan relationship with Israel would tend to make U.S. forces a "favorite target" of many groups. Fifth, if U.S. forces got into trouble in Lebanon, there might be a tendency in U.S. public opinion to blame Israel for having created the situation in which U.S. Marines could be killed.

The advantages of a United Nations peacekeeping force were equally clear. There already was a U.N. force in Lebanon. Expanding the mandate and size of this force to cope with the situation in 1982 would have required very difficult negotiations among the parties concerned, including both superpowers. However, supporters of the U.N. peacekeeping idea argued at the time that it was precisely such negotiations that would be essential to providing a basis for effective peacekeeping in Lebanon. In this view, a peacekeeping force which was supported by both superpowers, as well as accepted by the major regional actors, would have had more of a chance to be successful than a U.S.-led force. A U.N. force would likely have had a more carefully defined mandate with less ambiguity, in part as result of the negotiations required to establish it. This would have made it less vulnerable and much less likely to be drawn into a partisan role than a U.S.-sponsored force. Even from a more pessimistic viewpoint, it was argued that a U.N. force was preferred in the sense that its failure would not jeopardize U.S. credibility. Taking a more optimistic and longer range view, support for the idea of an expanded United Nations peacekeeping role in Lebanon could have helped to delegitimize military intervention and enhance the role of world law. Tragically, none of these arguments carried much weight with most U.S. leaders in 1982.

United Nations response to the Israeli invasion of Lebanon in June 1982 was formulated in two Security Council resolutions, 508 and 509, supported at the time by the United States. The U.N. Security Council demanded that:

> Israel withdraw all its military forces forthwith and unconditionally to the internationally recognized boundaries of Lebanon; and that all parties to the conflict cease immediately and simultaneously all military activities within Lebanon and across the Lebanese-Israeli border.[14]

The U.N. Security Council position essentially represented a call to return to the situation of the ceasefire agreement which had been negotiated by Ambassador Habib a year earlier and which had worked for ten months. If the United Nations had been given the opportunity to develop a role in the new crisis, the Security Council position would likely have been incorporated into the framework for a peacekeeping mission.

By the end of June 1982, however, the Reagan administration clearly was no longer interested in reviving the Habib ceasefire arrangement, despite its vote earlier in June for Security Council Resolutions 508 and 509. The Israeli invasion had radically changed the situation. The Reagan administration now saw possible U.S. "gains" from the invasion and openly opposed the idea of an expanded U.N. peacekeeping role. There was practically no debate in the Congress or in the media about these issues.

On June 26 the United States vetoed a Security Council resolution calling for limited Israeli and Palestinian military withdrawal from the center of Beirut and the stationing of U.N. military observers "to supervise the ceasefire and disengagement in and around Beirut." Explaining the U.S. vote, Charles M. Lichenstein, the acting delegate, said Washington opposed the resolution because "it did not eliminate from Beirut and elsewhere the presence of armed Palestinian elements."[15] The United States thus adopted one of Sharon's goals for the invasion. On the same day, the United States voted against a non-binding resolution in the U.N. General Assembly which demanded immediate withdrawal of Israeli forces from Lebanon and asked for punitive actions to be considered if Israel did not comply. Lebanese representatives at the United Nations were reported to be "bitterly disappointed" over the U.S. position, especially the negative U.S. vote in the Security Council which blocked the insertion of a United Nations presence into Beirut.[16]

The U.S. failure to press for effective negotiations to resolve the Palestinian issue during the previous year was an important contributing factor to the eventual breakdown of the Israeli-PLO ceasefire in Lebanon. Yet during July the United States twice blocked efforts by France and Egypt to introduce a resolution in the U.N. Security Council which would have linked a ceasefire and withdrawal of Israeli and Palestinian forces from Beirut with a political framework for negotiations to resolve the Israeli-Palestinian conflict.

The Franco-Egyptian formula called for negotiations based on the substance of U.N. Security Council Resolution 242, plus the principle of the right of the Palestinian people to self-determination. This was an attempt to formulate a more balanced and comprehensive framework for negotiations than Resolution 242 by itself, which only indirectly refers to the Palestinians and only as a problem of refugees. The initiative also would have asserted a U.N. role in the Beirut crisis and in wider peace negotiations. The Reagan administration opposed both the substance of the resolution and the idea of a United Nations role. One

U.S. diplomat at the United Nations, using rather undiplomatic language, described the initiative by Egypt and France as "confusing garbage." When it surfaced again in late July, U.S. Ambassador Jeane J. Kirkpatrick rejected the initiative as a "one-sided appeal in a two-sided conflict" and warned that it could complicate Ambassador Habib's mediation efforts, which the United States clearly viewed as the best way to resolve the crisis in Lebanon.[17]

In early August, in response to escalating Israeli military pressure on West Beirut, there were new moves to assert a U.N. peacekeeping role. On August 1 the Security Council unanimously demanded a ceasefire and again asked for U.N. military observers to be sent to Beirut to insure that the ceasefire was maintained.[18] The government of Lebanon and the PLO agreed to implement the plan. The Israeli government refused, indicating that it preferred U.S. observers and that it feared the presence of U.N. observers might become the basis for an expanded U.N. role.

Following increased Israeli bombing of Beirut on August 11, the Security Council renewed its demand that U.N. observers move into the city to monitor the ceasefire. While the United States voted in favor of these resolutions in the Security Council, it showed little interest in them and exerted no pressure on the Israeli government to accept them. U.S. officials made it clear that the U.S. priority was Ambassador Habib's mediation efforts and that the peacekeeping forces envisioned in these talks would be organized by the United States, not by the United Nations. It was clear by this time that, while the Reagan administration might vote for certain resolutions calling for an enlarged U.N. role, it was fundamentally committed to a process which would keep the United States in the diplomatic driver's seat.

The next opportunity to support an expanded U.N. role in Lebanon came in September after the assassination of President-Elect Bashir Gemayel. On September 17 the U.N. Security Council unanimously condemned the Israeli incursion into West Beirut and demanded "an immediate return to the positions occupied by Israel before September 15 (i.e., the Habib-negotiated Beirut agreement), as a first step towards full implementation of Security Council resolutions." The council also renewed its call for additional U.N. observers to be sent to Beirut to supplement the ten already there. The Israeli government rejected the resolutions. The United States, once again, voted for the resolutions, but showed no serious interest in them.

On the night of September 18, as news came out about the massacres in Sabra and Shatila, the U.N. Security Council convened in an urgently called closed-door session to consider what the United Nations should do. The idea of an expanded U. N. peacekeeping mission in Lebanon was raised again, this time by Jordan, which proposed sending a force of five thousand. Arab states and the Soviet Union, in general, expressed support for the idea, while Israel and the United States opposed it. In fact, U.S. officials indicated that, if an actual resolution was introduced calling for a U.N. peacekeeping force to go to Beirut, the United States would veto it. At a time when the United States was actively considering sending U.S. Marines back into Lebanon, U.S. officials rather disingenuously cautioned other nations against risking their soldiers in such a mission. In an apparently contradictory argument, U.S. officials also maintained at the time that a U.N. force was not needed because "the Lebanese army would soon be able to assume responsibility for maintaining order."[19] The Reagan administration showed no more interest in a possible expanded U.N. role in Lebanon after Sabra and Shatila than it did before.

There is a tendency, among both defenders and critics of U.S. policy, to explain U.S. opposition to the idea of a U.N. peacekeeping role in Lebanon as a response to or a reflection of Israeli policy. In one version of this explanation, U.S. policymakers, after taking account of adamant Israeli government opposition, opposed a U.N. role on the grounds that it was unrealistic. In another and cruder version, U.S. policy toward a possible U.N. role was simply a reflection of Israeli policy and the influence of the "Israeli lobby" in the United States. While it is true that the Israeli government was strongly opposed to an expanded U.N. role and, obviously, this had some influence on the thinking of U.S. policymakers, it is a mistake to view this factor as determinative. Both of these explanations fail to take account of reasons for U.S. opposition to a U.N. role which are deeply ingrained in U.S. foreign policy worldwide; these were fundamentally unrelated to Israeli interests or influence. They also fail to take sufficient account of the sharp divisions of opinion within Israel and among strong U.S. supporters of Israel over the invasion of Lebanon. These divisions created a context in which the Reagan administration politically had a wider range of policy options than is generally assumed.

U.S. opposition to seriously exploring the possibility of an expanded U.N. role in Lebanon in 1982 reflected the deep biases in the Reagan administration against the United Nations and against any cooperation with the Soviet Union. The U.S. position also reflected the view within the Reagan adminstration that the Israeli invasion had created an opportunity for the United States to gain unilateral advantage in Lebanon and in the region. Given the hostility and suspicion of the Reagan administration toward the United Nations, it was not surprising that the United States showed little interest in various initiatives in the Security Council to develop an expanded U.N. role. The idea of seeking a possible basis for cooperation with the Soviet Union in relation to Lebanon directly contradicted a major policy goal of the Reagan administration, i.e., to create a strategic consensus in the Middle East *against* the Soviet Union. Moreover, the U.S. preference for sending the marines to Lebanon, rather than supporting a U.N. peacekeeping force, also conformed to President Reagan's commitment to overcome the "Vietnam syndrome" in U.S. foreign policy, in part by taking advantage of opportunities to reassert U.S. military power around the world.

In relation to developments in Lebanon, as most Reagan administration officials saw it, the Israeli invasion offered several important gains for U.S. policy and now it was up to the United States to consolidate and build upon these gains. According to this view, Syria, the Soviet Union's surrogate in the Middle East, suffered a "bloody nose" from the invasion, weakening its own and the Soviet position in the region; the PLO's military defeat left it weakened and more likely to have to accommodate to a U.S.-mediated peace settlement with Israel; furthermore, the invasion had changed the internal balance of power in Lebanon in a way that would allow pro-western Christian forces to maintain political dominance. Israel had dirtied its hands by the invasion and by its role at Sabra and Shatila. The United States, however, had clean hands and a responsibility to act. A U.S.-led multinational force in Lebanon combined with the Reagan initiative for peace in the Middle East could consolidate these favorable developments. From this point of view, an expanded role for the United Nations in Lebanon might complicate or even reverse some of these gains. Given its ideological orientation and policy goals, the Reagan administration did not require pressure from Israel to appreciate the advantages of sending the U.S. Marines into Lebanon rather than supporting an expanded role for the United Nations.

The Reagan administration's preference for a U.S.-led multinational force and U.S.-mediated negotiations in Lebanon was reinforced by a broad consensus in Washington policymaking circles that this was "America's moment in the Middle East." Henry Kissinger wrote that the war in Lebanon had created a "window of opportunity" for the United States in Lebanon and in the Middle East region as a whole.[20] A senior State Department spokesman boasted at the time, "We have moved into the diplomatic driver's seat."[21]

This view was not limited to officials of the Reagan administration. William Quandt, who was National Security Council advisor on the Middle East to former President Carter and was frequently critical of Reagan administration policies, said, "A lot of things are in flux and we are in a position to dominate the diplomatic scene."[22] Eighteen months later, after the forced withdrawal of U.S. Marines from Lebanon and the failure of the Reagan initiative, this initial optimism about the United States role appeared extremely unrealistic. To be fair, however, in October 1982 many well-informed observers in the Middle East shared the belief that the United States could play an important and constructive role for peace. Perhaps, if U.S. policy had been different, it could have.

Israelis were deeply divided over the invasion of Lebanon. They also were divided over the U.S. response to the invasion. These divisions meant that a different U.S. policy, i.e., one more firmly opposed to the invasion and less willing to send U.S. military forces, could probably have found support within Israel. While then Israeli Defense Minister Sharon and other Likud leaders were generally pleased by U.S. acquiescence and increasing identification with the goals of the invasion during the summer of 1982, major Israeli opposition leaders were troubled. Obviously, no Israeli leader favored a continued PLO military presence in Lebanon and none was sorry to see Syria suffer a military setback, even if it was only temporary. But, while Sharon and many Likud colleagues believed that Israel was now in a position essentially to dictate the terms of a peace settlement with the Beirut government in Lebanon and with Palestinians in the West Bank and Gaza, other Israeli leaders feared that these ideas represented short-term illusions of military victory and that in the longer run Israel's invasion of Lebanon would prove disastrous. Israeli leaders, including some within the Labor Party, who held this view were troubled by the extent to which the Reagan administration appeared to share Sharon's illusions about Lebanon and by the fact that U.S. policy was reinforcing, rather than challenging, the policies of Prime Minister Begin's government.

It is true that no prominent Israeli leader openly favored an expanded U.N. peacekeeping role in Lebanon at the time, although some were open to the idea later. It is not clear, however, what the outcome would have been if the United States had chosen to support this alternative, given the divisions among Israelis over their government's policies. What is clear is that the United States did not seriously oppose the Israeli invasion, increasingly saw the crisis in Lebanon as an opportunity to expand its own influence in the region and preferred a U.S.-led rather than a U.N. peacekeeping role. All of these emphases in U.S. policies tended to undermine Israeli opposition to the invasion and occupation. Just as Sharon's policies would eventually lead to disastrous results for Israel in Lebanon, so the Reagan administration's policies would lead to a situation where over two hundred fifty marines would lose their lives and U.S. credibility in the region would be weakened.

In September 1982, after the massacres at Sabra and Shatila, the Reagan administration rejected new initiatives in the U.N. Security Council and decided to send U.S. military forces back into Lebanon. It did not take long before problems with the U.S. role in Lebanon began to appear.

Early Warning Signs

United States Marines reentered Lebanon on September 29, 1982 as part of the U.S.-led multinational force. This followed the election by the parliament of Amin Gemayel (brother of assassinated Bashir Gemayel) as president of Lebanon and the withdrawal of Israeli forces from West Beirut. Most Lebanese welcomed the return of the multinational force. The prevailing mood at the beginning of October was one of anxious hopefulness about the new government headed by Amin Gemayel and the possible helpful role of the United States.

The mandate of the U.S.-led multinational force was to help preserve the ceasefire and restore Lebanese sovereignty, initially in the Beirut area and then throughout the country as foreign forces were withdrawn. As simple and straightforward as the goals sounded, the complex realities of Lebanon made them extremely difficult to implement.

It was clear to most observers at the time that the success or failure of U.S. policy in Lebanon would be measured by progress, or lack of it, toward three interrelated conditions. *The first condition, restoration of Lebanese sovereignty*, depended not only on rebuilding an effective Lebanese army, but even more fundamentally on the ability of the new government in Beirut to win the confidence and loyalty of Lebanon's diverse communities. The challenges to achieving this goal were complex and difficult. The Lebanese army had to reassert control in Beirut, replacing both the Israeli forces which had controlled the area since June and a variety of local Lebanese militia. Lebanon's confessional system, which since 1948 assured dominance by Maronite Christians, had to give way to growing demographic and political pressures from the Muslim majority. An important test for the new government would be what signals it sent to Lebanon's Shiite Muslims, who benefitted least from the current division of political and economic power and who proportionately suffered most from the PLO-Israeli war in southern

Lebanon. Policies were needed to begin to close the growing gap between the rich and poor, a disproportionate number of whom were Shiites. Especially after the massacres at Sabra and Shatila, Palestinians in Lebanon needed tangible assurances of their security.

Paying lip-service to these objectives, as most Lebanese officials did at the time, was a lot easier than implementing policies to achieve them. An early warning sign of problems in the role of the United States was that no one seemed very clear exactly what the U.S. commitment was to any of these objectives, although it seemed that the Reagan administration put priority on rebuilding the Lebanese army.

Restoring Lebanese sovereignty was interrelated with a *a second condition, the withdrawal of foreign military forces*, including those of Israel, Syria and the PLO. Listening to what Israeli and Syrian leaders were saying about this issue should have served warning of just how daunting a challenge this goal would be. On the one hand, leaders of both Syria and Israel said that they had no territorial ambitions in Lebanon and that they were prepared to withdraw their military forces. However, the Syrian government, invoking U.N. Security Council Resolutions 508 and 509 (which the United States had voted to support), consistently demanded that, before Syria would withdraw, Israel must withdraw completely without achieving any concessions from its invasion. In contrast, the Israeli government sought a peace agreement with Lebanon or, at least, new security guarantees and steps toward normal relations, as well as simultaneous withdrawal of Syrian and PLO forces as conditions for the withdrawal of Israeli forces. For its part, the PLO, which still had several thousand troops in northern Lebanon, was unlikely to agree to any further withdrawals without substantial progress toward a political settlement of the Palestinian issue.

The U.S. strategy was to pursue an agreement between Israel and Lebanon for withdrawal of Israeli forces and then to depend on Lebanese and Saudi pressure on Syria and the PLO to withdraw. The optimism of U.S. leaders that this strategy could work apparently was based on the view that Israel and the dominant Christian elements in Lebanon favored it and, after the Israeli invasion, Syria and the PLO were too weak to oppose it.

The success of U.S. involvment in Lebanon also would be influenced by *a third condition, progress toward a wider peace process aimed at resolving the Palestinian issue and achieving a comprehensive peace*. President Reagan's September 1 address to the nation outlined U.S. views on these issues and appeared to signal a new high-level U.S. commitment to work for peace in the Middle East. Progress toward a wider peace process would relieve pressures that the Arab-Israeli-Palestinian conflict imposed on Lebanon, encouraging both internal reconciliation and withdrawal of foreign military forces. U.S. leaders were optimistic about the chances for the Reagan initiative, although there was ample evidence for a more sober view of what was possible.[23]

As early as October-December 1982, there were important warning signs about major problems with the U.S. role in Lebanon. On several occasions during this period, the Reagan administration failed to press the government of Amin Gemayel to take steps that would have encouraged greater confidence in the new government among Palestinians and Lebanon's Muslim majority. When President Gemayel visited the United States in October, senior U.S. embassy officials in Beirut counselled the Reagan administration on the urgency of pressing Gemayel to take action against the role of the Phalange militia for the Sabra and Shatila massacres, but this advice was not followed in Washington.[24]

During October, the Reagan administration acquiesced as the Lebanese army, which the United States had taken major responsibility to support and train, moved into predominantly Muslim West Beirut and disarmed local leftist and Muslim militia, while it made no moves to disarm or replace Christian militia in East Beirut or anywhere else.[25] Washington also remained silent when President Amin Gemayel, despite warnings by Lebanese Muslim and some Lebanese Christian leaders, ordered army bulldozers to destroy shantytowns in Beirut—shantytowns inhabited primarily by poor Shiite villagers who had fled from southern Lebanon because of the war. A *New York Times* report by Thomas L. Friedman warned that unless the grievances of the Shiites were addressed they would "represent an explosive problem for the new government."[26] Neither the Gemayel government nor the Reagan administration appeared to take the warning seriously.

The prevailing view in Washington during this period was that "if Lebanon was to have stability, it would be with Christian military dominance, with most Muslims preferring that to a resumption of civil war."[27] In light of subsequent events, and even in light of warnings at the time, this U.S. view was remarkably shortsighted and unrealistic.

By the end of December 1982, the anxieties of Beirut's Shiite and Sunni Muslim communities had already been exacerbated to the point that religious leaders of both communities joined in calling for a large march on the eve of the Prophet Mohammed's birthday.[28] Banners and placards carried by the marchers asserted that they, too, were citizens and an integral part of Lebanon. Many of the marchers protested what they viewed as harassment of Muslims by the Gemayel government and demanded that all militia, including the militia of Gemayel's own Phalange Party, be disarmed. Muslims expressed fears of what might happen in talks, just then beginning, between Lebanon and Israel. Specifically, they feared that the Gemayel government might agree to incorporate Phalange militia, or the militia of Saad Haddad in southern Lebanon, into the Lebanese army, thereby seeking to perpetuate Christian domination of Lebanon. Rather than use the occasion of this march called by religious leaders to impress upon Gemayel the need for steps to reassure the Muslim communities, the United States apparently did nothing.

Fighting in the Shouf, a mixed Christian and Druze area, east and south of Beirut, significantly increased intercommunal tensions. Lebanese Christian forces had entered several predominantly Druze villages along with invading Israeli forces and now refused to leave. Whereas President Gemayel was calling for the Lebanese army to begin moving into these areas, Druze leaders, fearing that the army would reinforce Christian control, wanted the Phalange forces disarmed or withdrawn first. A few days after the march in Beirut, Walid Jumblatt, political leader of the Druze community, accused not only the Phalange Party but also Israel of instigating sectarian warfare in the central mountains. Jumblatt's charge was based, in part, on the fact that it was Israeli forces which had allowed the Phalange militia to enter the area several months earlier.

Nabih Berri, leader of Amal, the largest Lebanese Shiite political organization, declared, "The only way to stop the fighting in the mountains is to collect all arms from all parties without exception."[29] Berri offered the same advice in many meetings with western diplomats in Beirut. Obviously, it was very difficult for Amin Gemayel to decide to disarm the Phalange, since it meant challenging his own power base. However, even in January 1983 it was becoming clear that, in the long run, the United States was compounding Lebanon's problems and its own by not pressing harder for more evenhanded policies of the kind Berri demanded.

Finally, on February 18 the Lebanese army did deploy in East Beirut, an event hailed by U.S. officials as an important sign of progress. A day earlier, however, Israeli forces had allowed the Israeli-backed Lebanese Christian militia of Saad Haddad to expand the area of its activity by deploying as far north as Sidon. On the same day, Israeli officials claimed that the Gemayel government already had agreed to incorporate Major Haddad's forces into the Lebanese army. Despite a strong denial of the Israeli claim by Elie Salem, Lebanon's foreign minister, these developments fueled growing Muslim fears about the future outcome of the Lebanese-Israeli negotiations. The Reagan administration did nothing to allay these fears.

Negotiations between Israel and Lebanon were an even more important arena for judging how the U.S. role in Lebanon was going, in part because the United States itself had said that it viewed progress toward Israeli withdrawal as the key to the rest of U.S. strategy. After four months, the United States had little to show for its efforts. In dramatic constrast to the target date of January 1, by which U.S. officials earlier had predicted foreign forces might be out of Lebanon,[30] Israeli and Lebanese negotiators did not even hold their first session until December 28.

Initially, the talks had been delayed because Lebanon rejected Israel's demand to hold some of the sessions in Jerusalem. (After the 1967 war Israel proclaimed united Jerusalem as its capital, but few nations recognize this claim.) Then the start of talks was delayed for many weeks over issues related to the content and structure of the agenda. Israeli government leaders wanted a Lebanese commitment to negotiate "normalization of relations," while Lebanese leaders wanted to focus on the withdrawal of Israeli troops. The U.S. compromise agenda, as mediated by Philip Habib, did not resolve this issue, but did provide a way for the talks to start. The agenda specified the following five issues to be negotiated concurrently by subcommittees:

> Termination of the state of war; security arrangements; framework for mutual relations, including issues such as liaison, ending hostile propaganda, the movement of goods, products and persons, commmunications, etc; program of complete withdrawals, conditions for Israeli withdrawal, within the context of the evacuation of all foreign forces; (and) possible guarantees.[31]

The compromise agenda reflected the balance of power in Lebanon at the time, as well as the U.S. orientation toward the negotiations. This compromise at least got talks started; it allowed Israeli government leaders to claim signficant potential gains from the invasion and Lebanese leaders to claim they had not conceded a single gain to Israel.

Despite agreement on the agenda, the Israeli and Lebanese governments were still far apart on what they wanted from the talks. While Beirut and Washington officials expressed optimism—in late December, President Reagan told King Hussein that Israeli forces would be out of Lebanon by March—almost no one else believed that an agreement was likely to be reached soon. The Israeli and Syrian positions were even further apart. Israel was still insisting on a military role in southern Lebanon, some steps toward normal relations and simultaneous Syrian withdrawal as conditions for its withdrawal. Syria, for its part, continued to insist that Israel withdraw without gaining any concessions, basing its demand on the U.N. Security Council position which called for Israeli forces to be withdrawn "forthwith and unconditionally."

At least implicitly abandoning its earlier support for the U.N. Security Council position, the U.S. position, as reflected in the compromise agenda, now supported Israel's achieving some version of its conditions for withdrawal. Specifically, the United States believed that Israel's withdrawal from Lebanon should take place "in the context of the evacuation of all foreign forces," clearly implying that Israeli withdrawal was conditional on Syrian and PLO withdrawal. Putting aside the differences in the political and legal bases on which the military forces of Israel, Syria and the PLO were in Lebanon, on a pragmatic level, the U.S. approach, in effect, gave Syria and the PLO crucial roles in the implementation of any agreement between Israel and Lebanon, even though neither Syria nor the PLO were included in the negotiations. Nevertheless, as negotiations proceeded, the United States appeared to take it for granted that Syria would acquiesce in whatever agreement Israel and Lebanon achieved.

Even after the Israel-Lebanon negotiations got started, during the first four months, i.e., January-April 1983, there was very little progress. On at least three specific occasions compromise formulas presented by the United States were rejected by the Israeli government.[32] Speculation increased that while President Gemayel needed a breakthrough as soon as possible to assure the Lebanese that his government could achieve Israeli withdrawal, Prime Minister Begin was in no hurry to conclude the talks. By late January, Israeli government responsibility for the lack of progress in the talks led to reports of a possible open confrontation between the Reagan administration and Begin's government. However, President Reagan clearly aimed to avoid such a confrontation and publicly pledged not to use pressure on Israel to speed up the talks.[33]

There were political risks in a U.S. confrontation with Israel, but there also were risks in not achieving Israeli withdrawal. As the talks dragged on, Lebanese support for the government of Amin Gemayel was eroding. Syria's position was becoming stronger, both politically as a result of Gemayel's problems and militarily as a result of substantial assistance from the Soviet Union. King Hussein and PLO leaders negotiating a possible positive response to the Reagan initiative were increasingly discouraged by the failure of the United States to achieve Israeli withdrawal from Lebanon as well as its failure to achieve a freeze on new Israeli settlements in the West Bank. Within Israel, the U.S. failure to press harder for Israeli withdrawal from Lebanon tended to strengthen the hands of harder-line Israeli leaders and undermine Israeli peace forces and the mainstream Labor opposition. There was open speculation in Israel and in Washington that a strong motivation for Begin's resistance to reaching agreement on Lebanon was to hurt chances of a breakthrough on the Reagan initiative, which the Likud government adamantly opposed.[34] By mid-March, the combination of these factors and the apparent lack of U.S. resolve led some analysts to question how much of a commitment the Reagan administration actually had to getting Israel out of Lebanon or achieving progress on its own initiative for peace.[35]

There was ample evidence in Israel, including public opinion polls and statements by Labor Party leaders, as well as large peace demonstrations, that Israelis were deeply divided over the invasion and occupation of Lebanon. As the talks between Israel and Lebanon stalled and the number of attacks on Israeli forces in Lebanon increased, Israeli doubts about the invasion deepened, even among many Likud supporters.[36] Within a month after the invasion began there were reports of unprecedented discontent and dissent among Israeli soldiers. By January 1983, Hirsch Goodman, military correspondent of the *Jerusalem Post*, reported that the discontent among Israeli soldiers in Lebanon was very high. Even within the Likud cabinet, Deputy Prime Minister David Levy and Communications Minister Mordecai Zippori were demanding a cabinet debate on whether Israeli policy in Lebanon was still appropriate.[37]

Former Prime Minister and Labor Party leader Yitzhak Rabin publicly argued that trying to achieve a formal peace agreement with Lebanon was "a mistake and an illusion" and urged the government to concentrate on achieving "Israel's minimum security needs in the north."[38] Ironically, while many Israeli experts on Lebanon and an increasing number of Israelis were becoming more critical of the occupation and becoming convinced that Israel ought to withdraw from Lebanon on the sole condition of security for its northern border, the United States had adopted several of Sharon's illusory goals for what the Israeli invasion could achieve. The Reagan administration apparently believed that Maronite Christian dominance in Lebanon could be preserved, that Syrian influence could be significantly reduced and that the United

States could become Lebanon's new "protector." Indeed, ideas about greatly increased U.S. influence in the area appeared to be much more important to the Reagan administration than Israeli opinion or interests.[39] The so-called "gains" for the United States turned out to be more illusion than reality.

Two events during April 1983 served as dramatic new warnings of the costs and the dangers of U.S. policy in Lebanon. On April 10 King Hussein announced that his talks with Yasser Arafat had failed and that he would not come forward for negotiations based on the Reagan initiative. Declining U.S. credibility, as a result of U.S. failure to achieve Israeli withdrawal from Lebanon or a freeze on new Israeli settlements, was clearly an important factor in why the PLO and Jordan finally were not able to agree on a positive joint response to the Reagan initiative.[40] On April 18 a bomb exploded at the U.S. Embassy in Beirut, killing thirty-nine people and wounding 120. The bombing, allegedly by a splinter Shiite group based in the Syrian-controlled Bekaa Valley, signalled the growing dangers for the United States in Lebanon as the U.S. role was increasingly perceived as being aligned with Christian Phalange forces against Lebanon's Muslim majority.[41]

Chapter Five

The Agreement That Didn't Work
May 1983-February 1984

Following King Hussein's announcement that he would not join negotiations based on the Reagan initiative, the focus of U.S. Middle East diplomacy shifted back to negotiations between Israel and Lebanon. There were still serious disagreements on issues related to the nature of security arrangements in southern Lebanon and the future status of relations between Israel and Lebanon. Even if these issues could be resolved, the chances of a positive Syrian response to a compromise agreement of the kind which seemed possible appeared problematic at best. U.S. officials remained "optimistic," just as they had about King Hussein until April 10, but most other observers were far more cautious or pessimistic.[1]

On April 22 the *New York Times* reported that Secretary of State Shultz would travel to the Middle East to press for a breakthrough in the Israeli-Lebanese negotiations and to seek support for the Reagan initiative. There were at least three major challenges to the Shultz mission.[2] The talks between Israel and Lebanon appeared deadlocked, with each side charging that the other was hardening its negotiating position. Syria, militarily stronger thanks to major Soviet assistance[3] and politically more self-assured as a result of Gemayel's problems and King Hussein's announcement, was showing no signs of softening its position on Israeli withdrawal. Furthermore, many Arab leaders, particularly in Egypt, Jordan and Saudi Arabia, on whom the Reagan administra-

tion was depending for support of a possible agreement between
Lebanon and Israel, were discouraged by the lack of effective U.S.
diplomacy during the preceding six months. U.S.credibility among Arab
leaders had significantly declined since the time when Ambassador
Habib successfully negotiated the Beirut agreement and President
Reagan had announced a new U.S. initiative for peace.[4]

The Shultz mission reflected the U.S. tendency to take Syria for
granted. Damascus was not even on the secretary of state's itinerary and
Ambassador Habib had not been there for several months. After talks
in Jerusalem and Beirut, where both Israeli and Lebanese leaders encouraged him to visit Syria, Shultz announced that he was prepared
to go to Damascus, but only when there had been sufficient "progress"
toward an agreement. Shultz explained that he did not want to give
Syria an opportunity "to raise objections that might imperil putting
the pact into effect."[5] However, to the extent that the United States
viewed Israeli withdrawal as conditional on Syrian withdrawal, it seemed
rather shortsighted for Shultz not to have given higher priority to visiting
Damascus. The U.S. Embassy in Damascus was well informed about
Syria's views and reported regularly to Washington, but apparently these
reports were not taken seriously by the Reagan administration. The
United States tended to ignore what Syria viewed as its vital interests
in Lebanon and in the region as a whole. The ultimate outcome of
Shultz' efforts demonstrated the dangers of this approach.

At the time of the Shultz trip, Syrian officials were pessimistic that
the United States was seeking the kind of agreement which Syria could
accept. In the view of Mohammed Heydar, a senior Syrian foreign affairs analyst, Secretary of State Shultz had come to the Middle East with
two alternate plans:

> The first plan is to create enough international support for
> a Lebanon-Israel agreement and enough disunity among
> Arab states that Syria would be forced to accept it. If this
> does not work, the United States will seek to impose the
> agreement by military force.

Heydar seemed confident that neither U.S. plan would work, but
he was concerned that an escalation of U.S. military action against Syria
could lead to a confrontation with the Soviet Union.[6]

Most Syrian officials interviewed during this period said Syria preferred a total withdrawal of all foreign forces from Lebanon over any
form of partition arrangement, but all of them emphasized that Syria
would never accept an agreement which allowed Israel to achieve gains
in Lebanon as a result of its 1982 invasion.[7] U.S. diplomats in Syria

also believed that this was the core of Syria's position. Compared with Sharon's vision of a full peace agreement with Lebanon, Israel's gains in the agreement Shultz was working on may have appeared to Washington as modest. However, there were clear indications that Syria viewed the gains as a threat to Syrian vital interests, including security, and was unlikely to accept them. There was urgent reason, therefore, for Shultz to go to Damascus before the agreement was in its final draft form, but he did not go.

Leading Israeli experts on Syria appeared more concerned and realistic about what Syria might do than most U.S. policymakers. According to Itamar Rabinovich, director of the Shiloah Center at Tel Aviv University, taking account of Syria's interests, which Rabinovich considered essential, made "Shultz' mission much tougher."[8] Rabinovich warned that conditions surrounding Israel's negotiations with Lebanon were more like those in 1977 when Syria rejected Sadat's unilateral approach to peace with Israel than like those in 1974 when Syria accepted Kissinger's disengagement agreement. Abba Eban, former foreign minister of Israel, described U.S. policy toward Syria as "naive" and was deeply skeptical that the kind of agreement Shultz was working on could work. Moreover, Eban believed that, by giving Syria a veto over Israeli withdrawal from Lebanon, the Likud government and the Reagan admininstration were creating "a more dangerous situation for Israel."[9] These Israeli views were ignored in Washington.

During the first week in May, the intense shuttle efforts of Secretary of State Shultz between Beirut and Jerusalem led to success in getting Lebanese and Israeli government approval of a draft agreement. From the first news about the agreement, however, the big question was whether it would work. In Lebanon, reactions to the proposed agreement reflected a mixture of desperate hope and deep skepticism. It was reported that the final talks among Lebanese leaders before Beirut gave its approval to the agreement "so strained the complex amalgam of Christians, Sunni Muslims, Shiite Muslims and Druze in the government of Gemayel. . . that the Lebanese system almost stalled out from an overload."[10]

In Israel also the proposed agreement was greeted by a mixture of hope and skepticism. Most members of the ruling Likud coalition supported the agreement, although several expressed disappointment that the terms appeared to represent only slight gains for Israel, compared with Sharon's much more ambitious goals for the invasion. Sharon himself denounced the agreement for precisely this reason. Shimon Peres, leader of the Labor Alignment, criticized the agreement from the opposite direction as potentially leaving Israel in a worse situation than before the June 1982 invasion and for giving Syria a veto over Israeli withdrawal from Lebanon.[11]

Syria's reaction was unambiguously negative. On May 7 the Syrian press criticized the draft agreement in harsh terms. This was the same day Secretary of State Shultz, after stopping in Jordan to brief King Hussein, made his first visit to Damascus, where he met for four hours with President Assad. After the meeting, a Syrian government spokesman denounced Lebanon's approval of the draft agreement as "an act of submission." From Damascus, Shultz travelled to Saudi Arabia to seek Saudi help in persuading Syria to accept the agreement. The next day President Assad visited Saudi Arabia to explain Syria's views. Shultz said he was "optimistic," but there were no indications that Syria was softening its opposition to the agreement or that Saudi Arabia was prepared to exert significant pressure on Syria to do so. It seemed clear that a workable agreement would require additional difficult negotiations. Instead, the United States apparently was relying on Lebanese and other Arab pressures to convince Syria to accept the agreement. In the meantime, the United States pushed ahead with Israel and Lebanon as if they had a workable agreement.

By the time the Israel-Lebanon agreement[12] was signed on May 17, there were additional important indications that the agreement was unlikely to be implemented. On the same day the United States signed a "confidential" understanding with Israel recognizing Israel's right to respond to terrorist attacks from Lebanon despite the agreement, and recognizing that Israel could delay its withdrawal from Lebanon until Syria and the PLO pulled out their forces.[13] On May 14 the Syrian government officially rejected the agreement. Despite growing divisions within the Palestinian movement, PLO leaders universally denounced the Lebanon-Israel agreement. In Lebanon, while the Gemayel government defended the agreement and it was almost unanimously approved by the parliament, public criticism of it increased, especially as it became clear that Syria's position was firm. On May 13 Walid Jumblatt, leader of the Lebanese Druze community, denounced the agreement as jeopardizing "Lebanon's sovereignty, independence and Arab affiliation."[14]

U.S. Secretary of State Shultz did make another trip to the Middle East at the beginning of July to explore a new idea, but failed to produce any progress. Shultz attempted to get Israel to set a timetable for complete withdrawal, in response to which it was believed Syria might be willing to announce a schedule for its withdrawal. On July 1 the *New York Times* reported that Israeli Foreign Minister Yitzhak Shamir had declared that Israel continued to insist on simultaneous Israeli and Syrian withdrawal.[15] Shultz then went to Damascus with essentially nothing new to discuss and came away quite discouraged, saying that the United States and Syria "had no agreement about the agreement."[16]

During the summer and early fall of 1983 there was debate within the Reagan administration between supporters of two different views of what to do next, particularly in relation to Syria. Supporters of the first view—a minority—believed that continuing real negotiations with Syria could make an agreement possible. At least some proponents of this view believed that the United States should broaden the agenda of discussions with Syria to include not only the situation in Lebanon but also U.S. views on the future status of the Golan Heights and Syria's role in wider peace negotiations. The second view, which clearly was in the ascendency by late July and conformed more with fundamental instincts of the Reagan administration, was that it was time for the United States to "close ranks with Israel" and "get tough" with Syria.[17] Secretary of State Shultz increasingly became a supporter of the second view.[18]

Secretary of State Shultz and other officials of the Reagan administration tended to "blame the Arabs," and particularly Syria, for the impasse over Lebanon and the failure of the Reagan initiative. This view found ready support in U.S. public attitudes. There was relatively little public debate in the United States about the May 17 agreement or U.S. policy in Lebanon and almost none about the failure of the Reagan initiative.

In Israel, however, debate about Israel's policy in Lebanon and the escalating costs of continuing occupation was vigorous in the period leading up to the signing of the agreement on May 17, and intensified after the signing.[19] If the Reagan administration wanted to pursue the idea of a workable negotiated agreement, it almost certainly could have counted on substantial Israeli public support. During several weeks in May, even as the Lebanon-Israel agreement was being finalized, an around-the-clock vigil was being held outside the residence of Prime Minister Begin in Jerusalem. On May 30 a demonstration of twenty-five hundred people took place at the Knesset, including many parents of Israeli soldiers killed in Lebanon. There were several spontaneous graveside demonstrations by parents who denounced former Defense Minister Sharon and the invasion. Sharon, reportedly, declined to attend funerals of Israeli soldiers killed in Lebanon to avoid the "political embarrassment" of such an incident. On June 4, only two weeks after the agreement with Lebanon was signed, more than one hundred thousand Israelis gathered in Tel Aviv for a demonstration sponsored by Peace Now, marking the first anniversery of the war in Lebanon and demanding immediate Israeli withdrawal and the resignation of the Begin government.

As it became clear that the May 17 agreement would not work, Israeli Labor Party leaders' criticism of the agreement became more intense and public. They began to offer an alternate policy. On June 2 the Labor Party Central Committee voted unanimously to demand an immediate pullout of Israeli forces from Beirut and the Shouf (a move also favored at the time by several members of Begin's own cabinet) and complete Israeli withdrawal from Lebanon within two or three months. By early July 1983 Shimon Peres was publicly advocating the plan for Israeli withdrawal which he actually carried out as prime minister in 1985.

In the United States on July 13 the *Washington Post* editorially urged the Reagan administration to consider adopting the Israeli Labor Party position as the basis for a new U.S. approach to Lebanon, despite the political problems that would almost inevitably have caused for its relationship with the Begin government.[20] The Reagan administration was not interested. In fact, it became more and more clear that the United States opposed the idea of unilateral Israeli withdrawal. The Reagan administration's view was that only if Israel kept its forces in Lebanon would there be sufficient pressure eventually to force Syria to withdraw and, thus, consolidate U.S. "gains" in Lebanon.

The problems caused for Lebanon by the impasse over the May 17 agreement were disastrous. Encouraged by the United States, the government of Amin Gemayel had staked much of its limited credibility on achieving an agreement for Israeli withdrawal from Lebanon. The U.S. strategy was that a successful troop withdrawal agreement coupled with a stronger national army would give Gemayel enough prestige and power to accomplish reunification of the country on terms that would perpetuate a western-oriented and, more specifically, a U.S.-oriented Lebanon. Instead, failure of the withdrawal agreement reignited sectarian strife, which already was fueled by Druze and Shiite bitterness over their problems with the Phalange forces, often supported by the Lebanese army. In contrast to the "momentum of hope" after Amin Gemayel first took office in the fall of 1982, by June 1983 the gaps in Lebanon between Christians and Muslims, between rich and poor, and between popular expectations and harsh realities had widened.[21]

Time for reconciliation and for a constructive U.S. role in Lebanon was running out. Fighting was escalating between Christians and Druze in the Shouf Mountains, in part in anticipation of a partial Israeli pullback. While President Gemayel insisted that the Lebanese army should take over positions abandoned by the Israelis, Lebanese Druze, Shiite and other Muslim leaders, fearful that the army would reinforce Christian domination in the area, continued to demand that the militias be disarmed first. Shiites in southern Lebanon were demonstrating increasing resistance to Israeli forces and to local Christian militia, which Shiite leaders blamed Gemayel's government for not controlling.

In the months following the May 17 agreement the problems facing the Gemayel government came more sharply into focus in the United States. In early July, David Ignatius wrote in the *Wall Street Journal*,

> To stabilize the Shouf and the rest of Lebanon, President Gemayel will have to convince the Moslems that he is sympathetic to their fears of Christian domination. In the short run, that means an understanding between Christian and Moslem warlords who now control Lebanese politics. But, in the long run it will probably require political reforms that replace the power of the warlords with a genuinely national politics in which Moslems will have more influence.[22]

The advice made sense, although it underestimated popular currents which even the "warlords" could hardly harness any more. If the United States had been determined to get Gemayel to follow this advice, it was still possible that the U.S. role could have been helpful, although more likely the situation had deteriorated to the extent that more drastic change was needed much more quickly than Ignatius' advice implied.

During early July in the Shouf region Druze and Christian militia fought fierce artillery battles, with the Druze increasingly getting the upper hand, despite support for the Christian forces by the Lebanese army. On July 16, following clashes between the Lebanese army and the Shiite Amal militia, Shiites in Beirut, Tyre and Baalbak held a general strike. On the same day, Syrian television strongly criticized President Amin Gemayel, ominously claiming that Gemayel had "lost his legitimacy."[23] On July 20 the Israeli cabinet unanimously approved a plan to redeploy Israeli troops in Lebanon to south of a line along the Awali River.

On July 23 Walid Jumblatt, the Druze leader, Rashid Karami, former prime minister and a Sunni leader, and Suliman Franjieh, former president and a Christian leader from northern Lebanon, announced the formation of the National Salvation Front to oppose the Gemayel government. Nabih Berri, leader of the Shiite organization, Amal, did not join the front but publicly pledged close cooperation. While Presi-

dent Gemayel tried to dismiss the front as unimportant, it was clear
that its formation represented another step in the direction of new civil
war or partition, unless there could be successful tough negotiations
among the warring factions.

During August-October, fighting in Lebanon intensified. Several
hundred people were killed and a few thousand wounded. The Lebanese
army was used by the Gemayel government in ways which more and
more irreversibly allied it with Christian militia against Druze, Shiite
and other Muslim militias. Syria provided essential support to forces
associated with the National Salvation Front, while at the same time
keeping lines open to the Gemayel government and trying to avoid a
direct combat role by its own forces in Lebanon. The United States continued to provide economic and military support to the Gemayel government and also tried to keep lines of communication open to the various
Lebanese factions and to Syria. It was becoming clear during this period,
however, that a combination of events and U.S. policy had increasingly transformed the multinational force in Lebanon from ''a peacekeeping force—welcomed by all Lebanese—into another warring faction.''[24]

During September and October there were a number of incidents
in which U.S. Marines, sometimes with support from naval artillery offshore, exchanged fire with Druze and Shiite forces on the southern side
of Beirut. Several marines were killed during this period and more were
wounded. Congressional leaders began to question the U.S. role in
Lebanon, although primarily on the basis of the War Powers Act and
other constitutional issues, rather than in terms of Middle East policy
issues. In fact, even though U.S. policy in Lebanon and in relation to
the Reagan initiative appeared not to be working, debate about what
U.S. policy ought to be was practically nonexistent. A column by Anthony Lewis in mid-September sharply focused at least a few of the issues
which ought to have been subject to major public debate but were not.
Lewis observed,

> The real question about the Marines. . .is what diplomatic
> and political strategy they are supposed to be supporting.
> . . .Are the Marines really there to support the Gemayel
> government right or wrong, as the Reagan administration
> has seemed to be signalling lately? If so, that is folly built
> on ignorance. . . .A policy without the political determina-
> tion to move toward a more inclusive Lebanese system is
> a recipe for disaster for Lebanon and the United States.[25]

If the Reagan administration did not have the vision or determination to press the Gemayel government for policies that were more in-

clusive when Gemayel first came to power a year earlier, it was doubtful that the administration would discover the determination now, when both Gemayel and the U.S. Marines were under attack.[26] The basic instinct of the Reagan administration in these circumstances was "to go for the gun." The suicide attack on the U.S. Marine barracks provided more than enough provocation.

On October 23 a truck loaded with explosives was driven into U.S. Marine headquarters near the Beirut Airport, killing two hundred fifty marines and wounding many others. A short time later, a second truck bomb destroyed French military headquarters, killing more than fifty French soldiers. In responding to the bombing, President Reagan not only threatened more forceful U.S. military action, but appeared also to raise the stakes of what was involved in the U.S. commitment in Lebanon. The president, for the first time, said that U.S. "vital interests" were at stake and, in an obvious reference to the Soviet Union, expressed his view that, if the United States does not prevent it, "a force is ready to take over the Middle East."[27] At the same time as the Reagan administration turned up its rhetoric about the U.S. commitment in Lebanon and prepared for military escalation, there were growing doubts about how long the U.S. commitment actually would last.[28]

Even at this late hour, the United States had political/diplomatic options which might have allowed it to recoup something of a constructive contribution for its role in Lebanon. Tragically, however, most debate in Washington was between "getting out" and various military options for staying in. In November 1983 the Reagan administration rejected a concrete new opportunity for creative U.S. diplomacy. Then, between November 1983 and March 1984 the Reagan administration dangerously escalated U.S. military involvement in Lebanon and then finally ordered a total withdrawal of U.S. forces.

From October 31 to November 4 leaders of all of Lebanon's major factions met in Switzerland at a national reconciliation conference. During several days of acrimonious discussions the Gemayel government was pressed hard by several Lebanese factions and by Syria, which had observer status at the conference, to abrogate the May 17 agreement with Israel. Finally, a compromise formula was accepted. It was agreed to suspend the conference temporarily, in order to provide time for President Gemayel to seek U.S. support to reopen negotiations on the agreement with Israel.

To many observers, this proposal offered the last chance to achieve a negotiated agreement for withdrawal of foreign forces from Lebanon. By this time there were six months of accumulated evidence that the

May 17 agreement not only had failed to achieve withdrawal of any forces but also was a major obstacle to political reconciliation in Lebanon. In addition to obvious Lebanese interest, there was evidence of growing public support among Israelis for finding a workable formula for withdrawal of Israeli forces from Lebanon. Despite these considerations, U.S. officials reacted to the news from the reconciliation conference by expressing concern that Lebanese leaders not take any steps that "might jeopardize the accord." State Department spokesman John R. Hughes said, "Our position on the May 17 agreement is very clear. We think it is an excellent agreement."[29]

A month later when President Gemayel visited Washington, the Reagan administration showed no interest in reopening negotiations over withdrawal of foreign forces and little concern about the possibility of compromise and reconciliation in Lebanon. The president and other U.S. officials simply reiterated U.S. commitment to the May 17 agreement. A few days earlier, during meetings with Israeli Prime Minister Shamir (Begin had retired by this time) and Defense Minister Arens, the United States had agreed to strengthen its "strategic cooperation" with Israel. Asserting a stronger U.S. military presence in the region was clearly a higher priority for the Reagan administration than seeking negotiated peace.

In relation to Lebanon, the United States was already escalating the military confrontation. The main debate in U.S. policymaking circles during December was between persons led by Henry Kissinger who favored reinvolving Israeli forces in escalating military pressure on Syria and those led by Defense Secretary Caspar Weinberger who favored acting alone so as not to "further complicate our relations with other Arab states."[30] Given the prevailing views in Washington at the time, Lebanese concerned with national reconciliation and Israelis concerned with getting their soldiers safely home from Lebanon could hardly expect much support from the United States.

The Final Phase

During November, following the breakdown of a ceasefire called at the time of the national reconciliation conference, resistance to Israeli occupation and fighting among various Lebanese factions increased again. On November 4 a truck carrying explosives crashed into Israeli military headquarter near Tyre, killing forty persons and wounding more than thirty. In retaliation, Israeli jets bombed Palestinian targets near the Beirut-Damascus highway, reportedly killing sixty people. During this period tensions between Israeli forces and Lebanese citizens were further exacerbated by tight Israeli restrictions on travel to and from

Israeli-occupied southern Lebanon. The measures were intended in theory to block Palestinian "terrorists" coming south to attack Israeli forces, although by this time almost all the attacks were by Shiites and other Lebanese resisting the Israeli occupation. Despite the tight travel restrictions, attacks continued to occur against Israeli forces and Israeli casualties from the occupation continued to increase.

In northern Lebanon anti-Arafat PLO forces, supported by Syria, fought Arafat loyalists near Tripoli. This was part of the continuing struggle over the leadership and direction of the Palestinian movement caused by the PLO's military defeat in Lebanon and exacerbated by the failure of Arafat's efforts with King Hussein to produce any significant movement toward a political settlement. In late December a plan was accepted for the evacuation of Arafat and many of his troops, under a U.N. flag.

During November fighting among Lebanese factions around Beirut escalated. The United States continued to provide support for the Gemayel government, while Syria supported the National Salvation Front opposed to Gemayel. On November 10 Syrian antiaircraft batteries fired on U.S. Navy reconnaissance planes flying over the Syrian controlled area of Lebanon. On November 13 the United States issued a sharp warning to Syria that U.S.forces could not "be attacked with impunity." Four days later *Pravda* declared that the United States and Israel were poised to attack "Lebanese progressive forces." Obviously, there was a danger of a U.S.-Soviet confrontation in the escalating U.S. conflict with Syria in Lebanon, although most experts believed it was unlikely that the Soviet Union would intervene unless Syrian territory was directly attacked. On November 19 Syrian Defense Minister Mustafa Tlas said Syria would respond to a U.S. attack with "kamikaze attacks on American warships."[31]

On November 29, as mentioned earlier, the United States and Israel announced that they were strengthening the U.S.-Israeli strategic cooperation. Syria denounced this decision in harsh terms, while leaders of Jordan and Egypt declared that the strategic cooperation agreement seriously undermined U.S. credibility in the region. Significantly, several Israeli Labor Party leaders also were critical of the strategic cooperation agreement with the United States on the grounds that the agreement drew Israel dangerously and unnecessarily into the superpower conflict and did not increase Israel's security in the Middle East. Despite negative reactions and consequences in the region, it was clear that this emphasis on strategic cooperation continued to be a high priority for the Reagan administration.

On December 4 U.S. Navy planes attacked Syrian positions in Lebanon in response to Syrian attacks on an unmanned U.S. reconnaissance aircraft the day before. Two of the twenty-eighty U.S. planes involved in the attack were shot down, with one pilot killed and another captured. A month later Syria released the captured pilot, Lieutenant Robert O. Goodman, Jr., to a delegation of U.S. black leaders, headed by the Reverend Jesse Jackson. On December 14 the U.S. battleship New Jersey and two other U.S. warships fired heavy artillery against Syrian anti-aircraft positions in the eastern mountains. On the same day President Reagan announced that U.S. Marines would remain in Lebanon until the Lebanese government resumed sovereignty over its territory or there was a total "collapse" of public order. While the administration was "talking tough" and escalating military action, there were other indications that the end of U.S. involvement in Lebanon was near.

On December 28, the Long Commission, organized by the Pentagon to investigate the bombing of marine headquarters, released a report critical of U.S. policy in Lebanon and calling for an urgent reassessment. The *New York Times* summarized the findings of the report:

> The Long Commission concluded that the American military's siding with the Lebanese army against the Druze and Moslem Shiite forces marked a fundamental shift from the Marines' original role. The commission urged a reexamination of alternative means of reaching U.S. objectives in Lebanon, including "a more vigorous and demanding approach to pursuing diplomatic alternatives."[32]

It was revealing that even a report commissioned by the Pentagon accused the Reagan administration of abandoning the original peacekeeping mission of the multinational force in Lebanon and insisted on greater use of diplomacy in U.S. policy.

Pressures also built in the Congress for withdrawal of U.S. forces from Lebanon, yet the administration's public position appeared to become even more determined. On January 22, President Reagan declared forcefully that U.S. withdrawal would call into question the U.S. commitment to "moderation and negotiations in the Middle East" and on February 1 that it would encourage "the forces of radicalism and extremism," according to the *New York Times*

On February 2 fierce fighting broke out between Druze and Christian militia in the mountains east of Beirut and between Shiites and the Lebanese army in Beirut's southern suburbs. On February 3 Nabih Berri called on Muslim members of the Lebanese army to refuse orders.

At least hundreds and possibly thousands of Muslim soldiers responded. On February 5 Prime Minister Shafik al Wazzan and Lebanon's cabinet resigned.

Two days later, on February 7, U.S. military forces in Lebanon were ordered to redeploy to ships off the Lebanese coast. At the same time President Reagan reaffirmed U.S. commitment to Lebanon and authorized air and naval attacks against militia in the Beirut area. On February 8 the U.S. battleship New Jersey fired more than two hundred fifty sixteen-inch shells from its largest guns into the mountains east of Beirut. On February 21 U.S. troops actually redeployed offshore and the next day President Reagan again reaffirmed his commitment to President Gemayel and said that the marines would return to Beirut if necessary.

On March 2 President Amin Gemayel and President Hafez al Assad reportedly reached an agreement on how to resolve the Lebanese crisis. On March 5 Lebanon formally abrogated the May 17 Israel-Lebanon agreement negotiated by the United States.

Lessons from Lebanon

Much could have been learned from the failure of the United States' role in Lebanon. Unfortunately, there was relatively little public debate over U.S. policy in the Middle East and what there was, for example during the 1984 presidential elections, did not address several of the most critical issues. Secretary of State Shultz and other senior officials in the Reagan administration basically blamed the Arabs, and especially Syria, for U.S. failures. The United States took steps to strengthen its strategic alliance with Israel and resisted taking any new peace initiatives until Israel and the Arab side demonstrated more movement on their own toward peace. In this author's view, the following list of lessons represents a more accurate picture of the reasons why U.S. policy in Lebanon failed and offers more reliable guidelines for constructive U.S. policy in the future.

The United States should have supported an expanded United Nations peacekeeping mission in Lebanon as preferable to a U.S.-led multinational force. In fact, as the role of U.S. Marines in Lebanon became more difficult and dangerous, there were more public calls in Washington for trying to replace the marines with a U.N. force, but by then it was too late. The idea that one country, and especially one of the superpowers, should send military forces to do "peacekeeping" in another country would be dangerous in any area of the world. In Lebanon the complexity and volatility of four interrelated conflicts (Lebanese-Lebanese with its religious dimension, Israeli-Palestinian,

Israeli-Syrian and U.S.-Soviet) made any peacekeeping mission extremely difficult. The fact that the United States was viewed as partisan in all four of these conflicts made a U.S.-sponsored peacekeeping mission even more problematic.

U.S. policy in Lebanon demonstrated a lack of understanding of the importance of local conflicts in influencing events and placed too great an emphasis on viewing Lebanon through the lens of U.S. conflict with the Soviet Union. While the former tendency consistently led the United States to exaggerate the legitimacy and strength of the Gemayel government and seriously underestimate the power of Muslims, the latter created a policy context in which whoever opposed the U.S. role in Lebanon was viewed (in President Reagan's phrase) as serving a "force from outside the Middle East," i.e., the Soviet Union. Given this orientation in U.S. policy, as the internal conflicts in Lebanon intensified, it was not surprising that the U.S.-led multinational force increasingly was transformed from a peacekeeping mission into "another warring faction."

Based on this writer's experience, many U.S. foreign service officers in Lebanon and in the region as a whole were knowledgeable and sensitive about local developments. While U.S. embassies reported regularly to Washington, much important information and advice appeared to be ignored or overridden by political considerations. For example, in late 1982 and early 1983 many early warning signs of growing Lebanese Muslim disenchantment with the government of Amin Gemayel were ignored by Washington, even when the warnings were reinforced by reports and recommendations from the U.S. Embassy in Beirut. President Reagan's tendency to view events in Lebanon primarily in the context of the U.S.-Soviet conflict did not appear to be reflected in much of the analysis one heard from U.S. officials in the region, but obviously it carried considerable weight with Washington policymakers, including Secretary of State Shultz.

United States policy in Lebanon (and in relation to the wider Arab-Israeli conflict) was flawed because it ignored or took Syria for granted. U.S. policymakers significantly underestimated Syria's vital interests in Lebanon and its commitment and capacity to pursue these interests, even after its military setback by Israel in June 1982. In part, U.S. underestimation of Syria was another reflection of U.S. lack of understanding of internal Lebanese conflicts and, in this case, Syria's stake in these conflicts. Furthermore, the U.S. tendency to view Syria essentially as a surrogate of the Soviet Union in the Middle East not only distorted the picture of Syria's interests, but also, in the context of U.S. anti-Soviet attitudes, delegitimized these interests. The Reagan initiative for peace of September 1, 1982 completely ignored Syria. Then, between September 1982 and May 1983, the U.S. took Syria for granted while it negotiated an agreement between Israel and Lebanon, the implementation of which depended on Syria's cooperation. The Reagan initiative failed. The May 17 agreement was never implemented and the costs to Lebanon and to Israel of this failure are still being paid. No one familiar with Syrian policy and diplomacy would suggest that negotiating with the Syrian government would be easy. After U.S. failures in Lebanon, however, the idea that a settlement in Lebanon or peace in the Middle East is possible without negotiating with Syria should be laid to rest once and for all.

U.S. policy in Lebanon failed to support Israelis, including prominent leaders of the Labor Alignment, who opposed their government's invasion and occupation of Lebanon. Among Israelis, the war in Lebanon was the most controversial war Israel ever fought. Even in the early months of the war there were large popular demonstrations led by Peace Now opposing the invasion and calling for immediate Israeli withdrawal. As Israeli forces remained in Lebanon and Lebanese resistance took an increasing toll of Israeli casualties, more and more Israelis wanted Israel to get out of Lebanon, on the sole condition of some form of security guarantees for their northern border.

In contrast, the United States did not actively oppose the Israeli invasion of Lebanon and there is some evidence that the Reagan administration, in particular Secretary of State Alexander Haig, gave a green light to the invasion. During the next two years the United States, even while it sought a formula for Israeli withdrawal, at the same time used the Israeli occupation as leverage to try to increase U.S. influence in Lebanon and reduce or eliminate the PLO and Syrian presence. In the fall of 1983, by which time a majority of Israelis simply ''wanted out of Lebanon,'' there was debate among Washington policy makers about trying to re-engage Israeli military forces in Lebanon in a way that would increase pressure on Syria to withdraw. Even the Likud government headed by Yitzhak Shamir saw little gain for Israel in such a strategy. Many Israelis who opposed their government's policies in Lebanon were deeply troubled by the U.S. role in this costly misadventure.

The U.S. failure to achieve progress toward resolving the Palestinian issue in the context of a wider Arab-Israeli peace process compounded the problems of the U.S. role in Lebanon. The primary goal of the Reagan intiative of September 1, 1982 was to encourage King Hussein of Jordan to come to U.S.-sponsored negotiations with Israel over the future of the West Bank and Gaza. However, the interrelationship of issues in the Arab-Israeli conflict meant that as long as the Reagan initiative was under active consideration by Jordan and the PLO, the United States had increased leverage in Lebanon, since progress on the Palestinian issue would relieve pressure there and undermine the rationale for Israeli, and to a lesser extent, Syrian military presence. (Based on a corollary of this argument, it was widely assumed that the Likud government in Israel wanted to delay any agreement in Lebanon until the Reagan initiative failed.) Just as the failure of the United States to achieve Israeli withdrawal from Lebanon negatively affected the chances of the Reagan initiative, so the failure of the Reagan intiative in April 1983 reduced U.S. credibility and political leverage with the major parties in Lebanon, including especially Israel and Syria.

Chapter
Six

The Reagan Initiative
Arab and Israeli Responses

This chapter goes back in time to examine the Reagan initiative of September 1982, a promising effort of the U.S. government to achieve peace in the Middle East. The background for the initiative and the responses from the various political currents in the area are important for understanding both the promise and the eventual failure of the initiative.

The war in Lebanon once again focused world attention on the centrality of the Palestinian issue in the Arab-Israeli conflict. The Israeli invasion demonstrated Israeli military superiority. But the consequences of the war and particularly the prolonged siege of Beirut generated increased sympathy for the Palestinians and, despite its military withdrawal, may actually have enhanced the PLO's political status for a time. The invasion intensified political divisions within Israel and caused new tensions in Israel's relations with the United States. Relations between Arab countries and the United States also were strained, since most Arab leaders held U.S. policy at least partially responsible for the Israeli invasion. By the end of the summer of 1982, in the wake of Israel's invasion, there was a widely shared sense that new initiatives were needed not only to restore order in Lebanon but also to resolve the Palestinian issue.

Several factors generated pressures for a greater U.S. role in the region. The special U.S. relationship with Israel led most people, including many Israelis, to believe that only the United States could convince Israel to withdraw its forces from Lebanon or to take steps in relation to reaching a peace settlement with the Palestinians. Bashir Gemayel, who was assassinated, and his brother, Amin Gemayel, who succeeded him as president of Lebanon, believed an expanded U.S. role in Lebanon was advantageous both in terms of getting Israeli and Syrian forces out and helping western-oriented Maronite Christians maintain their dominant position. President Sadat and King Hussein looked to the United States to play the key role in achieving movement toward a wider peace process with Israel. PLO leaders, including Arafat, who viewed the war in Lebanon as possibly creating conditions for a new political strategy, viewed the U.S. role as the most important factor. President Assad of Syria was deeply suspicious of unilateral U.S. peacemaking moves (as was the Soviet Union), but after its military trouncing by Israel in Lebanon, Syria appeared to be in no position to block an expanded U.S. role in the region.

During the summer of 1982, as a larger U.S. role in Lebanon was taking shape, a consensus developed in the State Department and the White House that the time was ripe for the United States to lead a new effort to resolve the Palestinian issue. This view had already been gaining strength in the administration before the Israeli invasion of Lebanon. In an important speech to the Chicago Council on Foreign Relations on May 26, 1982, a month after Israeli withdrawal from the Sinai and less than two weeks before the invasion of Lebanon, then Secretary of State Alexander Haig declared, "Now is America's moment in the Middle East." He promised new U.S. efforts to help end the Iran-Iraq war, to achieve results in the Camp David autonomy talks and to resolve the crisis in Lebanon.[1] As we saw in Chapter 2, in contrast to these pledges of a more active and positive U.S. role for peace, the United States did very little in the spring of 1982 either to achieve a breakthrough in the talks between Israel and Egypt or to prevent a new war in Lebanon. In any event, two weeks after Haig sounded these positive notes in U.S. policy, hopes for movement toward peace were crushed by Israel's invasion of Lebanon.

The war in Lebanon created a new set of circumstances by September 1982 which underlined the urgent need for new peace efforts and appeared "to put the United States in the diplomatic driver's seat." Senior officials in Washington agreed with Henry Kissinger that the war had opened a new opportunity for the United States. There also were risks, but most U.S. policymakers believed the opportunity outweighed the risks. Problems would arise to the extent that there was a conflict between the requirements for peace and what the United States saw as its strategic interests but in September 1982 most U.S. leaders and many others believed the two were compatible.[2]

The White House chose September 1, while U.S. Marines were overseeing the PLO military withdrawal from Beirut, as the date for President Reagan to deliver a nationally televised speech outlining a new U.S. effort for peace. The speech was carefully crafted and convincingly delivered ("A New Opportunity for Peace in the Middle East," Department of State Bulletin, September 1982). President Reagan said there were two basic issues the United States had to address in the Middle East: "First, there was the strategic threat to the region posed by the Soviet Union and its surrogates, best demonstrated by the brutal war in Afghanistan; and second, the peace process between Israel and its Arab neighbors." Emphasizing the unique importance of the U.S. role in the Middle East, the president explicitly reaffirmed U.S. commitment to "the Camp David framework as the only way to proceed," and reiterated the special role of the United States as mediator.

At the same time, the president pointed out how the Camp David talks had become stalled in part because both Israel and Egypt "felt free to express openly their views as to what the outcome should be," and "understandably, their views have differed on many points." The president said that it had become evident to him "that some clearer sense of America's position on the key issues is necessary to encourage wider support for the peace process."

In the administration's view, this was the essential purpose of the speech: to demonstrate, at the highest level possible, renewed U.S. commitment to the Camp David framework, and to the U.S. role as mediator within this framework. The president did not suggest any significant changes in U.S. policy toward the Arab-Israeli conflict, but he did publicly spell out U.S. views on several key issues as a way, hopefully, to break the stalemate in the autonomy talks and to encourage Jordanian and Palestinian involvement in the peace process.

The Main Points

It is important to summarize the major points of President Reagan's speech. The president called for "a fresh start" on resolving "the root causes of conflict between Arabs and Israelis." He explicitly urged:

- Israel to make clear that the security for which she yearns can only be achieved through genuine peace, a peace requiring magnanimity, vision and courage;

- the Palestinian people to recognize that their own political aspirations are inextricably bound to recognition of Israel's right to a secure future;
- the Arab states to accept the reality of Israel and the reality that peace and justice are to be gained only through hard, fair, direct negotiation.

The president declared that "the United States has a special responsibility," according to his view, because "no other nation is in a position to deal with the key parties to the conflict on the basis of trust and reliability." Declaring that "the Camp David agreement remains the foundation of our policy," the president then sought to clarify the U.S. position on several key issues related to the autonomy talks:

- During an essential transition period Palestinians in the West Bank and Gaza would have full autonomy over their own affairs with due consideration to self-government of the inhabitants and security of the parties involved.
- The United States would not support use of any additional aid for settlements during the transition period; furthermore an immediate settlement freeze by Israel, more than any other action, could create confidence for wider participation in negotiations.
- The purpose of this transition period would be the peaceful and orderly transfer of authority from Israel to the Palestinian inhabitants of the West Bank and Gaza. At the same time, such a transfer must not interfere with Israel's security requirements.
- Beyond the transitional period, the United States would not support the establishment of an independent Palestinian state in the West Bank and Gaza, and the United States would not support annexation or permanent control by Israel.
- The final status of these lands must be reached through the give and take of negotiations. But it was the firm view of the United States that self-government by the Palestinians of the West Bank and Gaza in association with Jordan offered the best chance for a durable, just and lasting peace.

The president reiterated U.S. commitment to U.N. Security Council Resolution 242 as "the foundation stone for America's Middle East peace effort" and said that, "in return for peace, the withdrawal provision of Resolution 242 applies to all fronts, including the West Bank

and Gaza.'' The president said, ''When the border is negotiated between Jordan and Israel, . . .the extent to which Israel should be asked
to give up territory will be heavily affected by the extent of true peace
and normalization and the security arrangements offered in return.''

Finally, on the status of Jerusalem, an essential and extremely sensitive issue not addressed in the Camp David agreement, the president
said, ''We remain convinced that Jerusalem must remain undivided,
but its final status should be decided through direct negotiations.''

Responses to the Initiative

Responses to the September 1 speech in the Middle East, western
Europe and the United States were encouragingly, although not universally, positive. On the Arab side, among parties most directly involved,
initial positive responses to the speech came from leaders of Egypt and
Jordan; there was mixed response from the leaders of the PLO. In Israel,
while the Likud government categorically rejected the initiative, Labor
Alignment leadership gave a positive response, consistent with their
pleas for more than a year that the United States needed to take a more
active and forceful role in the peace process.

The effects of the Lebanon war were complex and contradictory.
However, one immediate effect was to reinforce the views of at least
some Arab and Israeli political leaders that new peace efforts were
urgently needed. The Reagan initiative evoked a sense of hope among
many people in Israel, the West Bank and Gaza, Egypt and Jordan,
and Lebanon that the United States would now play a leading role in
pressing for movement toward negotiations. The failure of the initiative
eight months later deepened people's sense of desperation and frustration and weakened U.S. credibility throughout the region. In order to
understand why the Reagan initiative failed, and what the United States
might have done to improve the prospects that it would succeed, it is
important first to look in more detail at the responses of various parties.

The U.S. strategy was to win support from key Arab leaders, particularly King Hussein, for negotiations with Israel. With this support
the United States hoped to be able to convince Israel that the president's initiative represented the best, and only realistic, chance for peace.
A very early indication that the United States was counting on King
Hussein to play the key role in its strategy was the fact that U.S.
diplomats met with Hussein before the speech to get a preliminary
reading on what his reaction would be. The day after the speech, a State
Department official referred optimistically to Hussein's response saying, ''We didn't go into this blind. We didn't have a clear green light,
but we did have an amber light.''[3]

Most Arab leaders withheld official responses to the Reagan initiative until after the Arab summit, which was scheduled to convene in Fez, Morocco on September 6, 1982. However, there were enough unofficial and semi-official responses for U.S. leaders to feel encouraged. On September 2, the government of Jordan indicated through "authorized sources" that its reaction was "favorable, with reservations about some points that have to be clarified."[4]

Jordanians were positively impressed by President Reagan's decision to state his own position instead of acting only as a mediator with no opinion of his own. Most Arab leaders felt that all too often U.S. officials echoed Israeli policy. As a senior Jordanian editor, who had been briefed by cabinet members, explained to U.S. journalists, "We are happy that someone at last spoke with a purely American voice, proclaiming an American policy and defining American interests."[5] What worried Jordanians now, according to him, was "whether Mr. Reagan has the will and the power to back up his words."[6]

King Hussein obviously viewed the Reagan initiative as a very important and positive development, but he also made it clear from the start that he would need Palestinian and broader Arab support in order to come forward for negotiations about the future of the West Bank. In a television interview after he learned of the new U.S. initiative but three days before the president's speech, King Hussein said, "I am not in a position of (having) a mandate, either from the Palestinians or from the Arab world, following the Rabat Summit conference, to handle the problems of the West Bank directly, and I would not do so until I was offered such a mandate."[7] At the Rabat Arab summit in 1974, Arab heads of state had declared that the PLO was "the sole legitimate representative of the Palestinian people."

Responses to the Reagan initiative from PLO leaders and from Palestinians in the West Bank and Gaza were varied, with most persons indicating that they saw positive and negative elements in the president's speech. Yasser Arafat made a brief statement in Athens after arriving by boat from Beirut, declaring that President Reagan's initiative "has some positive aspects." Farouk Qaddumi, head of the Political Affairs Department of the PLO, hearing the main points of the president's speech from reporters just after he arrived in Athens, responded several times, "that's good," and "not bad," concluding with the comment, "not bad altogether." Dr. Hanna Nasir, the deported president of Bir Zeit University in the West Bank and in 1982 a member of the PLO Executive Committee, also indicated to reporters that he saw "positive aspects" in the Reagan initiative. Leaders of the more radical factions within the PLO, including George Habash of the Popular Front for the Liberation of Palestine (PFLP) and Nayef Hawatmeh of the Democratic Front for the Liberation of Palestine (DFLP), issued statements in Damascus on September 2 rejecting the Reagan plan. The PFLP statement described the plan as an attempt "to link the Arab area to American imperialist policy and to obtain political and national concessions from the PLO."[8]

Two of the most negative aspects of the U.S. initiative in the view of Palestinians were U.S. rejection of the idea of an independent Palestinian state and U.S. refusal to accept a role for the PLO in negotiations. In spite of these negative elements, the PLO Executive Committee did not adopt a position on the Reagan plan when it met, but rather concentrated on reaching agreement on positive points to present at the upcoming Fez Summit to form the basis of a unified Arab stand. Even before Arab leaders gathered at Fez, it was assumed that the PLO would be in a strong position to shape the Fez Declaration, especially after its stand against Israeli forces in Lebanon with little Arab help.

Many Palestinians in the West Bank and Gaza were encouraged by the Reagan initiative, although the daily problems caused by Israeli military rule and prohibitions against political activity severely limited the ways Palestinians under occupation could respond. Mayor Elias Freij of Bethlehem, the sole elected Palestinian mayor in a large West Bank city remaining in office by September, 1982 (the others had all been deposed and/or exiled by Israeli authorities), responded very favorably to the Reagan initiative and believed that the PLO should make a priority of seeking to open talks with the United States about next steps toward peace negotiations. Freij also believed that the PLO should revise its charter to bring it into line with PLO policy which reflected Palestinian willingness to accept a state in the West Bank and Gaza, alongside Israel.

Palestinian leaders in the occupied territories who had close ties with Jordan generally felt that the PLO should agree to some form of joint approach and joint delegation with King Hussein for peace negotiations. Other Palestinians, viewed as stronger nationalists, were much more skeptical of a joint approach and insisted that the Palestinians should be represented exclusively by the PLO in any negotiations. Palestinians with a more leftist orientation were the most critical of the Reagan initiative, not only because it rejected an independent Palestinian state and a role for the PLO in negotiations, but also because they did not accept the idea that the United States should be the sole mediator in peace negotiations.

The Egyptian government responded very favorably to the Reagan initiative, although officials indicated Egypt also had some "observations" about the plan it would share privately with the United States. Since President Sadat signed the Camp David agreement, Egypt had made a major, and from an Arab point of view dangerously unilateral, commitment to peace with Israel. Having become increasingly dependent on U.S. economic and military aid, Egypt also depended on the United States to help "make good" on the second half of the Camp David agreement, i.e., a settlement of the Palestinian issue in the context of negotiations over the future of the West Bank and Gaza. In the face of these realities, President Mubarak, whom some suspected of wanting to distance himself from Camp David after the Israeli invasion of Lebanon, saw the Reagan initiative as a hopeful sign that the United States was now ready to do what President Sadat had urged on his visit to Washington one month before he was assassinated, i.e., not only publicly state the U.S. position on what would be an acceptable settlement, but work hard to achieve it.

Syria, among the Arab states directly involved in the conflict with Israel, reacted the most negatively to the Reagan initiative. While President Hafez al Assad did not comment publicly on the initiative before the Fez summit, Damascus radio, which reflects official attitudes, denounced the Reagan plan as "a new maneuver in an established American policy that supports Israel's aggression, expansionist plans and racist goals."[9] As viewed in Damascus, the Reagan initiative essentially was aimed at achieving a second Camp David agreement, this time between Israel and Jordan, while excluding Syria and rejecting the right of self-determination for the Palestinians.

In the period following President Reagan's speech, the State Department issued clarifications saying that the reference in the speech to the U.S. view of U.N. Resolution 242 as applying to all fronts meant the United States did support negotiations over the Golan Heights as well as over the West Bank and Gaza. However, the omission of any explicit reference to Syria in the speech, combined with U.S. rejection of a Palestinian state and refusal to deal with the PLO, gave credibility to the Syrian view. Moreover, the fact that President Reagan's speech ignored Syria was an huge insult to President Assad, who viewed his country as having the most important role of any Arab country in the conflict with Israel, especially after Egypt signed the Camp David agreement.

The Fez Declaration

At the Arab summit meeting held in Fez, Morocco only a few days after President Reagan's speech, Arab leaders reached a new consensus on what was required to resolve the conflict with Israel. Based essentially on the eight-point plan put forward by King Fahd of Saudi Arabia a year earlier, the Fez Declaration, while unacceptable to Israel, went further toward a realistic basis for peace than the Arab states had ever gone before. Significantly, both the PLO and Syria, which opposed the Fahd plan in 1981, supported the Fez Declaration in 1982.

The following are the eight points of the Fez Declaration announced by Moroccan Foreign Minister, Mohammed Boucetta on September 9, 1982:[10]

1. Withdrawal of Israeli forces from all Arab territories occupied in 1967, including Arab (East) Jerusalem.

2. The removal of all settlements established by Israel on the occupied Arab territories after 1967.

3. Guaranteed freedom of worship and religious rites for all faiths in the Holy Places.

4. Emphasis on the right of the Palestinian people in determining their destiny and in exercising their inalienable national rights under the leadership of the Palestine Liberation Organization (PLO), their sole and legitimate representative, and compensation to those who are not willing to return to their homeland.

5. Placing the West Bank and Gaza Strip under a United Nations mandate for a transitional period not exceeding several months.

6. The establishment of an independent Palestinian state with Jerusalem as its capital.

7. The U.N. Security Council to be requested to agree on guarantees for peace among the region's states, including the independent Palestinian state.

8. The Security Council to undertake to guarantee the implementation of these principles.

The Arab summit decided to send a six-member commission comprised of representatives of Saudi Arabia, Jordan, Syria, Morocco, Tunisia and the PLO to seek responses to the Fez Declaration from the five permanent members of the U.N. Security Council. A delegation representing this commission was expected to go to Washington to discuss the Fez Declaration and to seek further clarification of President Reagan's initiative.

The United States publicly welcomed the Fez Declaration, which U.S. officials described as "remarkably moderate."[11] At the same time, however, the United States offered no indications that it would be willing to modify its own position at any point in response to the Arab plan. Indeed, the United States said it would refuse to receive a delegation from Fez if the delegation included a representative of the PLO and U.S. officials declared in advance of the meeting with Arab leaders that there would be no changes in the Reagan initiative.

Hussein and Arafat

Recognizing the limitations of moving on the Fez Declaration without some sign of flexibility from Israel or the United States, King Hussein opened talks in October with Yasser Arafat in Amman to discuss a possible joint response to the U.S. initiative; this would include the idea of seeking agreement in principle to a confederation between Jordan and a future West Bank/Gaza Palestinian entity and the possibility of a joint Jordanian-Palestinian delegation for negotiations. From the start of the Hussein-Arafat talks, these two ideas were viewed as positive ways to respond to the U.S. suggestion for self-government by the Palestinians in the West Bank and Gaza in association with Jordan and the U.S. rejection of a role for the PLO in negotiations. King Hussein clearly wanted to respond positively to the Reagan initiative, if he could do this in the context of a coordinated positive response with several Arab states and/or with the PLO.

The United States appeared eager for King Hussein to come forward for negotiations and many U.S. officials seemed to believe that the king could manage somehow to speak on behalf of the Palestinians. However, no one who knew the king well believed he would enter negotiations on his own. As one report at the time described the purpose of the Arafat-Hussein talks:

> The Jordanian monarch has the ear of the United States. The chief of the Palestine Liberation Organization has the Arab negotiating mantle. So the two are attempting to fashion a joint approach to President Reagan's peace initiative.[12]

Yasser Arafat and other PLO leaders also seemed genuinely interested in finding a way to respond positively to the U.S. initiative. After three days of Hussein-Arafat talks in Amman, on October 12, PLO spokesman Mahmoud Labadi said that the PLO was ready to negotiate with Washington on the basis of the Reagan plan, despite its explicit opposition to the idea of an independent Palestinian state or a role for the PLO. Addressing the question of possible confederation of the West Bank and Gaza with Jordan, Labadi said,

> Our basic aim is to secure an Israeli withdrawal, get Israel

to recognize our right of self-determination, set up a Palestinian state on the returned territory, and then talk of a federation or association with Jordan.[13]

While this position differed from the U.S. plan, and was unacceptable even to the Labor-led opposition in Israel, PLO leaders clearly were sending signals of positive interest in the Reagan initiative. The United States, however, was not willing nor really interested in talking with the PLO. As one U.S. Middle East diplomat put it, rather candidly, "The political psychology of the Reagan initiative was entirely based on the presupposition that it is possible to get someone else to speak for the Palestinians."

In October, a senior correspondent for *Al Ahram*, the largest daily newspaper in Egypt, said to me, "If the United States is really serious about the Reagan initiative, it should 'jump on' the Fez Declaration and on the Arafat-Hussein talks as very encouraging developments."[14] Mohammed Salmawi went on to say that the United States would have to engage in real give-and-take dialogue with various Arab parties, including the Palestinian leadership, if there were to be any chance of a breakthrough. Six weeks after President Reagan's speech, there were no signs that the United States was prepared to engage in this kind of diplomatic effort.

Israeli Responses to the Reagan Initiative

Prime Minister Begin told U.S. Ambassador Samuel Lewis that the day he learned of the Reagan initiative was "his saddest as prime minister." Begin was reported to have told the Israeli cabinet that any Israeli who accepted the Reagan plan would be "a traitor." On September 2, 1982, the Israeli cabinet voted unanimously to reject the U.S. plan for Palestinian self-government in the West Bank and Gaza, claiming it would lead to a Palestinian state and "could create a serious danger" to Israel's security. The cabinet also rejected President Reagan's appeal for a freeze on settlements in the occupied territories and decided to continue establishing settlements to consolidate Israel's control over the areas. The cabinet announced that Israel would reserve the right to apply sovereignty over the territories at the end of the five-year transition period of Palestinian autonomy called for in the Camp David agreement. While the official cabinet statement charged that the Reagan initiative explicitly contradicted the Camp David agreement, the real issues appeared to be related to different views of the meaning of Camp David.[15]

In dramatic contrast to the responses of the Likud government, Shimon Peres, leader of the opposition Labor Alignment, described

President Reagan's speech as "a most realistic basis for negotiations and for the continuation of the peace process in the Middle East." On September 14, Peres spelled out his views in the *Washington Post*, saying that he saw the Reagan initiative as an attempt "to create partners for negotiations even though no general trend for the negotiations has crystallized." Peres praised President Reagan's approach because it avoided "laying out a final program," while it "attempted to respond to the principal issues in a way that will reassure each side in the opening phases of the negotiations." Not surprisingly, Peres strongly concurred with President Reagan's preference for Jordan, rather than the PLO, as the primary negotiating partner and welcomed Reagan's explicit opposition to the creation of a Palestinian state. Emphasizing that "negotiations for peace are built on patience, on discussion and on compromise, including territorial compromise," Peres concluded by expressing his hope that Arab responses to the Reagan initiative would also be "directed at avoiding wars and building a peace on the basis of compromise."[16]

As encouraging as Peres' response was, of course the Labor Party was not in power in Israel and, even if it had been, there was still a large gap between Peres' position and what might be acceptable to King Hussein or the Palestinians. On one of the big issues, however, i.e., the role of Palestinians in the peace process, there were signs of more flexibility among Labor Party leaders than appeared in Peres' official response. From a political point of view, it was not surprising that Peres focused his response on Jordan's role, rather than on the Palestinians. Historically, the Israeli Labor Party had always favored what was called the "Jordan option" for a peace settlement related to the West Bank. One important effect of the Reagan initiative, according to some Labor Party leaders, was that, inasmuch as it recognized the centrality of the Palestinian issue and the need for Palestinian participation in negotiations, albeit not as the PLO, the initiative could help Israelis face the fact that a "pure Jordan option" no longer existed. As Abba Eban expressed it, commenting on the positive importance of the talks between King Hussein and Yasser Arafat, "We no longer speak of a 'Jordan option.' Negotiations will have to be trilateral, not bilateral. There must be a Palestinian component."[17]

On a popular level, as well as at the level of political leaders, Israelis were deeply divided in their responses to the new U.S. initiative for peace. On October 8 the *Jerusalem Post* reported an opinion poll conducted by the Modi'in Ezrachi Research Institute, showing that 38.6 per cent of Israelis polled believed their government should reject the

Reagan plan and 38.8 per cent believed the government should accept it as a basis for negotiations. After the massacres of Palestinians at Sabra and Shatila in Lebanon, the poll showed greater support among Israelis for accepting the Reagan plan and also a larger number of respondents who were undecided.

In relation to Israeli support for territorial compromise in the West Bank and Gaza in exchange for peace, the poll showed 52 per cent of Israelis opposed any territorial compromise, while 45.4 per cent supported compromise that would entail giving up all or part of the West Bank and Gaza, although only a very small percentage were willing to include East Jerusalem in the compromise. The results of this poll in late September 1982, in comparison with a poll in August before Sabra and Shatila, also showed that there was a trend in Israeli opinion toward both more "hawkish" and more "dovish" ends of the political spectrum at the expense of the center.

On the willingness of Israelis to support negotiations with the PLO, a poll by Modi'in Ezrachi in August showed results which indicated more flexibility in Israeli attitudes than is often assumed in the United States. While sixty per cent of Israelis opposed negotiations with the PLO, it is interesting that thirty-eight per cent supported negotiating with the PLO, including twenty per cent who accepted the idea of talks without any conditions.[18]

Many Israelis believed that if there were a real Arab peace offer, Israel would demonstrate even greater flexibility than these polls suggested. Each poll indicated Israeli views at the time and under the circumstances when it was taken. This obvious fact takes on particular significance because of the dramatic shift in Israeli opinion which occurred in response to the 1977 initiative of President Sadat. Before Sadat announced he was prepared to come to Jerusalem, only a small percentage of Israelis said they were willing to give back the Sinai to Egypt. After Sadat's visit, a majority of Israelis supported return of the Sinai in exchange for peace. Even among Likud supporters, who reflect more "hawkish" views in the polls cited above, there is evidence to suggest that some would show greater flexibility if they became convinced that peace were possible. As one Likud worker in Kiryat Shemona, near the border with Lebanon, told me, "Look, I don't believe the Arabs really want peace. If I became convinced they do want peace, then holding on to the West Bank and Gaza wouldn't be so important to me." While there was no accurate way to predict what Israeli opinion would be under different circumstances, some estimate of a potential for greater Israeli flexibility appeared to be realistic.

The Peace Movement View

The Israeli peace movement played an important role after Sadat's visit to Jerusalem and during the Camp David process. In response to the war in Lebanon, and especially after Sabra and Shatila, which provoked a demonstration by four hundred thousand Israelis, the peace movement was stronger than it had been for some time.

In addition to peace groups mentioned earlier new organizations were formed, including "Soldiers Against Silence" and "There Is A Limit" (Yesh Gevul) among Israeli soldiers, a movement of parents of Israeli soldiers who served in Lebanon called "Parents Against Silence," and "East for Peace" among Sephardic Jews. A new peace movement among Orthodox Israelis was formed to complement the older "Peace and Strength" (Oz ve Shalom). Called "Pathway to Peace" (Netivot Shalom), its founding conference in December 1982 attracted more than two thousand Orthodox Israelis, most of them young. Teach-ins organized by Peace Now, the largest Israeli peace movement, attracted several hundred and, in a few cases, several thousand Israeli youth. During the fall and winter months of 1982-83 there was an upsurge in the numbers of Israelis wanting to do volunteer work with the peace movement, to the extent that Peace Now, which prided itself on the looseness of its organization, had difficulty absorbing the volunteers.

As do peace movements in other countries, the Israeli peace movement tended to respond to events rather than generate its own political momentum. Just as events in Lebanon served as a negative impetus for the peace movement, the Reagan initiative was a positive impetus. Among other things, it helped to provide new motivation and energy for popular educational work about the realities of Israeli military occupation in the West Bank and Gaza and the advantages, from an Israeli point of view, of a negotiated settlement that would involve exchanging occupied territories for peace.

Israeli peace movement leaders, on the one hand, were encouraged by the Reagan intitiative. On the other hand, they were worried when the United States failed to follow up in ways to keep debate about the initiative alive in Israel and to increase pressure on the Begin government to adopt a more flexible position. The U.S. strategy was aimed at obtaining a breakthrough on the Arab side, specifically with Jordan, and then using this breakthrough to encourage a more flexible response from Israel. The problem with this approach was that it very soon became apparent that, without greater Israeli and/or U.S. flexibility, a breakthrough on the Arab side would be unlikely. There were some Israelis, as well as many Arabs, who understood this at the time and tried unsuccessfully to get the United States to modify its approach.

On the Arab side there were quite specific suggestions for what the United States might do to improve the chances of success for the Reagan initiative. The main advice Israeli supporters of the Reagan initiative offered was that the United States needed "to keep the pressure on," i.e., on Israel as well as on the Arabs. The first indication that the United States might not do this was the very low-key U.S. response to the rejection of the Reagan initiative by Prime Minister Begin and the Israeli cabinet. In fact, U.S. officials insisted that the United States would not seek to bring overt pressure on Israel to respond more positively to the Reagan initiative.[19] Whereas many Israelis believed that increased pressure by President Reagan would have increased debate in Israel over the initiative, they believed that the lack of U.S. pressure tended to defuse public debate and made Prime Minister Begin appear politically stronger than he actually was.

U.S. Views

Responses to President Reagan's speech within the United States were generally positive, including those of former President Carter, the Congress, the press and nongovernmental leaders of public opinion. Once again, as during the period immediately after the assassination of President Sadat, it appeared that President Reagan had "political room" to do something for peace in the Middle East, if only he would use it.

Former President Jimmy Carter, who had been briefed in advance by administration officials, responded quickly and publicly to charges by Prime Minister Begin and the Israeli Cabinet that the speech contradicted the Camp David agreement: "There is absolutely nothing in the president's speech last night," said Carter, "which is contrary to either the letter or the spirit of the Camp David agreement. It is absolutely compatible."[20] Carter's views of the speech were strongly endorsed by Zbigniew Brzezinski, former White House national security advisor who said, "I find it fully consistent with the spirit and letter of Camp David. And I know, because I was there."[21]

Carter spelled out his views in an interview with *Newsweek's* Vincent Coppola. Commenting specifically on the Israeli government charge that the United States had violated its role as "honest mediator," Carter said,

> What President Reagan said is not inconsistent with Camp David. The Camp David agreement just said that everybody who was part of the negotiating team can express his own view. And of course, the United States is a specifically designated part of the negotiating team. . . .President

Reagan has very properly said that our country feels that the best solution might be for the West Bank and Gaza to be affiliated in the long run with Jordan. But it's just an expression of opinion. He's not trying to short-circuit the negotiations. The final status of the West Bank and Gaza will have to be determined by negotiations among all the parties involved.[22]

Sol Linowitz, who served as President Carter's special Mideast negotiator from 1979 to 1981, also supported the Reagan initiative, if in somewhat more cautious terms. He said, ''. . .without the strong leadership of the United States, progress toward peace will not be made, nor will the Palestinian problem be dealt with effectively. The president's speech, therefore, is a welcome effort to move forward aggressively with a firm commitment to Camp David—even though his address may have created some problems that may make negotiating progress more difficult.''[23]

Response in the Congress to the president's speech by both Republican and Democratic party leadership, on the whole, was favorable. Indeed, in the area of foreign policy no major initiative by the Reagan administration during its first two years in office generated more positive bipartisan support.

U.S. media responded very favorably to the Reagan initiative. Wolf Blitzer reported in the *Jerusalem Post*, ''The Reagan plan has received an almost unanimously favourable reaction in major U.S. newspapers.''[24] The *New York Times*, in a lead editorial entitled, ''A Call to Moderates,'' declared,

> President Ronald Reagan's formula for new Arab-Israeli negotiations is reasonable and well-timed. Israel's rejection is lamentable but is not unchangeable. . . .Far from betraying the Camp David accords, Mr. Reagan aims to restore the promise that Mr. Begin drained from them.[25]

The *Washington Post*, in an equally strong and positive editorial, wrote,

> Finally President Reagan has a Mideast policy worthy of the name. . . .Mr. Reagan drew exactly the correct conclusion from the Lebanon crisis and from the earlier virtual collapse of the autonomy negotiations: the United States cannot afford to let the Palestinian question fester more.[26]

Response by ''opinion makers'' in the United States was also positive. Secretary of State Shultz had worked hard during several weeks of preparation to consult with key leaders of business and labor, from the former du Pont Chairman Irving Shapiro to AFL-CIO President Lane Kirkland. Shultz also met with several influential former U.S. policymakers, including Henry Kissinger. The careful preparation paid off when most of these leaders responded favorably to the president's speech.

In meetings between heads of U.S. Jewish organizations and the White House shortly after the president's speech, most of the Jewish leaders offered cautious support for the Reagan initiative, while some were more positive and some more negative, roughly corresponding to the division in Israeli opinion between Likud and Labor. Officials of the Reagan administration consistently sought to reassure Jewish leaders and others who questioned the U.S. public declaration of its views that the initiative was "not carved in stone and was intended primarily to break the stalemate in the peace negotiations."[27]

Western European and Soviet Responses

In general, responses of western European governments to the new U.S. initiative were positive, despite differences on some points related to what would be required to achieve a Middle East peace settlement. In particular, the Venice Declaration by the ten nations of the European Economic Community in 1980 explicitly endorsed the "right of the Palestinian people to self-determination" and called for the PLO to be "associated with negotiations" for peace. Furthermore, western European governments were more flexible than the United States on a role for the Soviet Union and more favorable to negotiations under the auspices of the United Nations. Despite these differences with the U.S. position, most western European governments tended to defer to the special role of the United States in the Middle East. Indeed, an immediate consequence of the Reagan initiative, and one which was welcomed by the United States, was that France withdrew its joint effort with Egypt to promote Middle East peace negotiations through the United Nations Security Council.

In contrast to reactions from western European governments, the Soviet Union bitterly denounced President Reagan's Middle East initiative, asserting that a "true settlement" would be possible only after Israel withdrew from all occupied territories and the Palestinians achieved their right to establish "an independent state." The USSR differed on the substance of a "fair peace settlement." Equally or perhaps even more important than these differences, the Soviet Union insisted that peace in the Middle East required a process of negotiations which involved both superpowers, not just one. *Pravda* editorially attacked the United States as a "self-appointed mediator" attempting "to arrogate to itself the right to determine'' the political map of the region.[28]

In order to resolve the differences between President Reagan's view and the views of western European governments on the requirements for peace or to overcome the very negative reaction of the Soviet Union, serious diplomatic efforts by the United States were obviously needed. The question was whether the Reagan administration would give these problems the attention they deserved, especially in light of the prevailing, rather simplistic view in Washington at the time that this was ''America's moment in the Middle East.''

Growing Problems

Events in Lebanon in the fall of 1982 offered early signs of the complex challenges to any new efforts for peace. The assassination of President-Elect Bashir Gemayel and the massacre of Palestinians at Sabra and Shatila, as well as the U.S. failure to make any progress on a plan for Israeli withdrawal, demonstrated that restoring order in Lebanon would be much more difficult than U.S. officials had estimated when they predicted that the U.S. and Israeli forces might be out of Lebanon by the end of 1982. (See Chapters 4 and 5.) Moreover, events in Lebanon diverted attention from the Reagan initiative and undermined U.S. credibility in relation to the prospects for wider peace negotiations.

For most Israelis during this period actual events in Lebanon commanded much more attention than the posibility of future negotiations over the West Bank and Gaza. Moreover, despite President Reagan's initial appeal for an Israeli settlements freeze, the United States did not appear to expect any help from Israel to encourage the peace process until after King Hussein agreed to negotiations. The absence of any U.S. diplomatic efforts to achieve a more positive response from Israel meant that even Israelis, including Labor Party leaders, who supported the Reagan initiative found it very difficult to stimulate public interest and debate. Since most Likud leaders wanted the Reagan initiative to fail, they were quite content with the low level of public attention.

Arab perceptions of and anger at U.S. responsibility for the massacres at Sabra and Shatila and for the failure to make progress on achieving Israeli withdrawal from Lebanon also diverted Arab attention from the Reagan initiative and undermined Arab confidence in the seriousness of the U.S. commitment to peace. For Palestinian leaders, including Arafat, who wanted the PLO to respond positively to the Reagan initiative, events in Lebanon made their task significantly more difficult.

All Arab leaders held the United States as partially responsible for the Beirut massacres and for Israel's refusal to withdraw its forces from

Lebanon. Even among Egyptian and Jordanian leaders who viewed the Reagan initiative as very important and positive, events in Lebanon undermined U.S. credibility. While King Hussein apparently saw no realistic alternative to looking to the United States, the mood in Arab countries, including Jordan, in November 1982 was already significantly more pessimistic about chances for a breakthrough than it had been immediately after President Reagan's speech.

In addition to events in Lebanon, there were other international and domestic developments, including serious U.S. economic problems, in late 1982 which diverted the Reagan administration from pursuing its peace initiative. At a deeper level, however, questions were beginning to be raised about whether the Reagan administration was committed to or capable of the kind of creative and intensive diplomacy in support of peace that had been so essential in achieving results in the Camp David process.

Chapter Seven

Why The Initiative Failed

*I*n order to succeed, an initiative for peace in the Middle East obviously required positive responses from the parties to the conflict. Given the complexity and depth of the conflict in the Middle East, however, it would have been naive to assume that any peace initiative would be immediately and universally accepted and, in fact, it is clear the United States did not expect such acceptance.

In September 1982 U.S. officials were pleased with the responses from Egypt and Jordan and welcomed the opening of a dialogue between King Hussein and Yasser Arafat. They were disappointed that Prime Minister Begin's response was categorically negative, but encouraged that Shimon Peres responded as positively as he did. The administration was also pleased by the positive response to the president's speech at home.

The U.S. strategy was based on the assumption that it could get King Hussein to announce Jordan's willingness to join direct negotiations with Israel and that this, in turn, would provide a basis for pressing Israel to demonstrate greater flexibility. By November 1982 there already were indications of serious problems with the U.S. approach. Important Arab and Israeli leaders who viewed the Reagan initiative as a positive development were appealing for more diplomatic help from the United States in order to keep alive the chance of a breakthrough to negotiations for peace.

In mid-November 1982 during a visit to Paris as head of the seven-member Arab League delegation from the Fez summit, King Hussein admitted to being anxious "lest the current momentum toward negotiation be allowed to fritter away."[1] The king blamed Israel for blocking progress by its rejection of the Reagan initiative and the Fez Declaration. More specifically, the king criticized the Likud government's decision to build more settlements in the West Bank and Gaza, a decision made in defiance of President Reagan's appeal for a settlements freeze. Hussein urged western, and especially U.S., pressure to halt the settlements.[2]

King Hussein was hopeful about the Jordan-PLO dialogue which he had initiated with Yasser Arafat but emphasized that he would not come to negotiations without the support of the PLO. In part reflecting his own interests and in part responding to President Reagan's view that self-rule for Palestinians in the West Bank and Gaza should be "in association" with Jordan, the king reported that there was fundamental agreement in talks with PLO leaders on the idea of a confederation after Israeli forces withdrew. In this arrangement, Jordanians and Palestinians would have their own parliaments, passports and flags, but be joined under a common higher assembly with responsibility for defense and foreign affairs.

The king said he believed Yasser Arafat could bring the PLO along, although he emphasized that Arafat and President Reagan had each lost credibility as a result of the Beirut massacres.[3] In an interview in Amman, Adnan Abu Odeh, the Jordanian information minister and close advisor to the king, also worried publicly about the credibility of the United States and moderate Palestinian leaders. Odeh said that U.S. pressure on Israel for a settlements freeze would increase the credibility of the Reagan initiative and strengthen the hands of leaders within the PLO who viewed the initiative as positive and favored a joint approach with Jordan.[4]

By this time, most Jordanian officals and even a few U.S. officials were nervous that Washington policymakers were underestimating the constraints on King Hussein. Many of those who were worried believed a more active and flexible U.S. diplomatic effort was urgently needed. Recalling the situation at the time of the Camp David negotiations, one U.S. diplomat in Amman said, "Carter kept thinking Hussein would participate—despite all our cables to Washington that this was impossible." Then, suggesting the dangers of this kind of unrealistic approach he said, "For the last two years of the Carter administration, it was not easy being an American in Jordan. We were lucky to even keep our relations with Amman."[5]

On December 1 the *Washington Post* headlined a story from Amman,

"Reagan to Receive Proposals: Jordan, PLO to Prepare Mideast Plan." According to this report and my own interviews with senior Jordanian and PLO officials, agreement had been reached on two alternate formulas for a joint delegation for negotiations. The first was for a joint Jordanian-Palestinian delegation and the second for a unified Arab delegation. In either, the Palestinian members would be appointed by and responsible to the PLO, although the PLO would not insist on having the PLO name at the table. Furthermore, PLO leaders suggested that the PLO was willing to name Palestinian representatives like Mohammed Milhem and Fahd Qawasme, prominent deported West Bank mayors, who in 1983 were still not PLO officials.

In mid-December there was additional confirmation of agreement that there would be a "special and distinctive relationship" between Jordan and a future West Bank/Gaza Palestinian entity. Jordanian officials emphasized that this point was a direct, positive response to President Reagan's idea for Palestinian self-government "in association with Jordan." While the PLO still insisted on the right of the Palestinian people to self-determination and to an independent state, Hani al Hassan, a senior political advisor to Yasser Arafat, said, "We are for the confederation," clearly implying that the PLO was willing, in advance of negotiations, to commit itself to a confederation of the West Bank and Gaza with Jordan.[6]

Despite progress, Jordanian officials recognized, on the eve of King Hussein's visit to Washington, that there still was no breakthrough. King Hussein and other Jordanian leaders hoped, however, that the United States would now be prepared to demonstrate some flexibility in its position, in response to what Jordan already had achieved with the PLO.

From King Hussein's viewpoint, there were at least four issues in relation to which the United States could help. First, the United States could support the principle of self-determination for Palestinians and/or show greater flexibility toward a PLO role in relation to peace negotiations. Second, the United States could use its influence to obtain a clearer commitment by the Israeli government to the principle of withdrawal from the occupied territories in exchange for peace. (King Hussein was convinced that in the years since the Likud came to power, there had been a definite erosion of commitment to U.N. Resolution 242 by the Israeli government and by the U.S. government as well.) Third, the United States could demonstrate greater commitment to guarantee the territorial integrity of Jordan, not only from a possible Israeli attack, but also from possible Syrian attack. This related directly to Jordan's request to purchase advanced U.S. arms. Fourth, the United States could insist on a freeze on Israeli settlements in the West Bank and demonstrate its effectiveness in achieving Israeli withdrawal from Lebanon.[7]

On December 21 King Hussein met with President Reagan. The president renewed his appeal for Jordan to enter Israeli-Egyptian negotiations over the West Bank and Gaza. King Hussein reportedly said that, although he shared President Reagan's desire for peace, conditions were "not yet ripe" for Jordan to make such a dramatic move. The king reported that his talks with Yasser Arafat had been very constructive, but he stressed the problems he faced and appealed to the president for help. According to reports, King Hussein raised concerns in relation to all of the issues mentioned above.[8] However, he emphasized specifically that he could not persuade the PLO or any Arabs to enter peace talks as long as Israel continued to defy President Reagan's call to halt new settlements in the occupied territories and as long as there was no progress on achieving Israeli withdrawal from Lebanon.[9]

In an editorial on December 22 the *Washington Post* credited these two points by King Hussein as "right and logical," although it said the king should not "use them as excuses." At one point, echoing the official U.S. position which focused pressure almost exclusively on Jordan, the editorial said, "Every new day he (King Hussein) stays away from the peace table gives Menachem Begin more time to harden Israel's grip on the West Bank." However, a few paragraphs later the editorial demonstrated more understanding of the king's situation and the problem with the U.S. approach by declaring, "If Washington cannot move Israel out of Lebanon, its credibility will be zero when it comes to advancing President Reagan's September 1 proposals."[10]

At the end of a second meeting between King Hussein and President Reagan on December 23, both said they were encouraged, although President Reagan sounded decidedly more optimistic. In his farewell remarks, the president said, "Your Majesty, we've had extremely productive talks and I think we've made significant progress toward peace." King Hussein spoke warmly of the meetings with the president and declared Jordan's commitment to "the cause of a just and durable peace." He said the Jordanian delegation would go back to the Middle East for further discussions "with our brethren" and expressed his hope "to be in touch again. . .before too long."[11] Neither leader spoke about an imminent decision by King Hussein to join negotiations or about the problems which Jordan faced in making such a move.

In the days following the talks, President Reagan maintained an upbeat, optimistic version of the talks, but other U.S. officials were more candid in discussing what had happened. They reported that, while the president agreed with King Hussein that Israeli settlements were "not helpful to the peace process," he offered to press for a settlements freeze only after the king formed a joint Jordanian-Palestinian delegation and announced his readiness to enter negotiations with Israel.[12] The president obviously was not prepared to press his September 1 suggestion that Israel adopt an immediate freeze on settlements to encourage the Arab side to come to negotiations.

President Reagan apparently did promise Hussein that the United States would achieve a breakthrough very soon on an agreement for Israeli withdrawal from Lebanon.[13] While an earlier U.S. estimate that the withdrawal could be accomplished by the end of year obviously was not realistic, the Reagan administration pointed to the fact that Israeli-Lebanese talks were about to start as a sign that an agreement on withdrawal could be reached soon. The failure of the United States to achieve progress in Lebanon had become an increasingly sore point in the Arab world. When King Hussein pleaded for some more tangible evidence of U.S. credibility, President Reagan reportedly urged the king to "watch what the United States does in Lebanon. Israeli forces will be out by March."[14]

By the beginning of March, however, there were still no signs that Israeli withdrawal from Lebanon was imminent. It was not until May 17, 1983 that the United States managed to get an agreement for Israeli withdrawal. It was an agreement that many people, including prominent Israeli leaders, viewed as unworkable from the moment it was signed.

After the December 1982 Hussein-Reagan meetings, U.S. officials tended to focus attention on the need to find a formula for a joint Jordanian-Palestinian delegation, with some more "optimistic" officials implying that this was the only remaining issue. Even on this issue, the United States was unwilling to offer King Hussein any help. Hussein was caught between the 1974 Rabat Arab Summit declaration which endorsed the PLO as "the sole legitimate representative of the Palestinian people," and the Camp David agreement, which, in effect, gave Israel a veto over any prospective Palestinian negotiators, except those residing in the West Bank and Gaza. The U.S. pledge that it would not talk with the PLO until it recognized Israel and accepted U.N. Security Council Resolution 242 further complicated Hussein's problem.

Essentially, the United States put the burden on King Hussein to find what one U.S. diplomat called "a way to wriggle through," i.e., to form a delegation with Palestinians whose presence would not drive Israel away from the table. From the Jordanian point of view, this position was not realistic and provided little help to King Hussein, who consistently said he could not come to negotiations without PLO support. When the PLO offered to name Palestinian representatives who were not PLO officials, the United States still insisted that the PLO have "no public role" in the peace process. Even Mayor Elias Friej of Bethlehem, a possible Palestinian representative for negotiations who was outspoken in his support of the Reagan initiative, refused to accept this condition. Mayor Friej told me several times, and said publicly that, in order to represent the Palestinian national cause, as compared with the municipality of Bethlehem, it was essential that he be named publicly by the PLO.

U.S. officials frequently explained U.S. inflexibility on this issue and on other issues in relation to the peace process by reference to what they believed Israel would or would not accept and, therefore, "what was practical." The political situation in Israel, however, actually was more fluid than the view of it in the Reagan administration.

Israeli Views

The debate in Israel over the Reagan initiative reflected deep divisions over the future of the Jewish state. Growing disenchantment with the invasion and occupation of Lebanon had brought these divisions to the surface in a way that many Israelis viewed as potentially providing an historic opportunity for movement toward peace. Israelis who supported their government's policy in Lebanon argued that, with the PLO militarily defeated and Syria weakened, Lebanon would be the next country to agree to peace with Israel. Furthermore, according to this view, there would not be any serious challenges to Israeli control over the West Bank and Gaza. In constrast to these views, many Israelis argued that the invasion of Lebanon was a tragic mistake which would cost Israel dearly and that exchanging land for peace in relation to the West Bank and Gaza was even more urgent than it had been earlier.

During late 1982 and early 1983 there were signs that Israelis who supported the Reagan initiative, including important leaders of the Labor Alignment, were increasingly worried about the fate of the initiative. Many of them believed that the United States had to push the initiative harder, in Israel as well as elsewhere. It certainly should have been an encouraging sign to the United States that key Israeli leaders were appealing to the United States to do some of the same things being urged by Jordanian and Palestinian leaders.

On November 1, a month before King Hussein's visit to Washington, former Prime Minister Yitzhak Rabin, known in Israel as holding relatively "hawkish" views within the Labor Party leadership, publicly proposed that the Israeli government undertake a six-month freeze on new settlements in the West Bank and Gaza as an inducement to Jordan to join the stalled autonomy talks.[15] This was a week before Prime Minister Begin was scheduled to meet President Reagan, a meeting which did not occur because of the sudden death of Begin's wife. During the same week Aharon Yariv, the former chief of Israeli intelligence, urged the government to adopt a more flexible stand toward the Arabs and warned that current government policies were creating a situation which would endanger U.S. support for Israel.[16]

Statements like these by important Israeli leaders could have been taken as opportunities for the United States to reiterate its own appeals for greater flexibility by the Israeli government. But the U.S. government gave little or no public recognition to the statements, thereby undermining the credibility of these views among Israelis. The Reagan administration's emphasis on strategic cooperation with Israel, plus its view that Jordan had to make the first move, meant that the Reagan initiative was not pushed in Israel even when important Israeli political leaders offered opportunities for the United States to do so.

The United States also failed to take advantage of growing Israeli public opinion which wanted Israel's forces to be withdrawn from Lebanon. (See Chapter 5.) By November 1982, the Israeli occupation of Lebanon already was quite unpopular in Israel, even among many supporters of the Likud government. On November 22, David Landau reported in the *Guardian* that two ministers in Begin's cabinet—Aharon Uzan, minister of agriculture, and Yitzhak Modai, minister of energy—were calling for consideration of unilateral Israeli withdrawal from Lebanon. Uzan urged that "Israel should return to its original objectives—procuring security for the Galilee—and should leave the Lebanese to solve their own problems."[17]

The United States, by this time, apparently was committed to a strategy which assumed that the Israeli invasion represented a permanent reshuffling of political power in Lebanon to the advantage of Israel and the United States. U.S. leaders believed the presence of Israeli forces provided important "leverage" in Lebanon to support continued Christian control and to pressure Syria to withdraw its military forces. While increasing numbers of Israelis were becoming disenchanted with the invasion and occupation, the Reagan administration apparently saw potential gains from the invasion, with the difference that the United States, not Israel, would be the primary beneficiary. Rather than press hard for early Israeli withdrawal, as President Carter had done successfully in 1978, the Reagan administration engaged in long and ultimately fruitless negotiations.

Israelis who wanted to see the Reagan initiative succeed were worried. On the eve of Prime Minister Begin's visit to the United States, a *Jerusalem Post* editorial publicly expressed doubts about U.S. commitment to pursue its initiative for peace.

> There is no evidence as yet that Mr. Reagan and his team are prepared to devote to the Middle East conflict the same single-minded effort which President Jimmy Carter brought to bear on it and without which peacemaking is probably impossible. . . .Thus despite the delicacy of his mission, Premier Begin can yet hope to emerge from the White House, as in the past, feeling free to pursue his ruinous policies further, while the U.S. temporizes, waiting and hoping, not comprehending that it has given him a green light and not having the will to be tougher.[18]

During Prime Minister Begin's visit to the United States, Israeli doubts about U.S. willingness "to be tougher" with Israel in pursuit of peace were confirmed. On November 14 Wolf Blitzer, who was travelling with the prime minister's party, wrote that Israel's ambassador to the United States, Moshe Arens, told him that "no Reagan administration official had ever alluded in his presence—even remotely—to the possibility of cutting U.S. economic aid to Israel because of the continued establishment of settlements on the West Bank."[19] A few days earlier, President Reagan himself, when pressed by a reporter to say how he would respond to another Begin rejection of the settlements freeze, said, "Well, I don't think it would be good diplomacy to be threatening or anything. And I don't believe that's necessary. . . .I think that all of us realize that peace is the ultimate goal there."[20]

The most dramatic revelation of the urgency Israeli leaders supporting the Reagan initiative felt came in the form of two columns on November 15 and 16 written by Max Frankel, the editorial page editor of the *New York Times*. The editorials were based on dozens of interviews with politically important Israelis, including top Labor Party leaders, arranged for Frankel by David Shipler, the *New York Times* correspondent in Israel. The first described the deep debate among Israelis about the "fateful choice" confronting Israel over its future relation to the West Bank and Gaza. Leaders of the Likud government explicitly called for permanent Israeli control from the Jordan River to the Mediterranean, while Labor Alignment opponents rejected this alternative as having disastrous consequences for Israel. They argued that absorbing 1.3 million Palestinians in the West Bank and Gaza will make Israel "either democratic and un-Jewish or Jewish and undemocratic." Frankel concluded this column by describing how those Israelis who opposed continued Israeli control of the occupied territories were counting on the United States to help break Mr. Begin's political power and that they were now advocating means of doing so "that would have been unthinkable even a few weeks ago."[21]

The second editorial, "Help Us by Cutting Aid," focused on Israeli opposition leaders' views of the relationship between U.S. aid to Israel and the power of Prime Minister Begin. In several "not for attribution" interviews with Frankel, high Labor Party officials had argued that Begin's "enormous strength" depended in large measure on "his capacity to evoke support—if not affection—at the White House and above all his use of American aid to fatten the Israeli consumer in an overstretched economy." According to these Israeli leaders, Frankel reported, "Mr. Begin will go on bribing the electorate until his West Bank ambition—underwritten by American taxpayers—is finally achieved."[22]

In this context, Frankel said that several Israeli opposition leaders counselled "sharp cuts in America's nonmilitary aid of $800 million a year" as a way of undermining support for the Likud government and forcing Israelis to take a harder look at the Reagan initiative as a basis for negotiated peace. The reason Israelis suggested nonmilitary aid as the focus for U.S. pressure was to blunt charges that the United States was threatening the security of Israel.

Frankel's two columns, not surprisingly, created a storm of controversy in Israel. Despite the absence of any reference to Shimon Peres in the columns, leaders of the Likud coalition accused Peres of having called for the cuts in U.S. aid and blasted such calls as "selling out Israel." Peres, who acknowledged having met with Frankel, denied having offered any such advice in the interviews. Other Labor Party leaders, including Abba Eban, also denied making the statements. Frankel himself attempted to defend Peres by arguing that "nothing in the article justifies the conclusion that the leader of the Labor opposition, Shimon Peres, gave me advice about American aid."

However, Frankel stuck to the accuracy of his columns as based solidly on the interviews he had conducted. Interviewed on the controversy, he said,

> My articles about a visit to Israel were based on conversations with several dozen leading politicians and Government

officials. As I wrote, I learned that many of the opponents of Prime Minister Begin's policies believe that American economic aid augments his political strength and is therefore underwriting his policy toward the West Bank. Thus many of them wish for reduction in that aid, though they feel they cannot safely urge it in public.[23]

On November 30, after the controversy had begun to cool, David Twersky, editor of the *Spectrum*, an Israeli labor movement monthly, wrote a guest column in the *Jerusalem Post* in which he argued that the substance of the debate should be kept alive. Twersky believed that it was not the idea of a cut in U.S. aid or U.S. pressure in behalf of the Reagan plan which threatened Israel, but rather, "It is this (Likud) government's policy in the (West Bank and Gaza) territories, their hands on the tiller charting our course, which should shake us to our depths." He warned against the anti-democratic nature of many of the attacks on Peres and argued that U.S. and Israeli interests were already too intertwined to say that raising the aid issue represented undue U.S. interference in Israeli politics.

Twersky reserved his main emphasis, however, for what he saw as the most fundamental question raised by the controversy, i.e., "What are the vital interests of Israel?" Twersky argued:

> The ideological minority which remains committed to the annexationist dogma, notwithstanding the political logic of compromise and compassion, is selling the nation a bill of goods. They equate Israeli security with the incorporation of all the territories into Israel. . . .They have a right to believe in this article of faith. . .but we cannot allow them to pass that equation off as sound moral mathematics. . . . They owe us an answer. Why should America pay for paving over the West Bank when Washington perceives this as running contrary to the very possibility of achieving peace? . . .Israel has a right to choose its own direction. But we cannot assume that Washington will underwrite it if it— and a large group of Israelis—believes the direction to be heading for moral and political disaster.

The fact that Israeli Labor opposition leaders were arguing these ideas publicly, despite the obvious political risks in doing so, clearly reflected their sense of great urgency. In Frankel's view the appeal for U.S. pressure to undermine Prime Minister Begin's power was also a sign of the opposition's weakness and desperation. If the Labor Alignment leadership were politically stronger or more courageous, it might have successfully challenged Likud without turning to the United States. Nevertheless, it should not be surprising that Israeli Labor leaders expected some help from the United States. More troubling is why the Reagan administration, if it was committed to supporting Israel and pursuing peace, did not respond to these appeals for help from politically important Israeli supporters of the Reagan initiative.

In fact, Israelis speaking out, albeit timidly, was a reflection not only of their sense of desperation but also their sense of hope that an important opportunity for movement toward peace existed and the United States could help by pressing Israel, as well as the Arab parties, to be more forthcoming. Many of these Israelis believed that a majority of the Israeli people would respond positively to U.S. pressure if they became convinced that there was a real chance for peace. In an interview in February 1983, Israel Gatt, a senior Labor Party official, said he was convinced that even Prime Minister Begin himself might come around to accept a negotiated compromise over the West Bank and Gaza if conditions could be created in which Israelis would demonstrate their overwhelming support for a settlement along these lines.[24]

Gatt did not view the necessary conditions as so difficult to imagine. In Gatt's scenario, King Hussein and Yasser Arafat would announce their willingness to name a joint delegation for negotiations, conditional on Israel's willingness to announce a freeze on settlements. In Gatt's view, this would provoke a fierce debate in Israel, a debate which he believed Israeli peace forces could win. He based his optimism on three factors: first, the greater fluidity in Israeli opinion as a result of the widespread disenchantment with the war in Lebanon, even among increasing numbers of Likud supporters; second, the almost equal division between Likud and Labor supporters in the Knesset, which meant that a crisis could easily bring down the government; and, third, the crucial role the United States could play in applying pressure on the Israeli government, for example, to agree to freeze new settlements for the sake of getting negotiations started. What troubled Israel Gatt was that the U.S. position as an advocate for peace appeared ambivalent and weak, at best.

In the middle of all the controversy sparked by Max Frankel's columns President Reagan and other U.S. officials went out of their way to reassure Israeli government leaders that the United States was not considering any form of pressure on Israel to advance the prospects of peace negotiations.

The problem was not simply a problem with the Reagan administration. In December 1982 a majority in Congress, both Democrats and

Republicans, responded even to hints of tension in U.S.-Israeli relations by taking what they viewed as "Israel's side" against the adminstration. Even though at the time Israelis were deeply and publicly
divided over what was best for Israel in relation to Lebanon and the
prospect of negotiations over the West Bank and Gaza, most members
of Congress appeared to pay little attention to these "complexities."
At the beginning of December, bipartisan congressional leadership insisted, against administration advice, on raising aid levels to Israel.

In an editorial on December 7 the *New York Times* tried to walk
a middle path on the issue of U.S. aid. On the one hand, the editorial
agreed with Secretary of State Shultz that "it would be counterproductive" for the United States to reduce aid to Israel but, on the other
hand, it argued that "now to increase aid to Israel. . .is a calamitous
signal to both Israelis and Arabs who favor negotiation on Mr. Reagan's
terms."[25]

Ironically, while in Israel political leaders publicly debated the relationship between Israeli interests and U.S. policy, most U.S. political
leaders made no reference to this debate in their public positions on
U.S. aid to Israel. The major themes sounded in Congress were that
increased aid levels were a testimony to the basic U.S. commitment to
Israel and that aid to Israel represented a real "bargain" in terms of
U.S. strategic interests in the Middle East. The argument made by
Israelis, that U.S. support for the Begin government was assisting Israel
to go in a direction which was disastrous for Israel—and, in the long
run, would be disastrous for the United States as well—was given almost
no public consideration in U.S. political discussions. Furthermore, except for a few individual Jewish leaders, this urgent concern of an important segment of Israelis also appeared to be given no consideration,
at least publicly, by the heads of most major U.S. Jewish organizations
or other strong supporters of Israel.

While some Israelis expressed profound concern for the future of
Israel, many U.S. leaders spoke of Israel as an "asset" in the global
struggle with the Soviet Union. Senator Rudy Boschwitz of Minnesota
reflected the views of many members of Congress when he wrote, "Increased U.S. cooperation with Israel—both economic and military—
can help enhance the American presence as a deterrent to the Soviets."
Completely ignoring the fact that important Israeli leaders were appealing for a more critical approach to U.S. aid to Israel based on the threat
to the future of Israel posed by the policies of Prime Minister Begin's
government, Senator Boschwitz argued that U.S. aid to Israel is a "metziah" (a bargain).[26]

A review of congressional consideration of aid to Israel in December 1982 reveals that the views of the new right in the United States appeared to have far more influence on Congress—even on members, like Senator Boschwitz, who have a deep commitment and affection for Israel—than the views of Israeli leaders such as Shimon Peres or Abba Eban. U.S. neo-conservatives, including many fundamentalist Christians, tended to disregard how Israelis perceived their interests and instead viewed Israel primarily as a proxy in the global strategy against the Soviet Union or in theological terms, as a "fulfillment of prophecy" in the approaching Armageddon.

A letter to the *New York Times* on November 21, 1982 by Joseph Churba, director of the Center for International Security, illustrated at least the secular variety of the neo-conservative approach. Dismissing the anguished appeals of Israeli Labor Party leaders as "leftist" and "parochial," Churba urged that these appeals "must not deter us from seeing Israel in the larger global picture," a perspective which certainly had a strong echo in the Reagan administration. In Churba's view, "Now more than ever before the Israeli defense forces' principal task is to deter Soviet military adventurism in the region."[27]

This is a view which many Israelis and U.S. supporters of Israel would have rejected in 1982—as they would reject it today. However, most remained silent then and still remain silent in order not to "rock the boat" of U.S. support for Israel. Tragically, during 1982-83, this was one reason there were only weak echoes in the United States of the appeals by important Israeli leaders for greater U.S. help in achieving movement toward negotiations for peace.

To many Israelis who supported the Reagan initiative, the U.S. decision to increase aid to Begin's government in December 1982 was a bitter disappointment even though most would not take the political risks of saying so in public. To King Hussein and other Arab leaders it was another blow to the already damaged credibility of the United States. It added to growing doubts about the commitment of the Reagan administration in support of its own peace initiative.

By early January 1983 there also was growing concern in Washington about the future of the Reagan initiative. The lack of progress in negotiations over withdrawal of foreign forces from Lebanon was particularly discouraging. While the United States had tried to keep from linking progress in Lebanon with progress on the Reagan initiative, by January U.S. officials were acknowledging that concluding negotiations in Lebanon was essential to getting King Hussein to join a wider U.S.-sponsored peace process. By this time U.S. officials were also acknowledging a view widely held among Israeli opposition leaders that the Begin government was stalling on the Lebanon negotiations, not only for the sake of getting the maximum from Lebanon but also as a way of undermining prospects for the Reagan initiative.

In January, the United States did exert some pressure on the Israeli government, including postponing arrangements for a visit to the United States by Prime Minister Begin.[28] By the end of January news reports were unanimous in describing increased tensions between the United States and Israel over the lack of progress on negotiations over Lebanon. There was speculation that the Reagan administration might consider using aid as a form of pressure on Mr. Begin. However, in a meeting with U.S. Jewish leaders on February 2, President Reagan once again ruled out pressure on Israel, despite U.S. frustration with the pace of the Lebanon talks. Edgar Bronfman, president of the World Jewish Congress, said after the meeting, "The administration is committed not to put pressure on Israel: no sanctions, no pressure, nothing like that."[29]

If the United States ruled out any form of pressure on Israel, either to advance the stalled Lebanon negotiations or to enhance prospects for President Reagan's initiative, it should not be surprising that top Israeli Labor Party leaders, particularly after the controversy over the Frankel articles, did not stick their necks out again to urge a tougher U.S. stand for peace. To the contrary, in January in response to speculation that the U.S. might threaten reduction in aid to Israel, former Prime Minister Peres announced that in such a confrontation he would side with Mr. Begin's government.

There were other Israelis, including other members of the Labor Party, however, who continued to address the issue in a critical way. Asher Maniv, editor of the Labor Party monthly magazine, *Migvan*, wrote in the *Jerusalem Post* on February 3 accusing Begin and Sharon of purposely blocking any progress on Lebanon in order to kill chances for the Reagan initiative. In the same article Maniv challenged Israel's Labor-led opposition to break more openly with Likud policies, even if it risked being "accused once again of lack of patriotism, of 'helping the goyim.'" Maniv argued that if the Labor opposition did not take a clear, strong stand, "it will have lost its raison d'etre." Maniv continued,

> The public outcry some months ago against any Israeli support for cutting or reducing American aid may have been understandable. But does the same logic apply to the exposure of the Begin-Sharon machinations to prevent the peace process? Is it not the duty of a responsible opposition to do everything in its power to further the vital Israeli in-

terest in peace? Does one always have to cheer one's own side, even when it plays foul?[30]

Following the release of the Israeli Kahan Commission Report in February 1983 on Israel's role in the massacres at Sabra and Shatila and the removal of Ariel Sharon as defense minister and Raphael Eitan as chief of staff, there were new hopes for progress in the Israeli-Lebanese negotiations. Israelis who wanted to see the Reagan initiative succeed hoped that the United States would achieve a breakthrough in the Lebanon talks in time to encourage King Hussein to come forward for negotiations, a scenario suggested by President Reagan in his meeting with Hussein in December. During the first three months of 1983 King Hussein continued his negotiations with Yasser Arafat and still hoped, especially if the U.S. could demonstrate progress in Lebanon, that these efforts would produce an agreement on a joint Jordanian-Palestinian approach to negotiations.

Palestinian Views

Despite the Reagan initiative's obvious shortcomings from a Palestinian viewpoint, Yasser Arafat and other PLO leaders viewed the Reagan initiative as important and potentially helpful in achieving a breakthrough to negotiations for peace. On November 4, 1982 the *Christian Science Monitor* carried a report by David Southerland of an interview with Khaled al Hassan, a senior PLO official and the one member of the Fez Arab summit delegation with whom the United States refused to meet. Hassan spoke candidly about the "positive points"and the "problems" in the Reagan initiative. "When he (President Reagan) said that the problem of the Palestinians is not a refugee problem, it's a national political problem, we are in agreement." And he said, the PLO agreed with the "five 'nos' in the U.S. initiative: no to new settlements, no to annexation, no to occupation, no to the Israeli concept of self-rule," and no to Israeli control over all of Jerusalem."

The basic problem with the Reagan initiative, in Khaled al Hassan's view, "was that it did not include any clear 'yesses' for the Palestinians. As a people," he continued, "we need a flag, we need a passport, and even, as one of our people said, we need the right to be arrested by a Palestinian policeman. This can be realized by what we call a ministate."

Khaled al Hassan said the PLO favored "mutual recognition and peaceful coexistence of two states—a Palestinian 'ministate' (in the West Bank and Gaza) and Israel." He insisted, however, that the PLO would not unilaterally recognize Israel. Hassan explained that, from the Palestinian point of view, the main problem with the Reagan initiative was that it did not acknowledge the right of the Palestinian people to self-determination and to some form of Palestinian statehood. Hassan said the PLO ''was for a confederation with Jordan but only after the Palestinians had established a state of their own.''

In order to explore next steps Hassan said ''the United States should talk with us. . .and if they find us reasonable, then a mechanism should be drafted as to what should be done.'' The Reagan administration wanted the PLO to authorize King Hussein to enter negotiations on behalf of the Palestinians. Hassan argued, ''If we are up to the standard to authorize a king to talk on behalf of the Palestinian people, why are we not authorized to talk on our own behalf? . . . There is no need for anybody to negotiate for us,'' said Hassan. ''We are old enough to negotiate for ourselves. We are over twenty-one.''

The United States apparently did view the PLO response to the Reagan initiative and Arafat's talks with King Hussein as encouraging. A basic problem in the U.S. approach, however, was its refusal to show any flexibility in diplomatic follow-up efforts to the Reagan initiative. The justification for U.S. inflexibility was that any shift in the U.S. approach to accommodate the Arab side would then make it less acceptable to Israel. This explanation appeared rather shortsighted since the Begin government had totally rejected the initiative from the start and the U.S. strategy was to convince King Hussein and the Palestinians to make a move toward negotiations. The rigidity of the Reagan administration's position despite appeals by Jordanian and Palestinian leaders for flexibility and by Israeli supporters of the Reagan initiative for greater pressure on Israel reinforced doubts on both sides about the seriousness of the U.S. commitment to peace.

Constraints on what Yasser Arafat and the PLO leadership could do unilaterally became clearer at a late November meeting in Damascus of the PLO's fifty-six member Central Council. (The Central Council is a larger body than the Executive Committee and representative of the much larger Palestine National Council, which is considered to be the Palestinians' parliament-in-exile.) At this meeting there were strong attempts by leftist and Syrian-oriented PLO factions to force the Central Council to reject the Reagan intiative because ''it did not openly acknowledge the PLO as the representative of the Palestinian people or the right of Palestinians to have an independent state.''[31] Arafat himself gave an emotion-charged speech assailing the inadequacies of the initiative while at the same time working hard to avoid its outright rejection and to allow him room to continue his negotiations with King Hussein.

The final statement of the Central Council criticized the shortcomings of the Reagan initiative, but did not reject the plan as such. Apparently, Chairman Arafat succeeded in keeping his options open, although the limitations on the PLO leader's maneuvering room also became clearer.

Commenting on the Damascus meeting, the State Department spokesman Alan Romberg said the meeting should be considered as part of the "process of consultations in the Palestinian community and also, of course, with other Arab communities."[32] Completely ignoring the substance of PLO criticism of the Reagan initiative, he went on to say, "we hope the preliminaries can be concluded in the near future so that the main event, the real peace negotiations, can begin." The United States demonstrated no appreciation of the real political problems the PLO faced and even less inclination to take steps that might have encouraged the PLO to be more forthcoming.

William Quandt, former National Security Council Middle East advisor to President Carter, offered a more reflective view on the PLO position. He said that what was happening was "a rather complicated diplomatic game" between the United States and the PLO. According to Quandt, by sticking to the precise formulation of the Reagan plan, the U.S. view was that the "Palestinians and Arabs will come closer to them." At the same time, the Palestinians "are constantly reminding Washington that there are some limitations on how far they can go," given the very important elements which were omitted or rejected in the plan.[33]

Quandt regarded the PLO response as demonstrating that they "are interested in peace, but it has to be a real peace and has to include self-determination and the right to a state." In his view, the PLO was clearly indicating its interest in a dialogue with the United States but not one "based on unilateral PLO concessions, without Israeli concessions." If the United States could not, or would not, achieve any Israeli concessions, e.g., a settlements freeze, prior to the start of negotiations, then the need for some flexibility in the U.S. position toward Jordan and the Palestinians became all the more important.[34]

After the meeting of the PLO Central Council in Damascus, Yasser Arafat left for Amman to resume his talks with King Hussein in preparation for the king's visit to Washington. Arafat left Damascus without meeting President Assad. There already were bitter feelings between Arafat and Assad over Syria's role—and PLO charges about Syria's role—during the Israeli invasion of Lebanon. The two leaders were also increasingly at odds over (1) Arafat's attempt to develop a joint approach with Jordan and (2) Assad's attempts to control or at least very strongly influence PLO strategy. Arafat's willingness to risk widening the split with Syria and with PLO factions based in Syria was important evidence that he believed there might be an opportunity for movement toward a negotiated settlement by working with Jordan, that Syria would not help in this process and that the United States could play a crucial role in the process.

During the Arafat-Hussein talks PLO leadership revealed more clearly the issues on which they were prepared to demonstrate greater flexibility and the issues on which they would likely stand firm. On the proposed relationship between the West Bank/Gaza and Jordan, Arafat emphasized that the PLO already had agreed with King Hussein to go beyond President Reagan's vague idea of "association" to the specific idea of confederation.[35] While on the one hand, in Arafat's view this still meant Palestinians would get their "ministate" first, on the other hand, it meant that the PLO was tentatively prepared to accept the idea of a "presidium" over the West Bank/Gaza and Jordan, headed by King Hussein. Several senior PLO leaders said the PLO was prepared to accept the demilitarization of the West Bank and Gaza, although clearly this was an issue to be decided in negotiations. In response to a question about Israeli security concerns, at one point Arafat himself suggested, "Why not put the MNF (U.S.-led multinational force) into the West Bank and Gaza as a first step?"

Arafat and other PLO leaders also made it clear that they were prepared to accept a compromise formula on the issue of representation in negotiations, i.e., the PLO would accept a joint rather than separate Palestinian delegation, but they insisted on the right of the PLO publicly to name Palestinian participants. While they appeared willing to name Palestinians who might be less objectionable to Israel, PLO leaders rejected the idea that Israel or the United States had a right to veto specific Palestinian participants. Nabil Shaath, a Palestinian businessman and member of the Palestine National Council (PNC) residing in Cairo, who was often mentioned as a possible participant in negotiations, explained that it was essential "to assure their legitimacy and authority that Palestinian participants be named publicly and be responsible to the PLO."[36] This basic point was reiterated to this writer in several interviews during this period with exiled Mayors Fahd Qawasme of Hebron and Mohammed Milhem of Halhoul, as well as Mayor Elias Friej of Bethlehem—all three also frequently mentioned as potential non-PLO officials who might be named as Palestinian negotiators.

U.S. officials acknowledged that the steps taken by the PLO in the talks with King Hussein were encouraging signs of greater PLO flexibility and realism. The United States, however, refused to demonstrate any flexibility in its own position. The Reagan administration continued to say no to the right of self-determination for the Palestinians, no to the idea of a Palestinian state, even in confederation with Jordan, no to PLO participation in negotiations or a public PLO role in naming Palestinian participants for joint delegation with Jordan and no to an international conference for peace. It almost seemed that as the PLO position became more flexible, the U.S. position became more rigid. By the end of 1982 there clearly was a tendency in the Reagan administration to adopt tougher, more confrontational policies toward parties viewed as adversaries of the United States.

Despite a growing sense of discouragement, Arafat and other PLO leaders hoped for more positive signs in early 1983 that would help create a context for the PLO to demonstrate further flexibility when the PNC convened in Algiers in mid-February. In the absence of any tangible signs of progress, tensions within the PLO over Arafat's cooperation with King Hussein and his positive interest in the Reagan initiative were increasing. During January at a meeting in Tripoli, Libya, the more radical factions in the PLO denounced the Reagan initiative and the idea of a joint PLO-Jordan approach to negotiations. In response, Arafat called a meeting of all the PLO factions in Aden, South Yemen, where he managed to get agreement basically reiterating the position of the PLO Central Council, criticizing but not outright rejecting the Reagan initiative.

Even at this point, there were indications, if the United States or Israel demonstrated some flexibility in their positions, that Arafat might propose that the PNC publicly endorse "mutual recognition with Israel."[37] Senior PLO leaders were confident that a majority of PNC members would support this step, if they saw any signs from the United States or Israel that such a move would be reciprocated.

In the absence of any encouraging signs from Israel or the United States by late January 1983, most PLO leaders who believed a breakthrough to negotiations might still be possible had reduced hopes for any dramatic move by the PNC. They now hoped that the PNC would at least endorse the concept of "confederation with Jordan" already advanced by Arafat and leave "the PLO's diplomatic options open" in relation to the Reagan initiative.

In general U.S. political leaders, as well most of the media, continued to express the view that the PNC should take a decisive step toward the positions of Israel and the United States, by either unilaterally recognizing Israel or at least tacitly authorizing King Hussein to negotiate for the Palestinians. There was some recognition of the flexibility already demonstrated by the PLO and of the problems for Arafat if he lacked more tangible encouragement from the United States. But most U.S. observers apparently believed that, to the extent the mainstream PLO leadership was seriously interested in a negotiated peace, its only realistic alternative was to demonstrate even more flexibility than it had so far. There was an almost universal tendency to see the division in the PNC as "between PLO moderates, who favor peace negotiations, and the radicals, who reject them."[38] According to this view, the choice for "moderate Palestinians" was whether the PLO would make the necessary further compromises to get negotiations started, essentially on U.S. terms, or become increasingly irrelevant as an organization. This was not the way most Palestinians, whether "moderates" or "radicals," viewed the alternatives facing the PLO.

The primary division in the Palestinian movement after September 1982 was not between those who favored and those who opposed the idea of negotiations for peace. The division was between conflicting evaluations of whether existing conditions, including especially the role of U.S. policy, offered the basis for negotiations which could result in a just solution of the Palestinian issue. Yasser Arafat, as well as other Fatah and independent PLO leaders, argued that the war in Lebanon had generated conditions, including the Reagan initiative, which potentially represented an historic opportunity for negotiated peace. In this context, Arafat and PLO leaders who shared his perspective believed that the PLO had to offer a creative and courageous response.

Other Palestinian leaders, including the major leftist and Syrian-backed factions, as well as some independents, argued that conditions did not yet exist for achieving a just peace and that the United States, in part because it was too closely tied to Israel, could not play a fair role as mediator for peace. On the eve of the PNC meeting, while Arafat remained committed to continuing his efforts with King Hussein and to exploring the positive potential in the current United States role, the lack of U.S. flexibility and U.S. failure to achieve any sign of flexibility from Israel tended to provide support for the more radical view within the PLO. There were members of the PNC who urged the PLO to show still greater flexibility in order to get negotiations going; and there were PNC members who rejected the idea of any negotiations with Israel. But these Palestinians represented relatively small tendencies at the Algiers meeting. Ironically, moderate forces in the PNC would likely have been much stronger if the 180 Palestinian members from the West Bank and Gaza had not been barred from participating by Israeli authorities.

By the time the PNC convened, it seemed clear that the fundamental issue would be whether Yasser Arafat would have enough support to pursue a coordinated strategy with King Hussein in response to the Reagan initiative or whether, in order to maintain his leadership over a unified PLO, Arafat would have to accept a narrowing of his political options. As it turned out, the PNC adopted a position on the Reagan initiative similar to the PLO Central Council position, thus providing Arafat some room to maneuvre, but not a strong mandate.[39]

The PNC rejected the idea that Jordan should be authorized to negotiate on behalf of the Palestinians, but affirmed a "special and distinctive" relationship with Jordan and approved the concept of a confederation between Jordan and an independent Palestinian state. Significantly, the idea of confederation with Jordan was endorsed across the board by almost all of the Palestinian political factions. Also significant, in terms of the PLO's acceptance of a limitation on its claim of territory, Khalid Fahoum, chairman of the PNC and generally assumed to support "pro-Syrian" views, publicly declared, "The Palestine Liberation Organization wants an independent state on the West Bank and Gaza Strip with Jerusalem as its capital." Fahoum added, in an obvious reference to Israel, "We do not want to destroy any state in the region."[40]

In an attempt to demonstrate continuing PLO interest in a potentially constructive U.S role, Abu Iyad (Saleh Khalef) a top, leftist-oriented PLO leader, gave an interview at the end of the Algiers PNC meeting in which he said the PLO would endorse U.S.-sponsored negotiations with Israel based on the Reagan plan if only "one word is added to the plan: 'self-determination' for the Palestinians." According to Abu Iyad, even PLO participation in negotiations was not a fixed requirement. Addressing the United States, he said,

> Let your government accept the right to Palestinian self-determination, including the creation of a state, not to us (the PLO)—but to the Palestinian people. I can assure you that Yasser Arafat and Abu Iyad would accept. The question of who is in a delegation is no problem to us.[41]

The Sixteenth Session of the PNC made it clearer to some observers that the fundamental issue for Palestinians was not whether or not to seek a negotiated peace settlement but rather how to achieve a peaceful settlement that did not surrender fundamental Palestinian rights.

Following the PNC meeting Arafat resumed his special negotiations with King Hussein. While most observers close to the Amman talks became increasingly skeptical that Arafat and Hussein could come up with anything that would satisfy the United States, U.S. officials continued to express optimism that the king was "on the verge" of obtaining "a green, or at least a yellow, light" from Arafat to enter negotiations. At one point in early April the U.S. ambassador in Jordan practically begged Thomas Friedman, correspondent for the *New York Times*, to stay in Amman because he (the ambassador) was certain that King Hussein would very soon announce his decision to enter peace negotiations with Israel.

Hussein and Arafat apparently did reach an agreement, but when Arafat took it to Kuwait to consult members of the PLO Executive Committee, it was rejected even by members who fully supported Arafat's efforts. The majority of PLO Executive Committe members believed that without some assurances from the United States, the draft agreement went too far toward compromising basic principles of the right of self-determination and the right of the PLO to be a direct participant in negotiations for peace. Arafat offered to resign as PLO chairman but was persuaded to continue. Most members of the PLO Executive Committee believed Arafat had gone too far in showing flexibility in order to reach agreement with King Hussein. Following his rebuff by the Executive Committee, Arafat did not return to Amman to continue his talks with Hussein. The Executive Committee appointed other members to carry the news to King Hussein.

On April 10, 1983, in a televised speech to the nation, King Hussein announced that he had been unable to achieve an agreement with the PLO on a common approach to peace and, therefore, Jordan would not come forward for negotiations. In the April 10 speech and in other public statements during this period, King Hussein openly expressed his disappointment at the PLO for not reaching agreement with Jordan and at the United States for failing to show greater commitment and flexibility in following through on the Reagan initiative.

To recapitulate, here are specific lessons the United States might have learned.

First, the U.S. tendency to assume that King Hussein could get the PLO to give a "yellow-light" or "look the other way" while he negotiated on behalf of the Palestinians misjudged Hussein's willingness to enter negotiations alone and the PLO's willingness to "give away" the role of speaking for the Palestinians. The United States fundamentally failed to understand the nature and depth of Palestinian nationalist aspirations and the impossibility, without guarantees about the outcome of negotiations, that the Palestinian leadership would give Jordan the mantle to negotiate for them, especially given the history of relations between Jordan and the PLO.

Second, although U.S. officials often spoke about the possibility that King Hussein could find "moderate Palestinian leaders" in the West Bank and Gaza who would agree to join with him in negotiations, Palestinian leaders, including those like Mayor Freij of Bethlehem and Mayor Shawa of Gaza who were outspoken in their support of the Reagan initiative, consistently said they would not participate in negotiations without being publicly asked to do so by the PLO. So far, the idea of finding an alternate Palestinian leadership to the PLO, no matter whether it is Israel, Egypt, Jordan, Syria or the United States which is looking for such leadership, has proven to be more illusion than reality.

Third, PLO refusal to go along with the draft agreement Arafat had reached with Hussein reflected the views of many mainstream Fatah and independent Palestinian leaders as well as more radical and Syrian-oriented leaders within the Executive Committee. Objections to the agreement reflected not only various PLO leaders' interpretations of the policies adopted by the PNC but also their expectations about likely outcomes of U.S.-sponsored negotiations based on the Reagan initiative. The United States should have recognized that the positions adopted by the PNC did fundamentally represent the limits of what the PLO leadership could agree to prior to negotiations, especially given the lack of any flexibility by the United States and Israeli at the time.

Fourth, the United States failed to understand the situation in Israel at the time and underestimated the potential popular support among Israelis for greater flexibility by their government in pursuit of peace. The United States ignored or rejected appeals by Israeli opposition leaders, including Labor Party leaders, for more pressure on Israel to take steps that would have encouraged prospects for peace negotiations.

Fifth, King Hussein's announcement on April 10 was viewed by many Arabs and Israelis as another failure of the "moderates" or "realists" on both sides. King Hussein would not come to negotiations without more support and he could not get it from the PLO or other Arab states. PLO leaders who favored a joint approach with Jordan failed to win sufficient support within the PLO, in part because they had so little to show to show for the flexibility the PLO did demonstrate. Israeli opposition leaders who supported the Reagan initiative were unable to generate greater support in Israel, at least in part, according to their view, because of the U.S. failure to exert any positive pressure on the Begin government in the seven months after President Reagan's announcement of the initiative. According to many of these Israelis, the United States expected almost nothing from Israel before negotiations. The failure of the Reagan initiative tended to strengthen hard-line forces on both sides, including Syria and Syrian-backed forces in the PLO, and the Likud and more extremist forces in Israel. (In a tragically ironic coincidence, Isam Sartawi, a well-known PLO leader who openly advocated peace with Israel, was assassinated in Portugal on the same day as King Hussein's speech.)

Sixth, the failure of the Reagan initiative resulted in significant damage to the credibility of the United States as a possible mediator in negotiations for peace. A few months after his April speech, King Hussein made another speech in which he called for an international conference for peace under auspices of the U.N. Security Council, a position which the king has urged since that time.

Chapter Eight

New Opportunities September 1984-January 1986

*D*uring late 1984 and early 1985 several developments in Israel and on the Arab side once again encouraged prospects for movement toward peace negotiations. Israeli elections in July 1984 led to the formation of a unity government headed by Shimon Peres. In the fall Jordan's decision to restore relations with Egypt and the meeting of the Palestine National Council in Amman, despite a boycott by more radical PLO factions, were viewed as encouraging. In early 1985 Israel finally announced plans for withdrawal of its forces from Lebanon. Both Prime Minister Peres and President Mubarak indicated their interest in improving Israeli-Egyptian relations, in part as a positive stimulus to the wider peace process. In February 1985 King Hussein and Yasser Arafat had agreed on a joint approach to negotiations, including the PLO endorsement of the principle of "exchange of territory for peace," the heart of U.N. Security Council Resolution 242.

These developments again encouraged Israeli and Arab, including Palestinian, leaders who believed there were fresh opportunities for movement toward a negotiated peace. Once again they looked to the United States to help coax all of the parties toward negotiations. All of the parties involved bear responsibility for the failure to make progress toward peace during this period, but the focus here is on how the United States responded to the opportunities which arose and to the appeals for help from Arab and Israeli leaders.

Elections in Israel

In Israel the national elections in July 1984 resulted in a deadlock between the Labor Alignment and the Likud coalition. The situation remained stalemated for two months while Labor and Likud each tried unsuccessfully to form coalition governments with the support of smaller parties. Confronted by the deteriorating situation in Lebanon and a massive economic crisis at home, by fall major leaders of the two blocs accepted the necessity of forming a national unity government. Since the Labor Party had won a larger number of seats it was agreed that Shimon Peres would serve as prime minister for the first two years, while Yitzhak Shamir would be deputy prime minister and foreign minister. In October 1986 the positions would rotate, with Yitzhak Shamir becoming the prime minister. Cabinet positions were divided between Labor and Likud, with a few going to representatives of the smaller parties. There was a deep sense of disappointment among those Israelis who had hoped for a clear Labor Party victory in the elections. There also was a widespread fear that the unity government would be totally deadlocked on crucial issues and not be capable of doing anything. At the same time there still was a sense of new opportunity with the formation of a government headed by Shimon Peres.

Israeli hopes that this government could make a difference to prospects for peace were based on the priorities of the unity government, which reflected popular sentiment at the time, and on the historic differences in the positions of Labor and Likud leaders toward the West Bank and Gaza. In late November the *Wall Street Journal* summarized interviews with top Israeli government leaders, including Prime Minister Peres, Deputy Prime Minister Shamir, Defense Minister Yitzhak Rabin and others, as indicating that Israel's priorities were: "to improve the economy, to get out of Lebanon, to warm the frosty peace with Egypt and, if possible, to arrive at a number of small agreements that would build on the present state of hostile but stable coexistence with Arab states."[1] Many Israelis believed that the chances of achieving these goals were significantly greater with a government headed by Shimon Peres, on the ground that Likud government policies had been largely responsible for creating the problems. While almost no one at the time believed there would be a major early breakthrough to peace, many Israelis did view progress on these goals as essential to laying a basis for a breakthrough. Everyone recognized that the nature of the unity government, as well as Prime Minister Peres' own cautious nature, would prevent Israel from taking any bold initiatives for peace.

In relation to Lebanon, most Likud leaders continued to insist on simultaneous Syrian withdrawal and some form of peace agreement with the Beirut government, in part as vindication for the Israeli invasion in 1982. The Labor Party emphasized that security for Israel's northern border was the only really essential requirement for Israeli withdrawal. By the fall of 1983 most Israelis believed that the Labor Party position offered more realistic hope of ending Israel's occupation of Lebanon.

On Israel's relations with Egypt, the Labor Party gave higher priority to restoring normal relations than did the Likud, even if it meant submitting the issue of Taba (a contested one square kilometer of the Sinai) to binding arbitration. While most Israelis felt bitter toward Egypt for withdrawing its ambassador and for its role in freezing the process of normalization of relations, there was no strong national commitment to hold on to Taba.

On the West Bank and Gaza, while Defense Minister Yitzhak Rabin authorized tough new security measures to control Palestinians, in terms of a possible future negotiated settlement, the Labor Party primarily emphasized Israeli security concerns, while the Likud emphasized Israel's historic claim to sovereignty over these areas as part of Eretz Israel. Israelis were deeply divided over the issue. Public opinion polls indicated that approximately forty per cent of Israelis opposed any Israeli withdrawal from the territories, while fifty per cent supported withdrawal from "some or all" of these territories in exchange for peace. Citing the dramatic shift in popular attitudes at the time of President Sadat's historic initiative, many Israelis believed that support for compromise over the West Bank and Gaza would be significantly greater in the context of actual peace negotiations.

On the one hand, the sharp divisions within the new unity government and the problems on the Arab side caused many Israelis to argue that there would not be early breakthroughs on any of these issues and especially not on the future of the West Bank and Gaza. On the other hand, there were Israelis who believed that breakthroughs were possible in relation to Lebanon and Egypt and that there were some encouraging signs, particularly in relations between Jordan and the PLO, which might enhance prospects for negotiations over the West Bank and Gaza. The latter view among Israelis was reinforced by early indications that Shimon Peres would welcome the creation of conditions that would make a breakthrough for peace possible during his tenure as prime minister. Peres apparently believed such a development could increase his political power to the extent that he would not have to turn over the government to Yitzhak Shamir in 1986. In this scenario, at some point Peres could dissolve the unity government and either form an alternate coalition without the Likud or call new elections that would provide a clear mandate for a Labor-led government. The problem was that while Peres could wish for a breakthrough to peace, he had relatively little political room to take steps which could encourage one.

Most Israelis who believed a breakthrough for peace was possible under Peres also believed the U.S. role in helping to create conditions for a breakthrough would be critically important. They were encouraged by President Reagan's address in the U.N. General Assembly in September 1984 in which he expressed U.S. interest in renewing peace efforts based on his 1982 initiative. As they did when the initiative was first announced, major Israeli Labor Party leaders publicly encouraged the United States to play a more active role for peace, including applying pressure on Israel as well as on the Arab parties to move toward negotiations.

Interviewed in *Parade* magazine in November 1984 Abba Eban, chairman of the Knesset Defense and Foreign Affairs Committee, observed,

> The U.S. is going to have to push us a bit more to finish this peace process. That is the greatest gift you Americans can still give to us. . . .America has given us all the money and weapons and diplomatic support we could ever hope for. Yet, to be frank, I think you have to risk getting us a bit angry at you. . . .President Jimmy Carter made us angry, but, as you remember, he also brought us peace with Egypt.[2]

Once again appeals for help from the United States came not only from Israeli peace movement leaders, but also from more centrist political leaders and were motivated fundamentally by their perceptions of the dangers to Israel of failure to take advantage of an opportunity to move toward negotiated peace. Once again these appeals were largely ignored in the United States. While Israeli leaders can certainly be faulted for not taking more courageous initiatives themselves, the failure of the United States to be more helpful, particularly after the 1984 U.S. elections, was a significant contributing factor to the lack of progress toward peace during this period.

Arab Developments

On the Arab side during this same period, there also were new developments, particularly between Jordan and Egypt, and within the PLO. The first came in late September 1984 when Jordan announced that it was restoring diplomatic relations with Egypt, severed at the time of the Egyptian peace agreement with Israel. In taking this step, Jordan broke ranks with other Arab countries, including Saudi Arabia, which had agreed that formal ties with Egypt should not be restored until Arab League members voted unanimously to lift the boycott. While the motivations for King Hussein's decision were complex, it was assumed in Jordan—and to a large extent outside of Jordan as well—that one reason for the move was to help end what the Jordanian Prime Minister Ahmad Obeidat called "the state of paralysis in the Arab world" in relation to many issues, including the Iran-Iraq war and the prospect of peace negotiations with Israel.[3]

It was widely recognized that King Hussein felt frustrated with the inability of the Arab states to come up with a practical approach to negotiations with Israel. In this context, restoring relations with Egypt, the only Arab country to have negotiated a peace agreement with Israel, served as a counter-pressure to the weight of harder-line Arab states such as Syria and, at least, opened up the possibility of developing a new Arab approach. Interviewed about Jordan's decision, Adnan Abu Odeh, Jordanian minister of court and close foreign policy advisor to King Hussein, said, "It strengthens the moderate camp of peace. It's a step that should have been taken and now is the time to take this step."[4]

Interviews with several Jordanian officials at the time indicated that the decision to restore diplomatic relations with Egypt had been under discussion for more than a year, but the timing of the announcement was related to King Hussein's perception that there might be a new opportunity for movement toward negotiations. King Hussein and his advisors believed that an Israeli government headed by Shimon Peres offered better prospects of a negotiated settlement than a government headed by Yitzhak Shamir. Furthermore, Jordanians were aware that the vast majority of Israelis had had enough of the Israeli occupation of Lebanon. That fact offered the prospect of Israeli withdrawal, a development which the king consistently had maintained would encourage prospects for wider peace negotiations.

More important to the king than developments in Israel, however, were indications, including President Reagan's September address to the United Nations, that the United States might be prepared to launch a new effort for peace. In several speeches and interviews during 1984, King Hussein indicated increasing frustration with the U.S. role. At the same time, the king continued to view the U.S. role as potentially the key to negotiations. While King Hussein did not expect the Reagan administration to make any dramatic moves until after the U.S. presidential elections in November 1984, according to one well-informed

Jordanian journalist and political commentator, "The king wanted to put the pieces (of the Arab world) back together and be ready to respond in case something happens after November."[5]

The United States and Israel welcomed Jordan's decision to restore relations with Egypt, although both governments appeared to overestimate the positive implications of the move and once again underestimate the limitations on King Hussein and other Arab leaders. Yitzhak Shamir, in his role as foreign minister, called Jordan's decision "a victory for the Camp David process." Alan Romberg, the U.S. State Department spokesman, said, "We hope other governments will see it in their interests to move in this direction."[6] U.S. and Israeli leaders tended to interpret Jordan's move as an indication that, if they held firm to their conditions for negotiations, the Arab side would eventually come around. An alternate view, voiced by some Israeli political leaders, was that, in order to encourage further positive steps on the Arab side, Israel and the United States had to make specific and positive reciprocal moves.

Reactions in the Arab world to Jordan's decision were mixed and revealed again the limitations on Arab flexibility, particularly without signs of reciprocal flexibility by Israel and/or the United States. Arab reactions gave credibility to the king's own emphasis that Jordan was not prepared to give up its objections to the Camp David process or to act independently of the PLO in entering U.S.-sponsored negotiations with Israel. Egypt's minister of state for foreign affairs, Boutros Ghali, warmly welcomed the Jordanian decision but carefully avoided referring to the Camp David process.[7] The Syrian government-owned daily newspaper, *Al Thawrah*, denounced Jordan's decision as "a treacherous stab in the back of the Arab struggle and an open plot against the Palestinian cause."[8] Syrian officials accused King Hussein of embarking on a second version of the Camp David process, a process Syria rejected both because it was solely sponsored by the United States (and excluded the Soviet Union) and because it ignored or rejected fundamental Syrian and Palestinian interests. Saudi Arabia maintained a studied silence. Later reports indicated that Saudi leaders would have preferred that King Hussein had waited to act in concert with other Arab states.[9]

Yasser Arafat and U.S. Deputy Undersecretary of State Richard Murphy arrived in Amman on the day after Jordan's announcement, but apparently the timing was coincidental. Arafat's visit was focused on trying to reach agreement among leaders of the PLO on convening the Palestine National Council, which had not met since February 1983 because of factional fighting within the Palestinian movement. There already were rumors that Arafat might be considering Amman as a possible site for the PNC meeting. The timing of King Hussein's announcement and Arafat's visit exacerbated tensions within the PLO by fueling speculation among Arafat's critics that he was cooking up a deal with the king to enter negotiations under the framework of Camp David.

Richard Murphy's primary purpose in visiting the region was to explore possible new moves to achieve Israeli and Syrian withdrawal from Lebanon. He went to Amman to inform King Hussein about his talks in Lebanon and to learn more about the king's view of prospects for a wider peace process. U.S. leaders, including particularly Secretary of State Shultz, felt badly burned by their experience in Lebanon and were wary of launching any new U.S. effort for peace. They believed the outcome was too uncertain and the political risks too high. U.S. wariness notwithstanding, the Murphy visit had the effect of providing encouragement to King Hussein that the United States might be prepared, after the November elections, to re-engage in efforts to promote a new peace process.

After the U.S. Elections

Following the re-election of Ronald Reagan in November 1984, both Jordanian and Egyptian leaders publicly declared their views about the urgency of movement toward peace and the need for a new initiative by the United States. As they saw it, President Reagan's impressive victory in the elections gave him greater latitude, as he would be less vulnerable to domestic political pressures. (Abba Eban also made his appeal for greater U.S. pressure for peace shortly after President Reagan won his second term.)

In a telegram congratulating President Reagan on his victory, President Hosni Mubarak of Egypt said, "We, in this vital part of the world, look in faith towards a resumption of the effective U.S. role to achieve the peace process and it is the role we consider essential to realize our efforts." Mubarak warned that "the deteriorating situation in the region calls for urgent action on the part of the parties most interested in achieving peace and security and furthering a just and lasting peace in the Middle East."[10] In an interview on the same day, President Mubarak's special foreign affairs advisor Osama Al Baz emphasized that a reiteration by U.S. leaders of their commitment to the Reagan initiative "could be a helping factor but not adequate. We need further steps . . .the situation now calls for a more solid position from the United States."[11] Specifically, Egyptian leaders, including the late President Sadat, had been urging for some time that the United States accept the principle of self-determination for the Palestinian people and open a dialogue with Palestinian leaders, i.e., the PLO.

The Palestine National Council

The second major development on the Arab side in the fall of 1984 was the decision by the PLO to hold the Palestine National Council meeting in Amman. For many months Yasser Arafat and leaders of the various conflicting factions within the PLO had been working to reach some form of political accommodation or reconciliation that would provide a basis for an agreement to convene the PNC. In June, 1984 a reconciliation agreement was reached between representatives of Fatah, the largest faction within the PLO and the one headed by Arafat, and representatives of the Democratic Front for Liberation of Palestine, Popular Front for Liberation of Palestine and smaller groups which were organized in a coalition they called the Democratic Salvation Front. During the summer more problems developed as leaders of Fatah and the Democratic Salvation Front could not agree on what to do about more radical dissident PLO factions grouped in what was called the National Salvation Front, which effectively had come under Syrian control and had engaged in military confrontation with Arafat's forces in northern Lebanon. By late summer 1984 Arafat was convinced that the PNC had to meet, even if it risked widening the split within the PLO. After compromise efforts failed to reach agreement on holding the meeting in Algiers, a location acceptable to most Damascus-based groups, Arafat accepted King Hussein's invitation to hold the PNC meeting in Jordan.

Palestinians across the political spectrum saw this decision as dramatic evidence that Arafat intended to develop a PLO strategy in coordination with Jordan. Those who favored Arafat's approach thought it the most realistic road to negotiations. Other Palestinians argued that a joint approach with Jordan to U.S.-sponsored negotiations was a mistake because it could not produce even a minimally acceptable outcome. They judged that it was less important to hold the PNC meeting immediately than to reunify the PLO. A reunified PLO, they believed, could again play a key role in uniting Arab, including Syrian, support behind a strategy based firmly on the Fez Declaration, without the risk of compromising the Palestinians' right of self-determination or the right of the PLO to participate in negotiations.

Most U.S. leaders interested in negotiations preferred to avoid having to deal with Syria and considered that Jordan-PLO cooperation was the next best thing to Jordan coming to negotiations alone. Therefore, in general, U.S. leaders welcomed the decision to hold the PNC in Amman, although there were no indications that the United States was prepared to take any concrete steps to encourage Jordan or the PLO to be more forthcoming. Some Palestinian supporters of Arafat questioned why he had pressed ahead when there were so few encouraging signs from the United States or from Israel. Other Palestinians believed it was essential for the PLO to press ahead diplomatically to pursue any possibility for negotiated peace which might exist, even if the chances of success appeared very small. Additionally, holding the PNC was important to Arafat to demonstrate that he could overcome opposition to his leadership and break the deadlock in the PLO.

On November 22, 1984 the Seventeenth Session of the PNC convened in Amman. Apparently a quorum was achieved despite a boycott by Syrian-based PLO factions and the refusal by Israel to allow West Bank and Gaza Palestinians to attend. Chairman Arafat delivered a long speech affirming the fundamental principles of the Palestinian struggle and reviewing its recent history, including the internal conflicts which had been greatly exacerbated in the period since the PLO left Beirut. Nothing in his speech ruled out rapprochement with factions boycotting the meeting and at one point Arafat declared, "Dialogue with all factions remains open because the heart of the revolution is very big."[12] At the same time, he took a tough line in blaming current internal problems on the dissident PLO factions and on Syria. On the central goals of the Palestinian struggle, he declared, "We shall fight for an independent Palestinian state, with Jerusalem as its capital through an international conference, with the Fez resolution as the basis for all our moves." In relation to what strategy the PLO should follow, Arafat favored the development of some form of coordinated Palestinian-Jordanian political initiative.[13]

After Arafat finished, King Hussein addressed the session. Affirming the right of the Palestinian people to self-determination and the PLO as the legitimate representative of the Palestinians, Hussein appealed to the PNC to develop a joint approach toward negotiations for peace, based on U.N. Security Council Resolution 242, which he called the "landmark which should guide us to an initiative to present to the world."[14] The king called for negotiations to take place in the framework of an international conference under U.N. auspices in which the PLO would participate. Arafat and Hussein embraced warmly after the king's speech.

The final communique of the PNC stressed fundamental principles of the Palestinian struggle, including the right of self-determination, the unity of the PLO and the independence of Palestinian decision-making. The statement condemned intra-Palestinian fighting in

Lebanon and interference by Syria and Libya in the Palestinian revolution. It called for an escalation of armed struggle and for increased political cooperation between the PLO and Jordan in finding an acceptable solution to the Palestinian issue.[15]

The PNC communique formally rejected U.N. Resolution 242, the Camp David accords and the Reagan initiative as inadequate bases for negotiations. The delegates instead reiterated the right of Palestinians to self-determination and urged the convening of an international conference to resolve the Middle East conflict, a conference in which the PLO would be a full participant.

Concerning relations with Syria, the PNC called for reconciliation based on the principles of "mutual respect" and "non-interference in the internal affairs of either party," even though it appeared doubtful that any reconciliation would occur soon. On relations with Egypt, which had been a source of controversy ever since Arafat's visit to Cairo in December 1983 and now were complicated by Jordan's decision to restore diplomatic relations, the PNC said that recent developments "demand that relations between the Palestinian and Egyptian peoples be strengthened." At the same time, the PNC cautioned the PLO to "follow a policy towards Egypt that corresponds with developments in Egyptian policy," which to most PNC members apparently meant developments which demonstrated Egyptian recognition that the Camp David process was inadequate for resolving the Palestinian issue.

On the central issue of relations with Jordan and the possibility of a coordinated Jordanian-Palestinian peace initiative which King Hussein had proposed, the PNC affirmed the special relationship of the Palestinian people with Jordan and instructed the new PLO Executive Committee to explore ways to strengthen this relationship, based on the Fez Declaration. While the PNC did not specifically endorse the development of a joint PLO-Jordanian initiative for peace, PNC members agreed that Arafat and the Executive Committee clearly were given the authority to do this.

Interviewed in Amman after the PNC meeting concluded, Khaled al Hassan, one of Arafat's closest senior advisors, reviewed what he thought were the important messages from the PNC to the world. "The first message of the PNC," he said, "is democracy, that is, despite all the obstacles Palestinians face, we have achieved a democratic movement, and the significance of this should be recognized, especially in the West."[16] The second message was that "Despite all the events in Lebanon and after Lebanon—despite all the attempts by Israel and certain Arab states to destroy us or control us—the PLO is still here and there will not be peace without us." Third, in relation to diplomatic efforts to reach a negotiated peace settlement, he said, "The PNC set clear limits beyond which the leadership cannot go, but within these limits the leadership was given flexibility to work out the details of a strategy." He emphasized that the right of the Palestinian people to self-determination once again was affirmed as a fundamental principle and one on which Palestinian leaders would likely stand firm, even if this meant no negotiations in the foreseeable future.

Joining the interview, Yasser Arafat responded to a question about what Palestinians want and what the PLO would do next:

> We will be more strong to fight for peace. We don't want more wars. We're fed up. We're tired of being treated like rats. We're not asking for the moon. . . . We're asking for our sacred right of self-determination. The United States and Israel are ignoring or rejecting the right of self-determination for Palestinians.

In an interview the next day, Khaled al Hassan said, "If the U.S. accepted self-determination, then, okay, we wouldn't need an international conference." Khaled al Hassan's emphasis on the fundamental importance to Palestinians of the principle of self-determination was reminiscent of the interview with Abu Iyad at the end of the Algiers PNC in 1983, when he said that the PLO would endorse the Reagan plan "if one word is added to the plan: 'self-determination' for the Palestinians."[17]

On the basic issues affecting a possible peace settlement, the policies adopted by the PNC meeting in Amman, like those of the PNC in Algiers, reflected two attitudes shared by most Palestinians: on the one hand, an apparently irreducible commitment to Palestinian national identity and national rights; on the other hand, a cautious willingness to explore various options on ways to achieve Palestinians goals.

After the PNC meeting, Palestinian and Jordanian leaders began a series of meetings to explore possible points of agreement for a joint Jordanian-PLO peace initiative. Based on the results of the Hussein-Arafat talks in 1982-83 and the outcome of the PNC, it seemed clear that any joint initiative would come only part of the way toward the Israeli and U.S. positions. By late November 1984, it appeared the United States was ready to revive the Reagan initiative; however, it was also relatively clear that, if the United States did not show more flexibility in relation to the principle of self-determination as applied to the Palestinians, there was not much chance of a breakthrough.

Chapter Nine

A New Effort For Peace

*B*efore the Israeli elections, it was reported that both the U.S. State Department and the White House, encouraged by the prospect of a Labor Party victory, were considering the idea of a new U.S. effort for peace in the Middle East. In the United States, the prevailing assumption in the media was that U.S. leaders favored a Labor Party victory because of the tensions with the Likud government and because a Labor government would be more amenable to taking the steps necessary for peace. Israeli Labor Party leaders chose to make this an issue in the election campaign, arguing that Likud policies in relation to Lebanon, the economy and the West Bank and Gaza were jeopardizing U.S. support for Israel. Likud leaders countered with claims that Israeli-U.S. relations were stronger than ever and with concrete evidence of increased U.S. support for the Likud-led government during the election period. The United States did increase support for Israel during the election period. Moreover, it was clear that, at least in terms of attitudes toward the Soviet Union, the ideological leanings of the Reagan administration were closer to Likud's views than they were to those of the Labor Party.

Nevertheless, when the Israeli elections resulted in a stalemate between Labor and Likud, most observers blamed this development for putting a new U.S. peace initiative on hold. A story in the *Wall Street Journal* on July 25, 1984 based on reports from Tel Aviv and Washington carried the headline, "Israeli Election Upsets U.S. Plan for Mideast: Inconclusive Results Dim Hopes to Push for Talks Between Israelis and

Arabs." Israeli pessimism about the effects of a possible unity government on prospects for peace was reported in the same news story. Knesset member Shulamit Aloni, leader of the Citizens Rights Party (Ratz) and a strong advocate of peace, predicted that such a government "would deal only with economic matters and would freeze action on anything else—peace included." At the conclusion of the news story, a State Department official reflected the cautious U.S. attitude at the time, saying, "We aren't going to take an intiative. We're willing to do things, but we're not in a position to force things."[1]

A day later, however, the *Jerusalem Post* carried a report that Assistant Secretary of State Richard Murphy told Congress that the United States planned to try to reactivate President Reagan's 1982 peace initiative as soon as possible. Murphy expressed U.S. commitment to "continue to encourage Lebanon to deal directly with Israel on the issue of Israeli withdrawal from south Lebanon and security arrangements along their border." He also referred to "welcome signs" of a more positive Syrian role in Lebanon and insisted that Syria would have to become involved in any revived negotiations. Murphy credited Jordan with having "maintained a continuing interest in seeking a political solution to the conflict with Israel" and expressed the hope that "upon larger reflection" both Jordan and Israel would drop their opposition to the Reagan plan and come to the negotiating table. While Murphy did not address the issue of Palestinian participation in negotiations nor suggest any new U.S. initiative, he did pledge that the United States "will work to ensure that no opportunity is lost."[2]

In the summer 1984 issue of *Foreign Affairs*, Alfred Atherton, a senior State Department official with twenty years' experience working on the Middle East, offered his views on the prospects for peace and the crucial role of the United States. Atherton regarded the Israeli-Egyptian peace treaty "as the one new and. . .irreversible reality in the thirty-year-old Arab-Israeli conflict. Without it, the prospects for a comprehensive peace in the region—dim as they may seem today—would be infinitely more distant." He singled out Anwar Sadat, Menachem Begin and Jimmy Carter for their respective roles in achieving this historic breakthrough.

In the current context, while recognizing the difficulties in getting negotiations started, Atherton insisted that the situation was not hopeless. He emphasized the fundamental importance of U.N. Resolution 242 and said,

> If Israel were again prepared to take that concept (territory for peace) as a point of departure, and if the Arabs were

prepared to make the hard decisions facing them, it should not be beyond human imagination to devise arrangements that would take into account the changes that have occurred since Resolution 242 was passed.

On U.S. policy toward the Palestinians, Atherton explicitly criticized the commitment made in 1975 by former Secretary of State Henry Kissinger that the United States would not recognize or negotiate with the PLO until it accepted U.N. Resolution 242 and Israel's right to exist. On the specific issue of the United States talking with the PLO, Atherton, who served under Kissinger in 1975, wrote,

It has long been my personal view that such a dialogue would have been an opportunity to exploit the latent divisions within the PLO, between those who advocate terrorism and reject the very idea of peace with Israel and those who are prepared to make a more pragmatic and less extreme approach.

Atherton maintained that the United States "remains the best hope for helping the nations of the Middle East find a peaceful future," and he believed "that most of the leaders in the area know this in their hearts. It is not too soon," Atherton counselled, "for us to start thinking now about the policies we will pursue in the new year to protect U.S. interests and to achieve U.S. objectives in the Middle East."

Atherton's critical view of U.S. policy took on added significance in relation to the political divisions within the Palestinian movment during 1984 and the efforts by Arafat to convene the Palestine National Council, even if it risked a wider split. Wolf Blitzer, the Washington correspondent for the *Jerusalem Post*, described Alfred Atherton as "one of the most respected Middle East specialists in Washington." While Atherton said that what he had written in *Foreign Affairs* were entirely his personal views, Blitzer observed that "the ideas presented by Atherton were known to be shared by many other career State Department officials."[3]

The combination of positive and uncertain developments led to debate among U.S. Middle East experts during the fall of 1984 about the prospects for peace and the usefulness of a new U.S. peace initiative. At a symposium on U.S.-Israeli relations at Haifa University in November, Sol Linowitz, President Carter's representative to the Palestinian autonomy talks, advocated a determined new U.S. peace initiative now "because time is not on the side of peace." Linowitz, who had been a cautious supporter of the Reagan initiative in 1982, believed that the unity government headed by Shimon Peres would be "more forthcoming'' than the Begin government and that the United States should revive the Reagan plan as a basis for negotiations. In contrast, Lawrence Eagleburger, former assistant secretary of state, and Sam Lewis, the U.S. ambassador to Israel, speaking at the same symposium, both argued that Israel should first deal with its economic crisis and that now is ''not the right time for a peace initiative'' because it might topple the new unity government. Lewis and Eagleburger implied that a better time for a new push toward peace would be mid-1985, after the new Israeli government had made some progress on the economic crisis.[4]

Speaking in Tel Aviv just before the U.S. elections, Ambassador Lewis had stirred up a controversy by explicitly criticizing the Reagan administration's failure to advance peace prospects by its ''lack of urgency about timing,'' particularly in relation to the autonomy talks during the period from spring 1981 until the Israeli invasion of Lebanon in June 1982. Lewis was also highly critical of the Reagan initiative, describing the timing of the initiative as ''abysmal,'' the tactics of presentation as ''worse,'' and the results so far, as ''nil.''[5]

Ambassador Lewis was quite specific in saying what he saw as the problems with U.S. policy in relation to peace prospects: 1) an insufficient sense of urgency; 2) a lack of a sense of personal involvement by President Reagan of the kind shown by Carter; 3) Reagan's emphasis on the superpower conflict in his approach to developments in the Middle East; 4) an earlier U.S. unwillingness to put forward its own specific proposals for a solution for the West Bank and Gaza; and 5) a tendency by the United States to attempt to perform a mediating role ''only with carrots.'' The White House was upset by Ambassador Lewis' speech, but reactions in Israel suggested that the speech reflected the thinking of a significant segment of Israeli political leadership in the Labor Party and in Israeli peace movement circles. Lewis' criticisms of the Reagan administration's approach to peace prospects in the Middle East seemed just as relevant to the situation in 1984-85 as they were to the earlier period.

After his re-election, President Reagan publicly expressed the view that an opportunity existed for movement toward peace negotiations and that the United States had an important role to play. Interviewed in the *Washington Times*, the president indicated that he saw signs that moderate Arab states were moving toward negotiations with Israel and he said the United States would ''do everything we can to hopefully (sic) encourage this trend.'' Among the signs which the president found encouraging were Syria's apparent acceptance of new talks between Israel and Lebanon on Israeli withdrawal, Jordan's decision to restore diplomatic relations with Egypt, the resumption of U.S.-Iraqi diplomatic relations in late November and the fact that the Palestine National Council meeting was held in Amman. The PNC meeting, according to the president's view, was a sign that the PLO was "taking on the radical factions in their own midst."[6] Despite his acknowledgment of these positive developments on the Arab side, President Reagan offered no indication of a shift in U.S. policy toward the Palestinians of the kind recommended by Atherton nor any willingness to follow the advice suggested in Ambassador Lewis' criticism. The lack of any shift in U.S. policy was an important factor in diminishing prospects for peace negotiations.

It was clear that two early tests of the seriousness of U.S. interest in pursuing the new opportunities would be what the United States did in relation to: 1) achieving Israeli withdrawal from Lebanon and 2) improving Israeli-Egyptian relations—developments which U.S. officials claimed were important goals of U.S. policy and essential to encouraging prospects for a wider peace process.

Israel's Decision to Withdraw

By fall 1984 the vast majority of Israelis wanted their army out of Lebanon. For most Israelis, including large numbers of Likud supporters, the illusory goals of Israel's invasion and occupation of Lebanon touted by Sharon and other Likud leaders had long since become less important than the very tangible and painful costs of continued occupation. Half the Israeli population were critical of their government's policies in Lebanon as early as July 1982. By late 1984 Israel's experience there was perceived by most Israelis to be a bitter confirmation of the opposition's worst predictions. Israelis preferred a negotiated withdrawal, but it became clear that this was unlikely to be achieved any time soon. Thus, most people favored Israel's getting out of Lebanon however it could, as soon as possible. By late 1984, some polls were indicating that nine out of ten Israelis favored unilateral withdrawal.[7]

On January 14, 1985, the Israeli Cabinet approved a plan for withdrawal of Israeli forces from most of Lebanon, to be accomplished in six to nine months. Announcing the decision, Defense Minister Yitzhak Rabin said, "After two and half years in Lebanon we have learned the hard way that Israel should not become the policeman of Lebanon."[8] He said that Israel would try to reestablish the situation in the southern border area of Lebanon which had existed prior to the Israeli invasion in June 1982. The fact that the PLO no longer had military bases in the area clearly would make this easier, but the Shiite resistance movement in southern Lebanon, in part a reaction to the

Israeli invasion and occupation, would make it much more difficult.

In the cabinet vote on the withdrawal plan, Labor Party ministers unanimously supported it. Six Likud ministers, including Foreign Minister Yitzhak Shamir and Minister Without Portfolio Moshe Arens, voted against the plan. Three Likud ministers, David Levy, Yitzhak Modai and Gideon Patt, voted for the withdrawal.

Most Israelis greeted the cabinet decision for unilateral withdrawal with a sense of relief, although many would have preferred even a more rapid withdrawal. Since the Israeli army invaded Lebanon in June 1982, Israeli casualties exceeded four thousand. While no precise figure was available, the numbers of Lebanese and Palestinians killed and wounded were estimated to be in the tens of thousands.

In an article entitled "Retreat from Lebanon," Hirsh Goodman, the defense correspondent for the *Jerusalem Post*, wrote,

> Six hundred and nine soldiers have been killed, and over 3500 injured, in a war that went too far, lasted too long, cost too much, and achieved too little. Too much blood has already been sacrificed on the altar of rhetoric for Israelis to care whether the decision to begin to end this war is a redeployment or a retreat. . . . "No more Katyushas on Galilee" was the battle-cry articulated by a prime minister who understood the power of words, but did not understand the limits of power. And it seems as if those ministers who still oppose the military's plan for ending this nightmare have yet to learn the lesson.[9]

Most Israelis, understandably, wanted to forget about Lebanon, just as most Americans after 1975 wanted to forget about Vietnam. But Israel lives and must struggle to find a way to survive in the Middle East. Therefore, of necessity, Israelis continued to debate the lessons from the Lebanon war. Beneath the surface of debate between hawks and doves, there was a widely shared sense that Lebanon represented some kind of watershed in the history of Israel.

Rabbi David Hartman, who is director of the Orthodox Shalom-Hartman Institute in Jerusalem and who lost his own son-in-law in Lebanon, offered his view of the meaning of the war.

> In Lebanon, the grandeur that started in 1967 was exploded. Reality is now hitting on the country, not just with Lebanon but with the economy as well, which was another form of this grandeur, living beyond our means. Just as the Six Day War was an overdose of fantasy, we are now getting an overdose of reality. It is almost too much at once—

Lebanon and the economy together.[10]

The same article in the *New York Times Magazine* which quoted Rabbi Hartman described Israel after the Lebanon war in the following way: "The post-1967 mood has been replaced today by a post-Lebanon mood of pervasive uncertainty about the future, whether that of the economy or the security of the northern border. Painful as it is, there is something healthy about the new mood, which is nothing if not pragmatic." The Israeli Cabinet decision for unilateral withdrawal from Lebanon fundamentally reflected this new pragmatism. As Prime Minister Peres said in defending the withdrawal plan, "There were no good options in Lebanon."

In the United States, editorials in most major newspapers expressed support for Israel's decision for unilateral withdrawal. The *New York Times*, in an editorial entitled "The Truth of Lebanon," praised the wisdom of the Israeli government's decision and counselled,

> The United States, too, has much to learn from the Sharon adventure. . . .It was negligent in not opposing his war plans and in later letting its "peacekeeping" force assume his political objectives. Once trapped, it invited further humiliation by sponsoring an unattainable coordinated withdrawal by Syria and Israel. It took months for Washington finally to pull back and let the Lebanese, Syrians and Israelis struggle by themselves for an unarticulated accommodation.[11]

Official U.S. government response to Israel's decision, however, indicated that the United States had not yet learned what at least some Israelis had learned from the Lebanon experience. The Reagan administration, like hardline ministers in the Israeli Cabinet, opposed Israel's decision to withdraw. Officially, the State Department declared that "we have consistently supported efforts to bring about the total withdrawal of all foreign forces from Lebanon, and we encourage the parties to continue their efforts to bring about a negotiated withdrawal." Privately, an administration official said, "We understand (Israel's) impatience, but we don't think this is the way to go about it."[12]

From the Reagan administration's point of view, Israel's continued occupation in Lebanon served U.S. strategic interests and cost the United States very little. The Israeli military occupation was providing what Washington erroneously viewed as "a calming effect in southern Lebanon" and it was keeping military pressure on Syria eventually to withdraw.[13] In the period immediately prior to Israel's decision to withdraw, Henry Kissinger was telling his friends in Washington that

"Israel should not budge from its current lines until the Syrians are ready to compromise." Kissinger's view, which many Reagan administration officials supported, was that a unilateral Israeli withdrawal would be a victory for Syria and that would translate into "a Soviet triumph over America."[14]

Between 1982 and 1984, the majority of Israelis and many of Israel's supporters in the United States had come, through a painful process, to view Israel's invasion of Lebanon as a political and military—and for some a moral—disaster. But even after all that had happened most U.S. political leaders appeared still to be operating on the basis of the same illusions that had led the United States to provide tacit support for the invasion in the first place and to see possibilities for U.S. strategic gains as a result of the invasion. The United States assumed it could manage the Lebanon crisis to U.S. advantage, in part using Israeli forces as proxies. This view did not augur well for U.S. support for the new Israeli pragmatism, whether in relation to getting out of Lebanon, or improving relations with Egypt, or the much more daunting challenge of developing a wider peace process which potentially could resolve the conflict with the Palestinians. Furthermore, U.S. support for the Israeli occupation in Lebanon, even after most Israelis opposed it, was a contributing factor to increased terrorist attacks, such as the TWA highjacking, directed against the United States.

Israeli-Egyptian Relations

The Israeli decision to withdraw from Lebanon heightened prospects of a thaw in the "frozen peace" between Israel and Egypt. Beginning in September 1984 there had been a series of signals and emissaries sent back and forth between Cairo and Jerusalem. President Mubarak sent a warm message of congratulations to Shimon Peres when he became the prime minister of Israel. In the message, Mubarak reportedly urged Israel to take "decisions that will remove obstacles on the path of the peace process."[15] Very soon after assuming office, Prime Minister Peres announced that improving relations with Egypt was a major priority for the new government of Israel.

The issue of Taba, one square kilometer of contested land on the Gulf of Aqaba near Eilat with an Israeli resort hotel on it, was acknowledged by both Egypt and Israel as the most specific issue which needed to be resolved if relations were to be improved. Egypt also insisted that Israel needed to withdraw from Lebanon and take steps to ease occupation policies toward Palestinians living in the West Bank and Gaza. Israel wanted a commitment from Egypt not simply to return its ambassador (the ambassador had been recalled in reaction to the massacres at Sabra and Shatila), but to get on with the fuller dimensions of normalization of relations promised in the Camp David treaty. The situation was further complicated, however, by political pressures and counter-pressures in both Egypt and Israel over how flexible or inflexible these governments should be in negotiations, in part reflecting how high a priority different leaders gave to improving relations.

Both Peres and Mubarak saw improvement in Israeli-Egyptian relations not only as important in itself, but also as essential to enhancing prospects for a wider peace process. As Ezer Weizman, Israeli minister-without-portfolio and a strong advocate of improved relations, put it, "If we don't reach a settlement with Egypt, we won't reach one with anyone. We won't reach any peace treaty with Jordan if we don't finish the business with Egypt."[16] On the Arab side, particularly after Jordan restored relations with Egypt, President Mubarak was eager to demonstrate that Egypt was in a position to help advance Arab interests vis-a-vis Israel.

Furthermore, progress in Egyptian-Israeli relations was seen on both sides as easing the way for a new initiative for peace by the United States, despite the very negative U.S. experience in Lebanon. Interviews with U.S. officials in the Middle East during this period consistently indicated that the United States viewed a breakthrough in Israeli-Egyptian relations as the single most important factor for improving the prospects of getting a wider peace process going.

As early as November 1984 there was evidence that, although Israel and Egypt needed U.S. help, the Reagan administration was not willing to make the kind of high-level commitment that probably would be necessary to achieve a breakthrough. Working against a full U.S. commitment were Secretary of State Shultz's extreme frustration over the U.S. experience in Lebanon and his tendency to blame the Arabs for U.S. failure. Shultz was reported still to be irritated with Egypt for not returning its ambassador to Israel after Israel and Lebanon signed the ill-fated May 17 agreement.[17]

In any case, Shultz' view reinforced the U.S. tendency to play a low-key role and to conclude that, if pressure was needed, it was needed primarily on Egypt. The U.S. attitude worried many Israelis who wanted a breakthrough in relations with Egypt and who believed that pressure also was needed on Israel. Once again it is possible to fault Egyptian and Israeli leaders for not taking bolder initiatives on their own to improve relations. Yet it is important to look critically at the U.S. failure to play a more timely and constructive role, particularly on this issue of getting relations between Israel and Egypt "back on track," which

U.S. Middle East diplomats stressed was critically important to U.S. policy.

At the end of November 1984 tensions between Prime Minister Peres and Deputy Prime Minister Shamir heated up over even the small, tentative steps Peres was taking to improve relations with Egypt. Shamir wanted Israel to take a very tough line in talks with Egypt and saw no great urgency in improving relations. Some Israelis accused the United States of taking "Shamir's side" of the internal Israeli debate, in part because U.S Ambassador Lewis' publicly expressed view that the time was not ripe for a new U.S. diplomatic push for peace appeared to contradict Peres' sense of urgency.[18]

Interviewed in the January 14, 1985 *U.S. News and World Report*, Peres and Mubarak not only indicated that they both felt a sense of urgency, but that they were optimistic that a breakthrough was possible. Peres warmly praised Mubarak as "a natural and powerful leader. . .whom the entire world learned quickly to respect and to trust." Mubarak described how during the Israeli elections he was "very anxious for Peres to take over," and said, "I am very optimistic since he came to power." Concerning the issue of Taba, Prime Minister Peres said, "We can easily solve such disputes. We must continue to work together for the expansion of the peace process in the Middle East." And President Mubarak said, "Let us negotiate and come to a decisive settlement of the Taba problem. It's nothing but a hotel. Why make an issue over it?"[19]

In late January Israel and Egypt held three days of negotiations over Taba at Beersheba in southern Israel. Enough progress was made to justify additional meetings. A major issue was whether the question of Taba should be submitted to "binding arbitration," a step called for in the Camp David agreement after negotiations and conciliation have been tried and failed. Egypt favored submitting the issue to binding arbitration; Israeli leaders were divided, with Peres' supporters leaning in favor and Shamir's supporters opposed. Foreign Minister Shamir, who had voted against the Camp David peace treaty in the first place, continued to urge a tougher Israeli line in the talks. Prime Minister Peres, seeing an opportunity for a breakthrough, favored greater Israeli flexibility in the negotiations. Many Israelis who supported Peres' view, but recognized the limitations imposed by the unity government, hoped for a more decisive role by the United States. Once again they were disappointed.

Sadly, while U.S. diplomats in the region continued to emphasize that a breakthrough in Israeli-Egyptian relations was essential to restarting the peace process, the U.S. role in the Taba talks was very low-key. For one thing, the United States was represented by very knowledgeable but low-level U.S. diplomats. The Reagan administration demonstrated no urgency even in early 1985, after announcement of the Jordan-PLO joint initiative for peace, to give higher priority to achieving a breakthrough in the Egyptian-Israeli talks by, for example, sending a higher-ranking State Department official or U.S. special envoy to participate.

The pattern of low-key U.S. involvement in the Israeli-Egyptian talks continued throughout 1985. To the extent that the Reagan administration was not prepared to re-engage wholeheartedly in the limited process of improving Israeli-Egyptian relations, it seemed even more unlikely that the United States would play an important and constructive role in launching a wider peace process which could deal with the Palestinian issue. The United States finally did send Assistant Secretary of State Richard Murphy to participate in the Taba talks in August 1986, but this was long after the Arafat-Hussein initiative for peace had broken down and too late to help Prime Minister Peres use the breakthrough in relations with Egypt as a step toward the much more challenging prospect of wider peace negotiations.

The Jordan-PLO Initiative for Peace

After the 1984 Palestine National Council session in Amman, Jordanian and PLO leaders held a series of meetings to explore possible points which could form the basis of a joint Jordanian-PLO initiative for peace. On February 11 Hussein and Arafat signed an agreement on a common approach to negotiations. The agreement was not officially released immediately by either Jordan or the PLO, at least in part because of last minute clarifications of wording. But the Democratic Front for the Liberation of Palestine, a radical faction of the PLO, released the text in Damascus and began to attack it. On February 24, the Jordanian minister of information, Taher Hikmat, officially released the text of the agreement in Amman.

The February 11 agreement represented a very important development in relations between Jordan and the PLO and reflected signficantly greater flexibility by the PLO in its approach to a negotiated peace settlement than it had demonstrated heretofore. Since there was a great deal of discussion about the agreement, it seems useful to reproduce the full text.

> Emanating from the spirit of the Fez summit resolutions, approved by Arab states, and from United Nations resolutions relating to the Palestine question, In accordance with

international legitimacy, and deriving from a common understanding on the establishment of a special relation between the Jordanian and Palestinian peoples, The Government of the Hashemite Kingdom of Jordan and the Palestine Liberation Organization have agreed to move together toward the achievement of a peaceful and just settlement of the Middle East crisis and the termination of Israeli occupation of the occupied Arab territories, including Jerusalem, on the basis of the following principles:

1. Total withdrawal from the territories occupied in 1967 for comprehensive peace as established in United Nations and Security Council resolutions.

2. Right of self-determination for the Palestinian people: Palestinians will exercise their inalienable right of self-determination when Jordanians and Palestinians will be able to do so within the context of the formation of the proposed federated Arab states of Jordan and Palestine.

3. Resolution of the problem of Palestinian refugees in accordance with United Nations resolutions.

4. Resolution of the Palestine question in all its aspects.

5. And on this basis, peace negotiations will be conducted under the auspices of an international conference in which the five permanent members of the Security Council and all the parties to the conflict will participate, including the Palestine Liberation Organization, the sole legitimate representative of the Palestine people, within a joint (Jordanian-Palestinian) delegation.[20]

In Israel, on February 17 the *Jerusalem Post* reported the text of the agreement. The news story, written by David Bernstein, the Post Mideast affairs reporter, was headlined, ''Arafat Seen Accepting 'Land for Peace' Formula.'' The story was positive in tone and recognized that the agreement represented a significant breakthrough. Bernstein confirmed that ''while Arafat did not accept U.N. Security Council Resolution 242, he did, for the first time, endorse the 'territory for peace' formula at the heart of that resolution.'' In the same news story Bernstein reported very favorable Egyptian reaction to the Jordan-PLO agreement and quoted President Mubarak as warning that Israel ''would commit a historic mistake'' if it ''failed to respond to this step.'' Mubarak, who was scheduled to visit Washington in the following month, said he would also do his best to persuade the United States to respond positively and to re-engage actively in the pursuit of peace in the Middle East.[21]

Official Israeli reactions to the Jordan-PLO agreement reflected the division between Labor and Likud in the unity government. Prime Minister Peres responded cautiously, saying, "There is no need for a hasty reaction. Let's wait and see what really happened."[22] Deputy Prime Minister Yitzhak Shamir disagreed and declared, "If Hussein really desires peace with Israel, he should sever his contacts with Arafat."[23] Abba Eban, taking a phrase reportedly used by King Hussein, described the agreement as "a narrow opening." However, he worried that "the opening is so narrow that if it is not widened, the Israelis will have a hard time noticing it." Eban believed that the United States could play a helpful role in "widening the narrow opening." He had spoken many times about the need for a more active and constructive U.S. role and about the need for positive U.S. pressure on Israel, as well as on the Arab side, to be more forthcoming.[24]

U.S. response to the Jordan-PLO agreement was very cautious.[25] Initial statements from White House officials suggested that President Reagan was encouraged by the agreement, but later statements by Secretary of State Shultz indicated that the United States would move very slowly in deciding how to respond. Initially, U.S. officials emphasized that the United States wanted answers to its long-standing questions: Did the February 11 agreement's endorsement of the "land for peace" concept mean the PLO was willing to accept U.N. Security Council Resolution 242? To what extent would the PLO be willing to name "non-PLO" Palestinians to a joint delegation, who would be acceptable to the United States and Israel? What was the role of the international conference, which up to this point the United States opposed, in favor of U.S.-sponsored direct negotiations between the parties?[26] On many occasions in the past, U.S. leaders had emphasized the importance of one or another side in the Arab-Israeli conflict taking positive steps toward negotiations, even if the whole picture was not in place. Now, the Reagan administration appeared to want clear positive answers to all its questions before the United States would make any moves.

Palestinian and Jordanian leaders—and most Arab leaders who believed an opportunity for peace existed—thought that the February 11 Jordan-PLO agreement represented a major breakthrough. To them, the U.S. response was very frustrating and confirmed fears among some of them that the Reagan administration lacked a commitment to pursue peace. In early March Yasser Arafat, who was defending the agreement with Jordan against criticism from some of his more radical colleagues within the PLO, denounced the U.S. response as "shameful." At the same time Arafat appealed again for U.S. help in achieving movement toward negotiations.[27] Adding to Palestinian frustration with U.S. policy, during the first week of March, the U.S State Department refused to allow Zehdi Terzi, the PLO's official observer at the United Nations, to visit Washington to meet with a group of members of Congress at their request to discuss and clarify the February 11 agreement.

Mohammed Milhem, the deported mayor of Halhoul in the West Bank who was named to the PLO Executive Committee in November 1984 and is viewed as a popular moderate Palestinian leader, also expressed deep disillusionment. "I thought the United States would change perhaps not 180 degrees, but maybe 90 or 100," he said. "Instead, Washington is beating around the bush." According to Milhem's view, in signing the February 11 agreement the PLO leadership had gone as far as it could without some reciprocal steps from Israel or the United States. Milhem said he now believed that the United States was attempting to extract concessions from the PLO that "will make us lose the confidence of our people and violate the resolutions of the Palestine National Council."[28]

By the middle of March 1985 King Hussein and senior Jordanian officials also were publicly expressing disappointment and frustration with the U.S. response. Interviewed by the *New York Times*, King Hussein called the February 11 agreement the "last chance for peace" and politely but firmly insisted that the United States must take a more active role in developing the peace process, a process in which the king believed the PLO also had to be involved. In order to keep the momentum alive, King Hussein said it was essential at a minimum for the United States to meet soon with a joint Jordanian-Palestinian delegation to explore next steps.[29]

Hopes for a breakthrough toward negotiations rose again in late March when it was learned that the United States would send Assistant Secretary of State Murphy to the Middle East in April. Murphy's trip included a meeting in Jerusalem with thirty prominent Palestinians from the West Bank and Gaza, representing a wide spectrum of Palestinian views. In the meeting, the Palestinians unanimously stressed that "the United States should establish contacts with the Palestine Liberation Organization" and that "peace will not be achieved as long as the Palestinians are ignored and as long as their right to self-determination and a state of their own is not recognized."[30]

A primary focus of Murphy's trip was to explore the possibility of a U.S. meeting with a joint Jordanian-Palestinian delegation. The United States still insisted that none of the Palestinians named could be PLO officials. It became clear during April that Arafat, aware of his own thin margin of support within the PLO for pursuing the joint agreement with King Hussein, was not willing to make any further concessions unless the United States offered something in exchange. Arafat put forward several suggestions, such as that Washington recognize the PLO as the legitimate representative of the Palestinian people, or recognize the right of the Palestinian people to self-determination.[31] There were no indications at this point, however, that the United States was prepared to show any flexibility in its positions on these issues or to take any concrete steps which might encourage the PLO to be more forthcoming.

In contrast, there were signs during the spring of 1985 that some Israelis who believed an opportunity for peace existed believed Israel should show greater flexibility toward the Palestinians. Shlomo Lahat, the popular, independent-minded mayor of Tel Aviv, told this writer March 1985, "If we Israeli Jews demand the right of self-determination, how can we deny this right to the Palestinians?" He emphasized that "Israel must negotiate with the PLO—precisely because the PLO is our enemy." When asked if this were something he was prepared to say publicly, he answered, "Of course, it is much too important only to say it in private."[32] Unfortunately, however, Lahat did not say this very often or loudly in Israel.

On March 10 Meir Merhav, a senior editor of the *Jerusalem Post*, wrote that the Israeli "consensus" against talking with the PLO is "utter nonsense, at least for those who do not want Israel to become a binational state, or worse still, an apartheid regime." Merhav argued against trying to find "proxy representatives" since, in his view, it is only the Palestinians "who can appoint their spokesmen, not us, not King Hussein, not President Mubarak." Merhav reflected a sense of urgency felt by many Israelis and he emphasized why it was essential to get the PLO into negotiations, rather than keep them out:

> How long must it take, how many more wars must we fight, how many lives must be wasted and how crushing must the economic burden become for the realization to sink in that the PLO, detestable as it may appear to us, is the representative of the Palestinians and holds the power of veto over anything that any Arab state or any group of Palestinians might agree on in an Arab-Israeli settlement.[33]

These views were anathema to many Israelis, but they also were increasingly accepted as realistic by others. No leader in the Israeli government (except for a few members of the Knesset) would have dared to espouse the views publicly, but some Israeli leaders acknowledged privately that Merhav was probably correct.

The Reagan administration clearly did not agree with the views of Israelis who believed it was necessary to talk with the PLO nor did it share their sense of urgency. In May 1985 Secretary of State Shultz was scheduled to visit the Middle East, but only Israel, primarily to smooth U.S.-Israeli relations after President Reagan's visit to a military cemetery in Bitburg in West Germany several months earlier. As a result of Murphy's trip in April and to avoid offending President Mubarak and King Hussein, Shultz was persuaded at the last minute to add Egypt and Jordan to his itinerary. His visit was another opportunity to explore a U.S. meeting with some form of Jordanian-Palestinian delegation. In the course of Shultz' discussions in Israel, Prime Minister Peres softened his opposition to the idea of such a meeting if there could be some assurance that it would lead to direct negotiations.

In the meantime, Jordan and the PLO had offered the United States a list of names of Palestinians who would participate in the joint delegation. Jordanian and PLO leaders hoped that Secretary Shultz would approve the names during his visit and that Richard Murphy would remain in the Middle East to hold an initial round of talks with the joint delegation. However, after the list of Palestinians was leaked in Israel, the United States objected to several of the names, including Mayor Mohammed Milhem and Anglican Bishop Eliya Khoury because they were members of the PLO Executive Committee. The United States refused to meet with the joint delegation.[34]

Despite this, during May when King Hussein was scheduled to visit Washington, there were new encouraging signs that a breakthrough was still possible. On May 14, interviewed in Amman, Yasser Arafat announced that the PLO was willing explicitly to accept U.N. Resolution 242, which recognized Israel, if the United States explicitly endorsed the right of the Palestinian people to self-determination.[35] Arafat's statement was consistent with the February 11 Jordan-PLO agreement and with earlier PLO support for a 1982 Franco-Egyptian initiative in the U.N. Security Council which would have added the principle of self-determination for Palestinians to Resolution 242 as the basis for Middle East peace negotiations. Coming on the eve of King Hussein's visit to the United States, the statement demonstrated Arafat's interest in helping to achieve a breakthrough, as well as the limitations on how far the PLO would go unilaterally without some reciprocal positive movement from Israel and/or the United States.

On May 29 King Hussein announced in Washington that the PLO was prepared to accept U.N. Resolution 242, although he did not repeat the PLO insistence on reciprocal U.S. acceptance of the Palestinian right of self-determination. In response to Jordan's efforts, the United States indicated that it might be willing to soften its opposition to King Hussein's view that negotiations should take place within the framework of some form of international conference. While U.S. officials continued to maintain that the international conference was merely "a cover" for the real, i.e., direct, negotiations with Israel, and that the conference would not have any authority in the negotiations, even this much U.S. flexibility was encouraging to King Hussein. King Hussein returned to Jordan pleased that, as a result of his discussions in Washington, it appeared relatively certain that the United States would now agree to meet with a joint Jordanian-Palestinian delegation later in the summer.[36]

At his June 1 press conference, Secretary of State Shultz reinforced the sense that things were moving in a positive way. Shultz announced that he expected U.S. officials would meet with a joint delegation "fairly soon." He added later that this would occur "assuming that we can put together the right structure of a delegation," making it clear that the United States still assumed a veto over Palestinian representatives. The issue of which Palestinians the PLO would name and whether the United States would accept them was obviously still an issue.[37] At the same time, there now was the encouraging new prospect, raised by Arafat's May 14 statement and King Hussein's announcement in Washington, that the PLO was prepared specifically to endorse U.N. Security Council Resolution 242. Senior Jordanian and PLO officials interviewed in June said that this issue should be addressed in the first meeting of the United States with a joint delegation.[38] In a meeting in Amman on June 22 with U.S. Christian and Jewish leaders, Arafat repeated his earlier statement. "I am ready explicitly to accept U.N. Resolution 242, if only the United States will accept the principle of self-determination for the Palestinians."[39]

In Israel, reactions to these developments once again reflected the divisions within the unity government and underlined the sense of urgency some Israelis felt to pursue whatever opportunity for negotiations existed while Shimon Peres was still the prime minister. Reacting strongly to the possibility that the United States would soon meet with a joint Jordanian-Palestinian delegation, possibly including PNC members, Deputy Prime Minister Yitzhak Shamir totally rejected the idea, saying that the PNC was the "brains and soul" of the PLO. Prime Minister Peres, eager to exploit the current opportunity and apparently accepting the need for some flexibility as to which Palestinians would be included, said that "Israel rejects the participation of PLO people and anyone who advocates the destruction of Israel." This was widely interpreted as accepting other Palestinians, possibly including some PNC members who were not "PLO officials" and, in general, giving the United State a little more room to maneuver.[40]

During July most of the signals continued to be positive in relation to the prospects for a meeting between the United States and a joint Jordanian-Palestinian delegation. On July 16 senior State Department officials expressed optimism that such a meeting would take place in August when Assistant Secretary of State Murphy planned to visit the Middle East and that the meeting could be very helpful in breaking the logjam in the peace process.[41] On July 18, reacting to reports that Israel had "vetoed" a list of Palestinians proposed to be participants in the joint delegation, U.S. officials said Israel did not have a veto in the matter and that this was "our decision. . . .If something will help the (peace) process, we will do it."[42]

During late July and early August, however, new uncertainty began to arise about whether the United States would actually go through with the meeting. The Reagan administration now began to indicate that it wanted more assurance that the meeting would lead quickly to direct negotiations with Israel. Obviously, this new emphasis presented a problem in that King Hussein's scenario projected several steps, including reciprocal statements by the PLO and the United States such as suggested by Arafat and then arranging for an international conference, in the context of which actual negotiations for peace would take place.

Assistant Secretary of State Murphy led a U.S. delegation to Jordan in August as planned, but Washington refused to allow him or any U.S. officials to meet with a joint Jordanian-Palestinian delegation, even though Palestinians who were to participate, including some from the West Bank and Gaza, had gathered in Amman in anticipation of the meeting. In announcing that there would be no meeting, Murphy said that the United States wanted "to chart a feasible and expeditious course for the entire process—not just one meeting."[43] This emphasis seemed to contradict earlier U.S. approaches to development of a peace process which emphasized the importance of taking small positive steps, even if the whole picture was not yet in view.

In any case, the U.S. refusal struck a hard blow to Jordanian and Palestinian hopes and tended to undermine support for those Israelis who were urging their own government to adopt a flexible position toward negotiations. There were indications that Murphy understood the damaging effects of the U.S. refusal to go through with the meeting.

After he returned from the Middle East, there were reports that he told Secretary of State Shultz that there was no chance of movement toward negotiations unless the United States agreed to meet with a joint Jordanian-Palestinian delegation.[44] The Reagan administration apparently was not prepared to take any political risks for peace. Even more troubling, however, the U.S. refusal to go through with the meeting reinforced growing doubts that peace in the Middle East was a priority for U.S. policy.

Secretary of State Shultz was sending signals that, if anything, the U.S. position against talking with the PLO had hardened. On September 7, after a meeting with Israeli Finance Minister Yitzhak Modai, Shultz declared in reference to the PLO that, "those who perpetuate violence deal themselves out of the peace process."[45] On September 12 Wolf Blitzer reported in the *Jerusalem Post* that the Reagan administration had formally communicated to King Hussein that the United States would "not meet with a joint Jordanian-Palestinian delegation without additional assurances that such a session will lead quickly to direct Arab-Israeli negotiations." Repeating a familiar pattern, while the Reagan administration was not willing to risk talking with a joint Jordanian-Palestinian delegation to explore peace prospects, it did take political risks by continuing to push for new arms sales to Jordan and Saudi Arabia, despite predictable and overwhelming opposition in Congress.[46]

During the fall of 1985, despite the awful events of the Achille Lauro hijacking and its aftermath, hopes for movement toward peace in the Middle East were kept alive, in part because of cautiously conciliatory speeches at the United Nations by King Hussein and Prime Minister Peres. In his speech, Hussein, while not dropping the demand for an international conference, said he was ready to negotiate peace directly with Israel. Foreign Minister Shamir insisted there was nothing new in the king's speech, but Prime Minister Peres publicly congratulated King Hussein for his "vision of peace."[47]

Three weeks later, in his address to the U.N. General Assembly, Prime Minister Peres challenged the United Nations "to depart from the tired and timid norm and to fullfill its destiny. . .by ushering the parties to the conflict into a new diplomatic initiative." While maintaining that negotiations needed to be directly between the parties concerned, Peres said that the negotiations "may be initiated with the support of an international forum," an obviously conciliatory response toward Hussein's insistence on the need for an international conference. Significantly, Peres also suggested that the negotiations could be broadened beyond the base of Resolutions 242 and 338 in order to "deal with the demarcation of boundaries as well as the resolution of the Palestinian problem."[48] Interviewed in Amman, King Hussein described Peres' speech as "the beginning of movement in the right direction" and "positive in spirit."[49]

Prime Minister Peres' speech to the United Nations occurred shortly before the U.S.-Soviet summit meeting in Vienna. To the extent that the United States was at all open to exploring possible Soviet interest in supporting a new peace process in the Middle East, Peres' speech provided new political space and even significant incentive for such an exploration. From the Soviet point of view, while Peres' speech may have been encouraging, the real test of the possibility for an international conference would be the U.S. position. There is no evidence that the Reagan administration viewed Peres' speech in this light. Indeed, there was speculation that Reagan administration officials saw it as creating a problem for the United States. When Richard Murphy came to Amman to brief Jordanian leaders on the summit meeting, he reported that the subject of the peace process in the Middle East was mentioned only briefly by the two leaders. While some U.S. officials claimed that the Soviet Union showed little interest in the Middle East, there was no evidence that the United States seriously offered to discuss the idea of an international conference. In fact, even after Peres' speech, Secretary of State Shultz and other U.S. officials continued to speak about the conference as little more than an "international cover" for direct negotiations between Israel and Jordan, still sometimes even omitting any reference to the Palestinians.

By early December 1985 most Jordanian leaders were discouraged and disillusioned by the U.S. role in the eleven months since agreement on the joint Jordan-PLO initiative for peace. In the view of Jordanian officials, while Jordan had been engaged for months in tough diplomatic efforts involving political compromise and political risks—with the PLO, Syria and other Arab states, the Soviet Union and, indirectly with Israel—the United States had taken no risks and no concrete steps to facilitate movement toward negotiations. Appreciating Peres' U.N. speech and the political limitations on what the Israeli unity government could do without more U.S. encouragement, one senior Jordanian official said, "Frankly speaking, Peres is moving better than the United States is moving."[50]

There was also considerable disappointment in Israel, although it was much more difficult for Israeli leaders to say so publicly, both because of Israeli dependence on the United States and because of the divisions and political balance between Labor and Likud. Several months earlier, however, David Shaham, director of the Tel Aviv-based International Center for Peace in the Middle East, the chairman of which is Abba Eban, wrote in the *New York Times,*

> In refraining from any initiative, to the point of almost total apathy, the United States is helping to perpetuate the deadlock. It pays lip service to the search for peace, encouraging the parties directly involved to enter into "direct negotiations." Yet even such talks could bear no fruit without active outside involvement. Meanwhile, American inaction lends support to the rejectionist fronts in both the Arab world and in Israel. . . .The Reagan administration must find ways of overcoming this inexplicable paralysis. The United States must resume its active role in the Middle East before it is too late.[51]

Shaham's views echoed the feelings of despair and frustration expressed by many Arabs and Israelis during several periods of opportunity since 1981. In this particular period, beginning with the Israeli elections in 1984, U.S. diplomats and political leaders had engaged in considerable discussion about what the United States should do for peace, but the United States had not really done anything. While Jordanian, Palestinian, Egyptian and Israeli leaders all had taken real, if all too timid, political risks to encourage peace prospects, the Reagan administration had taken none.

During January 1986 there was another flurry of diplomatic activity. Richard Murphy met in London with King Hussein and then in the Hague with Prime Minister Peres in an attempt to reactivate movement toward possible negotiations. These discussions apparently focused on possible ideas for an international conference, although there was still no indication that the United States was exploring ideas with the Soviet Union or any other permanent members of the U.N. Security Council, who would obviously have to be involved.

During the last week of January and first week of February there were intense discussions in Amman between the United States and Jordan and between Jordan and the PLO to try to help break the impasse. The United States reluctantly agreed to the idea of an international conference, while still rejecting the idea that the conference would have any authority and continuing to view it as a "cover" for direct negotiations between Jordan and Israel. Furthermore, U.S. officials indicated U.S. willingness to accept a PLO role in the negotiations if the PLO would first announce its endorsement of U.N. Security Council Resolutions 242 and 338. The United States pressured King Hussein to accept this formula. King Hussein, who apparently believed it was useless to seek more of a shift in U.S. policy, pressured the PLO.

There were intense, all-night discussions among PLO leaders which produced three alternate counter-proposals to break the deadlock.[52] Essentially, all three proposals offered PLO conditional acceptance of U.N. Security Council Resolution 242, in exchange for a U.S. commitment in support of the Palestinians' right of self- determination, in the context of confederation of the West Bank and Gaza with Jordan. King Hussein declined to press these proposals with the United States and the United States showed no interest in them. On February 7 Yasser Arafat and the special U.S. envoy, Wat T. Claverius, left Jordan, signalling the collapse of the Amman talks.

On Febuary 19, King Hussein, in a three-hour televised address, offered the official Jordanian version of events during the recent period. The king expressed frustration and deep disappointment at the PLO for its unwillingness to make further compromise, especially in the last round of talks when Jordan did manage to achieve some shift in the U.S. position. But Hussein also expressed deep disappointment in the U.S. role during the twelve months that had elapsed since the agreement on the joint Jordanian-PLO initiative for peace. (The king's frustration with the PLO was widely reported in the United States, while his frustration with U.S. policy received almost no attention.) A short time later, the PLO offered its version of why the Amman talks broke down. While its view differed from King Hussein's version, and some PLO leaders were very critical of the king, the PLO directed most of its criticism at the failure of the United States to respond positively to the February 11, 1985 Jordan-PLO joint peace initiative

After the breakdown in the Amman talks and King Hussein's public attack on the PLO leadership, tensions between Jordan and the PLO increased. Jordanian officials talked of possible alternative Palestinian leadership to the PLO and Jordan committed larger amounts of development funds to the West Bank, apparently in part to enlist greater support among Palestinians. There were no indications, however, that support for the PLO declined. If anything, in response to Jordanian challenges to the PLO leadership—and offical Israeli expressions of support for these challenges—Palestinians in the West Bank and Gaza seemed to rally more to the PLO.

In August 1986 Jordan closed the PLO office in Amman. Abu Jihad (Khalil Wazir), Arafat's deputy commander, and several other PLO officials were forced to leave Jordan. This move, combined with Jordan's decision to pump more development funds into the West Bank and its support for Israel's appointment of pro-Jordanian Palestinian mayors in three West Bank towns, apparently reflected an attempt by Jordan to challenge PLO leadership with more flexible, pro-Jordanian Palestinians in the West Bank and Gaza. However, distancing itself from the current PLO leadership can also be viewed as Jordan's way of trying to protect itself from the threat of Israeli retaliation for a predictable increase in Palestinian terrorist attacks after the failure to get negotiations started. The move also was likely another step in King Hussein's efforts to improve relations with Syria's President Assad, who definitely is opposed to Arafat's leadership. Furthermore, to the extent that King Hussein does not see any early prospect for negotiations, it was important from his viewpoint to encourage Palestinians to remain in the West Bank, in part to avoid the additional economic pressures on Jordan if more Palestinians emigrate across the Jordan River. Despite the current cool relations between Jordan and the PLO, given the interdependence of their interests, it is difficult to imagine either Jordan or the PLO making any serious moves toward peace without some degree of coordination.

In the United States, at both an official governmental level and in the media, the simplistic tendency was to blame the PLO for the breakdown in movement toward negotiations in 1985-86. A more objective review of events during this period reveals that while each of the parties involved could have done more for peace than it did, Israeli and Arab leaders, including leaders of the PLO, did take tangible steps based on their views that an opportunity for peace existed and did appeal to the United States to help open the way toward negotiations. The United States failed to develop any new effort for peace and, specifically, failed to take steps, any one of which could have encouraged the parties themselves to be more forthcoming. It is essential to pinpoint these steps, not only to understand the U.S. role in what happened—and what did not happen—during 1985-86 but also to identify the likely issues for any future constructive involvement by the United States in the search for peace in the Middle East:

First, the United States failed to act positively to take advantage of several developments in late 1984 and early 1985 which encouraged prospects for movement toward peace, including Jordan's decision to restore relations with Egypt, the PNC meeting in Amman, the Israeli decision to withdraw from Lebanon and the tentative steps by Israel and Egypt to resolve the Taba issue and restore normal relations

Second, the United States refused to meet at any time with a joint Jordanian-Palestinian delegation named by Hussein and Arafat to explore possible next steps toward negotiations for peace, despite King Hussein's appeals that such a meeting was the minimal essential step to keep the momentum alive and Prime Minister Peres' cautious acceptance that such a meeting might be useful.

Third, the United States rejected the principle of the right of self-determination for Palestinians, even in the context of the proposed confederation with Jordan and in exchange for PLO offers to accept U.N. Security Council Resolutions 242 and 338. Acceptance of their right of self-determination is the minimum virtually all Palestinians would insist on before they would accept U.N. Resolutions 242 and 338.

Fourth, the United States refused to recognize the PLO as representative of the Palestinian people or meet with any PLO leaders, even though U.S. officials said Palestinians had to be involved in the negotiations and Palestinians almost unanimously say the PLO represents them. In the final rounds of talks in Amman in January 1986, U.S. willingness to accept a PLO role in the U.S. version of an international conference was still conditional on PLO acceptance of U.N. Resolution 242 as the sole basis for negotiations, with no U.S. recognition of the Palestinian people's right of self- determination.

Fifth, the United States opposed the idea of an international conference for peace and refused to explore the idea seriously with the Soviet Union and other permanent members of the U.N. Security Council. Even in January 1986, the United States was still not willing to consider a conference with any authority in the negotiations. An international conference which would, in effect, be a "cover" for U.S.-mediated negotiations is unlikely to be accepted by other permanent members of the U.N. Security Council, especially the Soviet Union.

The opportunities for movement toward a negotiated wider peace which occurred during 1985 were not nearly as dramatic or unambiguous as the opening created by President Sadat's historic visit to Israel in 1977. There were no leaders in power in Israel or on the Arab side in 1985 prepared to make such a bold initiative without prior assurance of a positive outcome. There were important political leaders on both sides, however, who made clear that they believed new opportunities for peace existed and that they were willing to help try to take advantage of the opportunities. They also made it clear that they hoped for U.S. help in encouraging the next steps toward peace.

The record of events during this period strongly suggests that, if the United States had taken any one of the steps discussed above, while initially the step would have been controversial, there would have been a greater possibility of movement toward negotiations for peace. Many

Arabs and Israelis who were critical of their own leaders for not taking more courageous initiatives for peace during this period believe that U.S. policy was a major contributing factor to why these opportunities for peace were missed. It is not clear now when or in what form new possibilities for peace may occur.

What is certain is that the search for a solution to the Palestinian problem and peaceful settlement of the Arab-Israeli conflict is as essential to Israelis as it is to Palestinians and other Arabs. The record of recent years demonstrates that the United States cannot impose peace, but also that without a change in U.S. policy there is little chance of progress toward peace. If there is no peace, the spiral of violence in the Middle East will almost inevitably escalate, posing grave new dangers to Arabs and Israelis as well as to the entire world.

Chapter Ten

What's Wrong With U.S. Policy?

*T*he United States has been the predominant outside influence in the Middle East since British and French power declined after World War II. From the late 1940s until today, the United States has been deeply involved in the Arab-Israeli conflict, both as the primary supporter of Israel and, at times, as mediator in seeking agreements between Israel and various Arab parties, notably the historic Camp David peace treaty between Israel and Egypt in the late 1970s.

On several occasions, U.S. military forces have been deployed in the region, most recently in Lebanon where more than two hundred fifty U.S. Marines were killed. At present, U.S. forces participate in the multinational force in the Sinai as a part of the Camp David treaty. U.S. economic and military aid to countries in the Middle East represents more than half of the total U.S. aid to all countries. Given the global importance of oil and the involvement of both the United States and the Soviet Union, the Middle East seems the most likely place where a local conflict could escalate into a superpower confrontation and, possibly, nuclear war. The Arab-Israeli conflict has produced five major wars in the Middle East in the last forty years.

Despite all of these factors attesting to the importance of the region, the central role of the United States and the urgency of resolving the Arab-Israeli conflict, there is little public discussion and debate about U.S. policy in the Middle East, in contrast to the relatively well-informed and intense public debate about U.S. policy in other areas of the world, including Asia, Central America and Southern Africa.

Since the war in Lebanon there appears to be somewhat increased public interest in a more critical look at U.S. policy in the Middle East. Among at least some strong supporters of Israel, policies of the Begin government, especially the 1982 invasion of Lebanon, as well as the growing divisions among Israelis, are causing a reappraisal of what support for Israel means. Also, in part as a result of the war in Lebanon, there is greater awareness of the suffering of the Palestinians and their need for a homeland. More people, including a significant segment of the U.S. Jewish community, are aware of increasing dangers and dilemmas facing Israel if a peace settlement with the Palestinians is not achieved. Furthermore, as a result of the Reagan administration's use of the marines in Lebanon, its bombing of Libya and the revelations about its arms deals with Iran, people in the U.S. peace movement and others, many for the first time, have begun to take a more active interest in the Middle East.

Why Special Treatment for the Middle East

There are several reasons for the low historic level of critical U.S. public discussion. First, the issues are complex. Even when viewed relatively narrowly, the Arab-Israeli conflict requires some working knowledge of at least five countries—Israel, Egypt, Lebanon, Jordan and Syria—the history of the Jewish people and the Palestinians, and three religions—Judaism, Christianity and Islam. The number of parties directly involved in the conflict is further complicated by divisions within each which have significant bearing on the prospects for resolving the conflict.

If one also seeks to understand other regional actors with important indirect roles, such as Saudi Arabia, Iran and Iraq, the discussion becomes more complex; if the other Gulf states, Libya, Tunisia, Algeria and Morocco, are added, the complexity grows. Moreover, because of the economic and strategic importance of the Middle East, the roles of various European states and Japan, as well as the Soviet Union and the United States must be considered. This is not meant to suggest that there cannot be informed, rational discussion, but only that the complexity inhibits such discussion.

A second difficulty for many people is that the Arab-Israeli conflict is not one in which they perceive all the right is on one side and all the wrong on the other. People sometimes describe the conflict in such terms, e.g., "Israel wants peace. The Arab states want to destroy Israel," or "The Arabs are ready to compromise, but Israel wants more land." It does not take much study before one is forced to recognize that the situation is more complicated than this and that views which imply that all the right is on one side are neither morally sound nor practically helpful.

A third reason is the fear that discussion of the Arab-Israeli conflict stirs up powerful and threatening emotions. For many Jews in the United States who may be critical of Israel in discussion with other Jews there is a real, though often unspoken, fear that U.S. support for Israel is not deeply rooted and that public debate about the Middle East might provide a basis for U.S. policies which could endanger the security or even the existence of Israel. To understand this fear, one needs to remember, as Jews do, the historic prejudice of Christianity against the Jewish people and the centuries of persecution of Jews, culminating only a few decades ago in the Holocaust. Contemporary examples of anti-Jewish bias and violence reveal that this deep prejudice is still very much alive. For many non-Jews who are concerned about peace in the Middle East there is a fear that speaking out in ways that may be critical of Israel or U.S. policy may be viewed by Jews as anti-Israel or anti-Jewish. Discussion about the Middle East, in order to be constructive and effective, must address persistent underlying prejudice against the Jewish people as well as the complexities of the Arab-Israeli conflict.

Prejudice against the Jewish people, however, is not the only prejudice which inhibits rational discussion about the Middle East. There also exist deep western, particularly western Christian, prejudices against Arabs and against Islam. Most people are not conscious of how these affect thinking about the Middle East, in part because little work has been done to expose them. The frequent stereotyping of Arabs and Muslims as "oil rich," "fanatics" or "terrorists," the degree of anti-Arab and anti-Muslim sentiment in U.S. public responses to the Islamic resurgence and to military raids against Libya, and incidents of violence against Arab-Americans indicate that these prejudices are a far more important factor in inhibiting and distorting discussion of the Middle East than often is assumed. Deep prejudices against Arabs and Muslims must be exposed and confronted as part of developing constructive discussion about the Middle East.

Frequently, when discussion critical of U.S. policy toward the Arab-Israeli conflict does occur, there is a tendency to blame Israel or "the Jewish lobby" for the failure of U.S. policy to promote a just peace settlement. This simplistic view of what determines U.S. policy, with its implicit and, sometimes, explicit anti-Jewish prejudice, is the fourth reason for lack of more rational public discussion of the Middle East. The organized lobby in support of Israel, specifically the American Israel Public Affairs Committee (AIPAC), is well organized and plays an important role on specific issues and sometimes in specific election campaigns. AIPAC certainly can be criticized for its tendency to define support for Israel to mean uncritical support of every Israeli government policy, including those, such as the invasion of Lebanon or the occupation of the West Bank and Gaza, on which Israelis themselves are deeply divided, and for using pressure tactics against those who criticize specific Israeli government policies. However, it is a mistake to suggest that the lobby for Israel determines the basic goals or strategies of U.S. policy in the Middle East. The view that it does obscures much stronger forces in U.S. society, e.g., the "new right" and Christian fundamentalists, which are influencing U.S. foreign policy everywhere in the world, including the Middle East, and fundamentally are not concerned with what is good for Israel. Moreover, the emphasis on the role of AIPAC tends to pit Jews against non-Jews in critical discussion about the Middle East. This, in turn, inhibits the prospects of developing broad public support for a more constructive U.S. policy for peace, which is as essential for Israel as it is for the Palestinians and the Arab states.

The fifth reason inhibiting discussion is the appearance that U.S. policy in the Middle East is "different" from its policy in other parts of the world. After all, it can be argued, "the United States supports Israel, the only democratic state in the region and, at the same time, attempts to be an honest broker for peace between Israel and the Arabs." The question this study raises is not whether these are good goals for U.S. policy, but whether they are the actual goals. While many people were satisfied with U.S. policy in recent years, other people, including some prominent Jewish leaders such as the late Nahum Goldman, became increasingly concerned that the United States not only was failing to help achieve peace, but also was reinforcing trends in Israel and the region as a whole which posed grave dangers for the future of both Arabs and Israelis, and for world peace.

United States policy in the Middle East is not fundamentally different from its policy in other areas of the world. Indeed, to anyone knowledgeable about U.S. policy in Vietnam, Central America or Southern Africa, the basic orientation of U.S. Middle East policy—and the problems with it—will be very familiar. The point is not that the Middle East conflict is the same as or even analogous to these other conflicts, any more than those conflicts are the same. What is being argued is that U.S. foreign policy worldwide rests on the same fundamental premises and that some of these premises or tendencies have serious negative consequences in the Middle East, as they do in other regions of the world. But most people have not considered how these premises affect U.S. policy in the Middle East. If that can be demonstrated, a useful critical framework for improved understanding of U.S. policy in the Middle East may emerge. That there already exists a relatively broad constituency, including important sections of U.S. religious leadership, critical of U.S. policy in other areas of the world, at least suggests the potential for significant public support for a more constructive United States policy for peace in the Middle East.

Overestimating Military Power

A fundamental problem in U.S. foreign policy is the tendency to overestimate the determinative influence of military power. This applies not only to U.S. military power, but also to the military power of others. This tendency often leads the United States to a reliance on military power to address political problems. It also causes the United States to emphasize the role of military aid and arms transfers as a way of allying itself with local military elites, supporting friendly governments and seeking to increase U.S. influence in different areas of the world.

The history of U.S. intervention in Vietnam demonstrated to many people the tragic consequences of overestimating what military power can achieve. For several years during the war, most U.S. policymakers and the vast majority of citizens believed that the United States simply could not lose in Vietnam. The United States dropped more tons of bombs in Vietnam, Laos and Cambodia than were dropped by all sides in World War II and provided billions of dollars in military aid to keep a series of "friendly governments" in power in Saigon. Despite all of this military power, after ten years during which more than 1.5 million Vietnamese and fifty thousand Americans were killed, the Saigon government collapsed and the United Staes was forced to withdraw.

The fall of the shah of Iran in 1979 is another clear and dramatic example of this dangerous illusion. In military terms, the shah of Iran had the strongest regime in the Middle East area. U.S. policy had played a decisive role in building up the shah's military and, over the years, the United States came to depend on it as a force for stability in a volatile area of the world. The problem was that the shah almost totally lost the support of the Iranian people and, finally, popular opposition to his regime became so massive and determined that all of the shah's military might was not sufficient to keep him in power.

In relation to both of these examples, Vietnam and Iran, there is much to discuss and debate about what has happened since the revolutionary movements took power and about how U.S. policy has affected subsequent developments. But we are not debating the merits of these movements. Indeed, it is quite possible that people who disagree about the relative positive and negative effects of the revolutions in Vietnam and Iran might agree that the tendency in U.S. policy to overestimate the determinative influence of military power had disastrous consequences on both countries and on U.S. interests.

This tendency in U.S. policy has had serious negative effects in the Middle East during the period 1981-86. Three examples will be cited, but they are part of a larger pattern. The first example is the U.S. role at the time of the assassination of Egyptian President Anwar Sadat in October 1981. Beginning in July 1981 with the ceasefire negotiated by U.S. Ambassador Habib between the PLO and Israel in southern Lebanon, many Arab and Israeli leaders, as well as leaders in the United States, urged the Reagan administration to step up pressures on the Arabs and on Israel for progress in resolving the Palestinian issue. In response to the assassination of Sadat, many leaders, including former U.S. Presidents Carter and Ford, repeated these appeals, with an even greater sense of urgency.

But the U.S. priority in the Middle East in 1981 was to strengthen military cooperation with friendly governments, as part of its announced policy of organizing a regional "strategic consensus" against the Soviet Union. In September 1981 when Israeli Prime Minister Begin visited Washington, the Reagan administration relegated the issue of the autonomy talks with Egypt to a low priority and focused, instead, on developing greater military cooperation between the United States and Israel. In October, in response to the assassination of Sadat, Secretary of State Haig hardly spoke about the unfinished business of Camp David, but he did announce that the United States would increase military cooperation and engage in joint military exercises with Egypt, including the possible use of B-52s. While showing no inclination to take political risks to achieve a breakthrough in the talks between Egypt and Israel over the West Bank and Gaza, in November 1981 the Reagan adminstration did risk confrontation with Israel and the Congress to win approval of its request to sell Airborne Warning and Control Systems (AWACS) to Saudi Arabia.

It is doubtful that these steps signficantly added to the long term security of Israel, Egypt or Saudi Arabia. What is clear, however, is that by emphasizing military power and strategic cooperation against the Soviet Union, the United States gave lower priority to pressing forward with the second stage of the Camp David peace process. (Ironically, even the Camp David peace agreement itself included provision for an increase in U.S. military aid to Israel and Egypt.) There is little doubt that progress on the central issue in the second stage of the Camp David agreement, i.e., resolving the Palestinian issue, would have increased stability in the region and enhanced the security of those states most directly involved in the conflict, including Israel. But pursuit of peace was clearly not the priority for the United States.

The United States and Lebanon

The second example of over-reliance on military force is the U.S. response to Israel's invasion of Lebanon in 1982. By early spring 1982 it was clear that Israeli Defense Minister Sharon had a plan for invading Lebanon and that Prime Minister Begin's government was only waiting for the right moment to launch an attack. While Israeli Labor Party leaders continued to argue against invasion—in retrospect, some Israelis would say not forcefully enough—U.S. leaders appeared to become more and more resigned to the idea, and even positively interested. Some officials began to talk about possible strategic gains for the United States from a "successful" Israeli military move.

In their book, *Israel's War in Lebanon*, Ze'ev Schiff and Ehud Ya'ari, two prominent Israeli journalists, argued that then Secretary of State Alexander Haig gave a green light to Israel's invasion. What is absolutely certain is that the United States did not put up a red light against the invasion. In June, during the initial weeks of the war, the United States voted for U.N. Security Council Resolutions 508 and 509 which called for Israeli forces to withdraw from Lebanon "immediately and without conditions." But by the end of June, the Reagan administration, impressed by possible U.S. "gains" as a result of Israel's invasion, supported several conditions for Israeli withdrawal, including the demand for Syrian withdrawal. The United States also made clear its strong preference for sending U.S. military forces into Lebanon rather than supporting an expanded U.N. peacekeeping mission.

The U.S. position was in harmony with at least some of Sharon's goals for the Israeli invasion of Lebanon, although U.S. leaders appear to have had their own reasons for supporting these goals in hope of the United States' gaining a position of much greater influence in Lebanon and in the region, at the expense of Syria and the Soviet Union. U.S. policy reflected not only ignorance about Lebanon and the dynamics of its internal divisions, but also fundamental illusions about the capacity of military power—in this case, Israeli and U.S. military power—to shape events in Lebanon.

It was not until after two hundred fifty marines were killed in a suicide attack on their barracks that the United States decided to pull its military forces out of Lebanon. Even in January 1985, after Prime Minister Peres won cabinet approval for Israeli withdrawal from Lebanon,

Reagan administration officials expressed disappointment at the decision. The United States would have preferred Israeli forces to remain in Lebanon as a continuing military pressure until Syria also agreed to withdraw. The U.S. role in Lebanon showed U.S. illusions about military force reinforcing Israeli illusions and vice versa. The voices of other Israeli leaders and all too few Americans who warned about the dangers of military intervention in Lebanon were ignored. While the problems faced by Lebanon today certainly cannot primarily be blamed on outside forces, it is clear that the Israeli invasion added significantly to the suffering and further complicated the internal conflicts. The attempt by the United States to seek U.S. advantage in the crisis and, in this context, the use of the multinational force, compounded Lebanon's troubles rather than helping to resolve them.

Military Aid and Arms Sales

The third example is simpler. It is almost taken for granted that the United States provides military aid to Israel despite the strains this causes in U.S. relations with Arab states. In recent years there also have been several occasions when the United States has been willing to risk political confrontation with Israel and U.S. supporters of Israel over selling advanced arms to Egypt, Jordan and Saudi Arabia. During these same years, however, even when there were encouraging signs that important Israeli and Arab leaders wanted U.S. help in seeking peace, the United States was unwilling to take comparable political risks.

There were at least two times, once in 1982-83 during the months following announcement of the Reagan initiative, and again, after the February 1985 Jordan-PLO agreement on a joint peace initiative, when it appeared that there were steps the United States could have taken which would have increased chances of getting wider negotiations for peace going. During both periods the United States basically refused to make any moves for peace which would cause controversy in U.S. relations with Israel. But simultaneously the Reagan administration did run the risks of public confrontation with Israel and with the U.S. Congress by pushing (unsuccessfully) for approval of the sale of advanced arms to Jordan. Public revelations in late 1986 began to indicate what risks the Reagan administration took during recent years in authorizing major arms deals with Iran.

Underestimating Popular Power

A fundamental corollary to overestimating the influence of military power is the U.S. tendency to underestimate the power of the aspirations and struggles of ordinary people. In Vietnam, if one problem was U.S. leaders' belief in the invincibility of U.S. military power, an equally important problem was the almost total failure of U.S. leaders to understand the determination and dedication of Vietnamese opposed to U.S. intervention. This tendency was also a major factor in the U.S. delay in recognizing that Anastasio Somoza and Ferdinand Marcos were finished as rulers in Nicaragua and the Philippines. Black South Africans have been warning the United States for years that underestimating the power of popular aspirations for ending apartheid consistently has led the United States to adopt policies which are "too little, too late."

This problem also has been evident in U.S. policy in the Middle East. During the 1970s many knowledgeable observers warned the United States that it was underestimating the potential of popular discontent against the shah in Iran. During 1982-84 in Lebanon, both Israeli and U.S. leaders seriously underestimated the power of the Lebanese people, especially Lebanese Shiites, to resist Israeli occupation and the U.S. military presence. As in the case of Iran, when as late as 1977-78 senior U.S. State Department officials knew relatively little about the Ayatollah Khomeini, so in relation to Lebanon, U.S. leaders knew little about Imam Musa al Sadr, a leader and hero of Lebanese Shiites, who disappeared in Libya in 1980 and whose photograph can be seen displayed in Shiite communities throughout Lebanon. (In his book about Musa al Sadr, *The Unfinished Imam*, Fouad Ajami reveals that the U.S. Embassy in Beirut actually did appreciate the importance of Imam Musa al Sadr and tried unsuccessfully to convince political leaders in Washington of his importance.)

Despite warnings from many Lebanese and at least some Israeli experts on Lebanon, Israeli Likud leaders and officials of the Reagan administration apparently believed that, by removing the Palestinian military forces as a factor, Lebanon could be patched back together with Christian political hegemony intact or even strengthened. The point here is not to suggest that there was an easy solution to Lebanon's problems, but that the U.S. tendency to underestimate the power of Lebanese struggling for change compounded the suffering in Lebanon and made a solution significantly more difficult. The tendency to underestimate the significance of popular movements in Lebanon also obviously generated new problems for Israel and the United States.

Turning to the core issue in the Arab-Israeli conflict, the struggle between Israeli Jews and Palestinian Arabs, this study suggests that during the period 1981-86 the United States consistently underestimated the aspirations of Israelis and Palestinians to achieve a fair peace settlement. This statement is likely to be controversial among many people, but, as documented in this study, there were several times during recent years when both Israeli and Palestinian leaders, representing the views of a substantial minority or even a majority of their peoples, believed there were opportunities for movement toward peace which were frustrated in part by the failure of the United States to act in ways they believed could have helped take advantage of the opportunities.

There were several important U.S. Middle East policy assumptions during 1981-86 which reflected the U.S. tendency to underestimate the power of the Palestinian people's national aspirations and the importance of the Palestine Liberation Organization. As examples, the United States assumed:

• that President Sadat or King Hussein could speak for the Palestinians;
• that, after the 1982 PLO military defeat in Lebanon, Palestinians would relinquish the principle of self-determination or the right of the PLO to represent Palestinians in negotiations;
• that, if PLO leaders were not willing to make the compromises necessary (from a U.S. point of view), then other more moderate Palestinian leaders would emerge;
• that if the United States stuck firmly to its position, e.g., in the Reagan initiative, given the power realities in the region, eventually, Palestinians would have to come around and accept it; and
• that, if Palestinians missed the boat of negotiations offered on U.S. terms, then it would be too late for the Palestinians.

All of these U.S. assumptions and expectations radically underestimated the power of Palestinian aspirations and the determination of the Palestinian national movement. All of them contributed to the failure of U.S. policy to promote negotiations for peace during recent years.

In relation to Israel, during this same period 1981-86, U.S. policy underestimated the aspirations of most Israelis for peace and the willingness of substantial numbers of Israelis to challenge their own government to do more for peace. Several U.S. policy assumptions in relation to Israel during these years illustrate this problem. For example, the United States assumed:

• that stronger U.S. opposition to Israel's invasion of Lebanon or its policies in the West Bank and Gaza would have been counterproductive;
• that, despite pleas by important Israeli leaders that the U.S. do so, it was not useful to press Israel for a positive response to the Reagan initiative, including the president's call for a settlements freeze;
• that, if the United States were to accept the principle of the right of Palestinians to self-determination as part of the basis for peace negotiations or if the United States were to talk with the PLO, the reac-

tion of Israelis would be universally and irreversibly negative;
• that appeals by Israeli opposition leaders for greater U.S. pressure
on Israel, as well as on the Arab side, were motivated primarily by an
interest in obtaining power, rather than by the belief that positive U.S.
pressure could help to encourage Israel to show greater flexibility of
a kind required for progress toward peace; and
• that there was no way to challenge U.S. supporters of Israel to accept the idea that both sides in the Arab-Israeli conflict must show flexibility and be willing to compromise in order to achieve peace.

These tendencies in the United States contributed during 1981-86
to a failure of U.S. policy to play a more constructive role in helping
Israel to move toward a negotiated peace with the Palestinians and with
other Arab states. Beneath the surface of U.S. failure to understand
and respond to the aspirations of Palestinians or Israelis for a just peace,
there are persistent, underlying western and Christian prejudices against
the Jewish people and the Arabs. While the changes required in U.S.
policy to enable the United States to play a more constructive role
sometimes seem relatively small, they are unlikely to occur without addressing underlying U.S. attitudes toward the peoples of the region.

U.S.-Soviet Conflict

A third fundamental problem with negative consequences in the
Middle East is the U.S. tendency to view local or regional conflicts
primarily through the lens of conflict with the Soviet Union. Since 1981
President Reagan has placed new emphasis on this view, but the basic
tendency has been deeply ingrained in U.S. foreign policy for decades.

Perceptual problems and the negative consequences of this tendency have been widely discussed and debated in relation to U.S. policy
in Vietnam, Central America, the Philippines, South Africa and other
areas of the world. There has not been nearly enough attention to its
harmful effects in relation to U.S. policy in the Middle East.

This ideological emphasis in U.S. policy actually presents not just
one problem, but at least three. First, this view clearly tends to ignore
or underestimate the importance of local and regional factors in conflict. In its more extreme version, this view simply reduces every local
conflict to little more than a stage for conflict between the United States
and the Soviet Union and assigns local actors specific roles in this global
war. Second, this emphasis tends to define relations between the United
States and the Soviet Union exclusively in conflict terms, practically ruling out the possibility of U.S.-Soviet cooperation. Especially when this
view is applied in a rigid way, as it has been by many in the Reagan
administration, it not only blinds U.S. policymakers to the possibility

that the United States and the Soviet Union might have common or, at least, compatible interests in a specific region at a particular time, but builds up domestic political constraints against the possibility of U.S.-Soviet cooperation even if it appeared to policy makers to be in U.S. interests. Third, the emphasis has a tendency to become self-fulfilling. The more the United States responds to a regional conflict this way, whatever degree of U.S.-Soviet conflict may objectively be involved, the greater the tendency for Soviet leaders to respond in a similar manner.

In the Middle East the three most serious negative consequences of this emphasis in U.S. policy are that it has helped to fuel a regional arms race, it has led the United States to ignore or to exclude Syria from development of a peace process, and it has contributed to the United States' missing opportunities for movement toward peace.

More than half of the world's arms transfers at present involve countries in the Middle East. The United States, the Soviet Union and several countries in Europe are major arms suppliers to the region. While the motivation for Middle Eastern countries to seek arms relates fundamentally to regional conflicts and the motivation for countries to supply arms is as much economic as political, the breakdown of detente and heating up of the U.S.-Soviet conflict clearly tends to escalate the regional arms race. Moreover, to the extent that conflict between the United States and Soviet Union is exacerbated, the chances of restricting or reversing the regional arms race are significantly reduced.

The tendency in U.S. policy, e.g., in the Reagan initiative, to ignore or exclude Syria, in part because of Syria's relation with the Soviet Union, is dangerously shortsighted. Syria is a major party in the Arab-Israeli conflict. Since Egypt signed the Camp David agreement, Syria represents the greatest military threat to Israel. Syria's military build-up since its big losses in the 1982 Lebanon war has caused many experts to predict that, if there is no movement toward a comprehensive peace, a major Syrian-Israeli clash is likely to occur within the next few years. As it has for a century, Syria plays a major role in Lebanon. Syria also plays a major role in relation to the Palestinian struggle and regional developments, including supporting Iran in the Iran-Iraq war. Like those of other countries, the goals of Syrian policies are complex and shaped by a combination of internal, regional and international considerations, probably in that order of importance. While Syria's role in the region and its tough position on what is required for a negotiated settlement of the Arab-Israeli conflict commonly are criticized in the West, realistically, Syria cannot be ignored if lasting peace is the goal.

Syria's relation to the Soviet Union is also complex. It is true that Syria has become increasingly dependent on the Soviet Union, especially for military support. This does not mean, however, that the Soviet Union controls Syrian policy. There have been indications at times that Syria would like to improve its relations with the United States. The government of President Hafez al Assad is the most insistent of all Arab governments that an international conference, involving the Soviet Union as well as the United States, is the *only* way of achieving a negotiated settlement of the Arab-Israeli conflict. But statements by Syrian leaders consistently suggest that the reason for Syria's position has little to do with any deep commitment to the Soviet Union, but is based on Syria's view that U.S.-sponsored negotiations would be heavily weighted in favor of Israel. There are signs, including its endorsement of the September 1982 Arab Fez Declaration, that Syria is prepared to accept a negotiated settlement with Israel. These signs ought to lead U.S. policymakers to pursue ways to include, rather than exclude, Syria in a wider peace process.

The sharp contrast between the views of Anwar Sadat and Ronald Reagan about the situation in the Middle East in August 1981 during Sadat's last visit to the United States was a dramatic example of how the emphasis on conflict with the USSR can blind U.S. leaders to opportunities for movement toward peace. President Sadat urgently pleaded for the United States to open a dialogue with the Palestinian leadership in order to take advantage of the opportunity created by the PLO-Israeli ceasefire in southern Lebanon. In his public remarks, President Reagan made no reference to the Palestinians at all and concentrated instead on how important U.S.-Egyptian relations were to the U.S. goal of containing Soviet influence in the Middle East. The views of Israelis who also saw the Lebanon ceasefire as an opportunity for peace were closer to Sadat's perspective than they were to Reagan's.

The problem of the U.S. concentration on excluding Soviet influence in the region is also reflected in the United States' negative response to the idea of an international conference for peace. In recent years, as the Camp David treaty and the Reagan initiative both failed to generate a wider Middle East peace process and as U.S. credibility as the sole mediator for peace has decreased among even pro-U.S. Arab leaders, the idea of some form of international conference for peace has begun to receive more serious consideration. Except for very brief interludes, for instance at the time of the "Vance-Gromyko Communique" in October 1977, the United States has opposed Soviet involvement in a Middle East peace process and, therefore, opposed the idea of an international peace conference which would include the USSR.

In 1984 King Hussein, who was widely assumed to favor a U.S.-mediated peace process, began to say that an international conference under U.N. auspices was the only realistic way to achieve peace. In part, this reflected King Hussein's own growing disillusionment with the U.S. role after the failure of the Reagan initiative and the U.S. failure to achieve Israeli withdrawal from Lebanon. In 1985 King Hussein reiterated this view and, while U.S. officials maintained that the king merely wanted an "international cover" for direct negotiations with Israel, there were significant indications that the king wanted more than this. During the second half of 1985 the United States began to show some flexibility, but still refused to accept King Hussein's view—a view held even more strongly by Palestinian leaders—that the international conference should have a real—not merely a ceremonial—role in mediating negotiations among the parties.

The United States frequently claims that its opposition to an international conference is based on the fact that Israel would refuse to participate and, therefore, the idea is simply not workable. However, there is evidence that at least some Israeli leaders take a more pragmatic view than the Reagan administration about a possible Soviet role. For example, when Prime Minister Peres addressed the U.N. General Assembly in October 1985 he expressed support for the idea of "an international forum" to "initiate negotiations." Israel's willingness to consider a Soviet role in the peace process has tended to be conditioned less by ideological concerns and more by pragmatic ones: to potential Soviet willingness to restore diplomatic relations with Israel, severed as a result of the 1967 war, and easing emigration policies for Jews who want to leave the Soviet Union.

At a minimum, Peres' speech at the United Nations, coming as it did on the eve of the U.S.-Soviet summit meetings in Vienna, provided a dramatic opportunity for President Reagan to explore an international conference seriously with General Secretary Gorbachev. Israeli hardline Likud leaders launched bitter attacks on Peres' speech, apparently worried that the United States could use the speech as an excuse for greater flexibility toward Soviet involvement in a Middle East peace process for which Peres would get the credit. There is no evidence that the United States was seriously interested in this idea. On the contrary, at the time it appeared that the Reagan administration gave higher priority to keeping the Soviet Union out of a peace process than it did to getting a peace process going.

The more time elapses, and especially if U.S. credibility among Arab leaders continues to decline, the more likely it is that an international conference for peace will become the only possible way of resolving the Arab-Israeli conflict. While there is disagreement among western experts about the level of Soviet interest in a Middle East peace settlement, many believe that the Soviet Union would support a reasonable peace settlement if it had a role in achieving it. U.S. a priori rejection of the international conference idea, in effect, has meant that Soviet interest has not been tested.

"Go It Alone"

A fourth underlying problem in U.S. foreign policy is that all too often the United States tries to be the sole arbiter of regional conflicts and tends to rebuff both advice and assistance from other governments and a role for the United Nations. In one sense, this problem involves attempts to exclude a Soviet role, but also the United States often ignores or rejects advice and/or assistance even from its allies and friends as well.

Whatever happens in Central America, in retrospect, the United States' rebuff of efforts at mediation by the Contadora Group of nations is likely to be viewed as shortsighted and as having compounded the tragedy of the conflict. For many years, U.S. administrations basically have ignored the advice of African governments in its relation to South Africa. In its dealings with the Soviet Union on arms control and other issues, the United States tends to expect its western European allies to line up behind the U.S. position on a particular issue, rather than respecting the independent interests of these governments and viewing them as a potential bridge between U.S. and Soviet positions.

This tendency to "go it alone" is a basic problem in U.S. foreign policy in many areas of the world. But it is especially unrealistic and dangerous in the Middle East, where so many countries have vital interests and where a superpower confrontation is likely and could possibly lead to nuclear war. In recent years there have been several occasions when the U.S. States ignored or rejected advice and assistance from its European allies which could have encouraged prospects for peace in the Middle East. The United States rejected the 1980 Venice Declaration by the European Economic Community which suggested that the principle of the right of self-determination for the Palestinian people needs to be included along with U.N. Security Council Resolutions 242 and 338 as the basis for negotiations and that the PLO has to be "associated with" the negotiations. Initiatives along these lines by France and Egypt in the U.N. Security Council were rejected by the United States in 1981 and 1982. The United States ignored advice of several European governments in 1982-83 on how to improve the chances for success of the Reagan initiative and in 1985 in relation to the need for a more active and creative U.S. response to the Hussein-Arafat joint initiative for peace.

European governments generally have been more receptive than the United States to proposals for a U.N.- sponsored international conference for peace in the Middle East, but they typically cite Israeli and U.S. opposition to the idea as making it unworkable. These governments and certain eastern European governments, e.g., Rumania, which has relations with Israel, potentially could play an important bridging role in helping to resolve differences over how an international conference would be organized and how it would work. So far, there is almost no evidence that the United States would welcome this kind of help. To the extent that the United States would engage in more genuine dialogue with western European nations, it is likely that both U.S. interests and prospects for peace in the Middle East would benefit.

The Future

The United States does have important responsibility in the Middle East and, even after all that has happened, could play a constructive role in helping to achieve a peaceful resolution of the Arab-Israeli conflict. At present, the possibility of peace appears remote. Indeed, missed opportunities in recent years have contributed to the present dangers of increasing violence and a possible new war in the region. But there will be new opportunities for movement toward peace, in part because there are large numbers of Arabs and Israelis, including leaders on all sides, who recognize that without peace there will be neither justice nor lasting security for any of the peoples in the Middle East. The prospects for peace will be significantly affected by U.S. policy. If U.S. policy remains the same, the prospects for peace will be dim. But if U.S. policy would change along lines suggested here, the U.S. could play a constructive role in helping to make peace possible.

Chapter Eleven

What If There Is No Peace?

*T*he situation in the Middle East in relation to the Arab-Israeli conflict will not remain the same as it is today. If conditions do not get better, they are very likely to get worse. Concretely, if there is no progress toward resolving the Palestinian issue and achieving a comprehensive peace settlement between Israel and the Arab states, the cycle of violence and the tendency toward extremism will increase. Since 1948 there have been five major Middle East wars related directly to the Arab-Israeli conflict. If there is no peace, there will almost inevitably be another war, probably even more destructive and dangerous than the last one.

There is a tendency in U.S. policy-making circles and among the public to assume that the status quo in the Middle East is more stable than it actually is and to underestimate the dangers if there is no resolution of the Arab-Israeli conflict. From a U.S. political policymaker's point of view, Middle East oil is flowing and at new low prices, Israel remains a strong, dependable and dependent U.S. ally, the Palestinians are scattered and weak, Soviet influence in the region is still marginal, and most Arab states, caught between secular leftist and Islamic militant pressures, have nowhere to turn except to the United States. This geopolitical view reflects little concern for what is happening to the peoples of the Middle East—Arabs and Israelis. Even in terms of "hard-nosed" calculations of U.S. interests, this view is foolishly shortsighted.

Without attempting a crystal-ball view of the future, it is possible to cite several current dangers related to the Arab-Israeli conflict which do not augur well for the prospects of people's security or political stability in the region if there is no peace.

Violence Between Palestinians and Jews

Since the 1982 war in Lebanon there has been a marked increase in violent incidents between Palestinian Arabs and Israeli Jews in the West Bank and Gaza, and also within Israel. On the average of once every few weeks there is a report of a Palestinian living under military occupation wounding or killing an Israeli, in response to which there often is retaliation by Israeli settlers and demands within Israel for tougher security measures. Organized Palestinian terrorist attacks appear to be increasing in frequency. Terrorist attacks by Jews against Palestinians in the West Bank and Gaza as well as outbursts of anti-Arab violence within Israel also have increased.

Palestinians living in the West Bank and Gaza appear to be more desperate and determined since the war in Lebanon. The PLO military defeat in Lebanon and its failure to achieve a political breakthrough in coordination with King Hussein, combined with the daily grinding realities of economic hardship and military occupation, have increased the Palestinians' desperation. The example of successful Shiite resistance against Israeli occupation in Lebanon and the natural evolution of Palestinian nationalism have increased their determination. Furthermore, in late October 1986 the PLO Executive Committee apparently decided once again to make armed struggle a priority after the failure of its political strategy to achieve positive results. Even in the absence of a strategy, however, the bitter frustration among Palestinians provides a basis for increased violence.

Many Israelis, for their part, also appear less hopeful that what appeared to them as "moderate" political solutions—the Labor Party's Jordan option or the Likud's autonomy plan—will work. There is increasing polarization of Israeli views. A growing minority of Israelis on one side are willing to acknowledge the necessity of negotiating for peace with the PLO and a growing minority on the other side are increasingly willing to support more extreme methods, including the death penalty (not currently a part of Israeli law) and increased use of deportation to control the Palestinians. While at one level these forces compete with each other for limited power and influence in relation to government policies, at another they express their views directly by increased cooperation with or increased violence against the Palestinians.

There is no evidence that violence between Palestinians and Israeli

Jews will decline unless there is progress toward resolving the underlying conflict between these two peoples. Ze'ev Schiff, a prominent Israeli correspondent, wrote in *Haaretz* newspaper on July 28, 1985:

> We should remember that we are in a state of war here with a people which has been pushed into a corner. The only thing extremists among us are saying to these people is that they must either become accustomed to Israeli occupation, commit national suicide, or leave their homes and villages. We shouldn't wonder, then, that the Palestinians have resorted to arms and sabotage.

Schiff's views were echoed by Raja Shehadeh, a Palestinian attorney who heads Law in the Service of Man, the West Bank chapter of the International Commission of Jurists. Interviewed in the *Christian Science Monitor* on July 30, 1985, Raja Shehadeh commented on the possibility of more violence.

> I see it increasing, and I think that we will ultimately all suffer. There is nothing worse than blind and arbitrary violence. . . .The root causes of it must be confronted.

The failure to resolve the fundamental conflict between Israel and the Palestinians not only exacerbates the suffering of Palestinians, but also deepens the dilemmas for the future of Israel as a Jewish state. Watching the recent trend of violent incidents, one is forced to the tragic conclusion that, if there is no breakthrough toward negotiated peace, violence between Palestinians and Israelis as well as political polarization within Israel are likely to increase.

Deterioration in Egyptian-Israeli Relations

Both Egyptians and Israelis feel frustrated by the unfulfilled hopes of the Camp David peace treaty, although at least for now both governments remain committed to the agreement and are engaged in a process to resolve the issue over Taba and proceed with normalization of relations. Many Israelis are angry and frustrated over the failure of normal relations to flourish in the ways they expected and over Egypt's "freezing" of the peace in response to the war in Lebanon. Egyptians are bitter over Israel's invasion of Lebanon and the failure to resolve the Palestinian issue.

As Egypt moves to restore normal relations with other Arab countries, severed at the time of the Camp David agreement with Israel, so far it has not backed away from the agreement, despite internal political pressures from the growing Islamic trend and other opposition forces. But most people believe that peace between Egypt and Israel is not permanently irreversible and that unless there is progress toward resolving the Palestinian issue and achieving a comprehensive peace settlement relations between the two countries will deteriorate.

As more time passes and there is no progress toward the broader peace envisioned by the late President Sadat, the psychological breakthrough achieved at a popular level among both Israelis and Egyptians is fading and being replaced by a combination of bitterness and old stereotypes, now fueled by new religious and secular fanaticism. If there is another war between Israel and the Arabs, there is much less certainty than there was in 1982 about what Egypt will do.

Syria's Military Build-Up

Since the peace treaty between Israel and Egypt, Syria represents the biggest military threat to Israel. The Syrian view is that there are only two ways that a just settlement of the Arab-Israeli conflict can occur. The first is that over time Syria and the other Arab states will achieve military parity with Israel and, either as a result of new war or the threat of war, there will be a negotiated solution. The other way is by means of an international peace conference in which the Soviet Union and the United States would have equivalent roles.

Based on Syria's view of its security needs and its view that in either of the above-mentioned scenarios military strength will be a crucial factor in protecting Syria's interests, the Syrian government has been engaged in a steady military build-up. After its defeat by Israel in Lebanon in 1982 Syria rapidly recovered and increased its military strength, thanks to large infusions of military assistance from the Soviet Union, including new long-range ground-to-ground missiles.

Most military experts believe Syrian military capability will be at a level within a few years that could tempt Syrian leaders to risk a new war with Israel. Realistically, experts say Israel would win in any such confrontation, but conceivably at significantly higher cost than in the past. What Egypt would do in response to a new war between Syria and Israel is a very important question and not one about which anyone can be very certain of the answer. Growing Syrian military strength is one important reason why any new effort for peace should seek to include, rather than exclude, Syria.

Growing Influence of Harder-Line Leadership

There are visible trends within Israel, among Palestinians and in the Arab states reflecting the growing influence of harder line popular attitudes and political leadership. In Israel the increased power of the Likud since the mid-1970s, combined with the growth of extreme tendencies represented by Tehiya and the Kach Movement of Rabbi Kahane, reflects this development. Among the Palestinians, the challenges to Arafat's leadership in recent years, as well as the decision to place increased emphasis on armed struggle, reflect the strength of harder-line influences in the PLO. In Egypt almost all of the internal opposition to the Mubarak government urges Egypt to take a harder line in relation to Israel. In Jordan King Hussein has taken steps to improve relations with Syria. On the issue of a possible peace process King Hussein's views have shifted from apparently favoring or, at least, accepting a U.S.-mediated process, to insisting on the need for some form of international conference. In Lebanon the growing political strength of the Shiites certainly means that Lebanon's conditions for accommodation with Israel will be tougher than in the past. And in Syria, while the government of President Assad already takes a very tough line on the conflict with Israel, one of the charges by Islamic militant and other radical opponents of Assad is that his government is ready to make a deal with Israel.

The reasons for the growing influence of harder-line leadership in the area are complex and clearly not all related to the Arab-Israeli conflict. However, it is true that continuation of the conflict is one important factor in the popular appeal and power of such forces. Conversely, if the Palestinian issue and the Arab-Israeli conflict could be resolved, the appeal and power of more moderate or realistic Arab and Israeli leaders would very likely be greater because they would have achieved something with very tangible positive benefits.

The Rise of Religious Militant Movements

The growing power of Islamic militant movements among Arabs and, to a much lesser extent, the increased influence and militancy of the orthodox religious trend among Israeli Jews, pose a danger that the Arab-Israeli conflict increasingly will be defined in religious terms and, thus, become even more difficult to resolve than it is now. Once again, it is important not to oversimplify. The causes (and potential positive and negative effects) of the Islamic resurgence and of the rise of new militancy among many Orthodox Israeli Jews are complex and related more fundamentally to economic, social and cultural developments and tensions than to the Arab-Israeli conflict. But the conflict is a factor in the growth of these movements and provides an important and very dangerous focal point for their religious "messianism" and militancy. Both Arab and Israeli political leaders are under increasing pressures from these religious movements.

Dangers of a Superpower Confrontation

In 1983 in Lebanon the U.S. military confrontation with Syrian forces could have escalated to involve the Soviet Union. In the 1967 and 1973

Arab-Israeli wars also the United States and Soviet Union came dangerously close to direct military confrontations.

U.S. economic and strategic interests in the region as well as U.S. support for Israel mean the United States will continue to be deeply involved in developments in the Middle East. The Soviet Union also has economic and strategic interests and allies in the Middle East as well as deep national security concerns about a region near its southern border.

Neither the United States nor the Soviet Union will abandon its interests in the Middle East. As the Arab-Israeli conflict continues and each side acquires larger arsenals of more advanced weapons, including the prospect that at some point both sides may have nuclear weapons, the danger becomes greater that a new war could escalate to a direct military confrontation between the superpowers and possibly to global nuclear war. Thus, the failure to achieve peace in the Middle East not only has profoundly negative effects on the fate of Arabs and Israelis but also on the future prospects of world peace.

Is Peace Possible?

This study has focused on the missed opportunities for the United States to encourage prospects for Arab-Israeli peace during 1981-86. But the purpose is not to cry over spilt milk. Rather it is to argue that there will be other opportunities and the United States can contribute to creating them. When new opportunities come, the United States can benefit from past mistakes and help the parties in conflict to find the way toward peace.

Arabs and Israelis who want peace will likely continue to look to the United States for help. It is certainly to be hoped that they will find ways to take more initiatives on their own. In any event, whether or not the United States puts a high priority on peace in the Middle East will certainly be a key factor in shaping what happens.

Notes

CHAPTER 1: ARAB-ISRAELI PEACE AND THE UNITED STATES

1. U.N. Security Council Resolution 242, *The Search for Peace in the Middle East, Documents and Statements, 1967-79*, U.S. Government Printing Office, 1979, p. 93.

2. Hebrew: Land of Israel. The usual and accepted Hebrew name of Palestine, roughly corresponding to Palestine within its boundaries (including Transjordan) under the British Mandate.

3. U.N. Security Council Resolution 338, *The Search for Peace in the Middle East, Documents and Statements, 1967-79*, U.S. Government Printing Office, 1979, p. 97.

4. See *Militarization of the Middle East* by Max Holland, a pamphlet published by the American Friends Service Committee, 1983.

CHAPTER 2: ISRAELI-PLO CEASEFIRE IN LEBANON

1. T. Elaine Carey, "Lebanon: Powerless to Protect Lebanese or to Keep PLO in Check," *Christian Science Monitor* July 12, 1981.

2. Ibid.

3. James McCartney, "Lebanon A Testing Ground for Superpowers," *Journal of Commerce* June 12, 1981.

4. Ibid.

5. "Sequence of Actions," *New York Times* May 24, 1981.

6. "Cashing In on a Crisis," *Newsweek* June 8, 1981.

7. David Landau, "Calls Mount for Ceasefire as Government Meets," *Jerusalem Post* July 21, 1981.

8. David L. Shipler, "Ceasefire in Mideast Fighting Declared by Israel and PLO: U.S. Sees Hope for Wider Peace," *New York Times* July 25, 1981.

9. Norman Kempster, "In the Lebanon Crisis, Israeli Policy Flounders," *Los Angeles Times* May 24, 1981.

10. Norman Kempster, "Begin Violated Agreement with Syrians, Rabin Asserts," *Los Angeles Times* June 4, 1981.

11. "Prime Minister of Israel Menachem Begin Speaks," *Jewish Press* June 12, 1981.

12. "A Respite," editorial, *Jerusalem Post* July 20, 1981.

13. Interview in *Yediot Aharonot*, July 19, 1981, quoted in *New Outlook* July 1981.

14. Trudy Rubin, "American Criticism Fails to Unite Israelis," *Christian Science Monitor* July 24, 1981.

15. Asher Wallfish, "Begin Says Israel Will Try To Keep Ceasefire Going," *Jerusalem Post* July 28, 1981.

16. John Kifner, "Radicals in PLO Refuse Ceasefire: Israel Front Quiet," *New York Times*, July 26, 1981.

17. John Kifner, "Leaders of PLO Denounce Faction That Broke Truce: Lebanon Border Is Quiet," *New York Times* July 27, 1981.

18. See Gideon Katz, "Minister: Israel Rejected PLO Offer of Non-Aggression Pact," *Davar* January 14, 1983.

19. "Ceasefire—For A While," editorial, *Washington Post* July 26, 1981.

20. "Beyond the Ceasefire," editorial, *Christian Science Monitor* July 27, 1981.

21. Anwar Sadat, "Arrival Remarks," *Department of State Bulletin* September 1981.

22. Ronald Reagan, "Remarks During Visit of President Sadat," *Department of State Bulletin* September 1981.

23. Terrence Smith, "Haig Thanks Begin and Two Key Arabs," *New York Times* July 26, 1981.

24. "Arafat Hails Saudi Initiative As Basis for Lasting Peace," *Jerusalem Post* August 18, 1981.

25. David Richardson, "White House Advisor Calls Autonomy Talks Major Issue," *Jerusalem Post* August 21, 1981.

26. Ibid.

27. "True Grit with Mr. Begin," editorial, *New York Times* September 6, 1981 and "Welcome, Mr. Begin," editorial, *Washington Post* September 8, 1981.

28. Bernard Gwertzman, "U.S.-Israeli Talks on Military Links Are

Reported Set," *New York Times* September 6, 1981.

29. David Friedman, "Background Report: Reagan Administration Does Not Expect Breakthrough in Autonomy Talks During Reagan-Begin Summit," *Jewish Telegraphic Agency* September 8, 1981.

30. See *Mideast Observer* September 15, 1981.

31. "Carrot Diplomacy," editorial, *Christian Science Monitor* September 14, 1981.

32. Sarah Honig, "Peres: Begin Traded AWACS for Pact with U.S.," *Jerusalem Post* September 18, 1981.

33. Asher Maniv, "A Suspect Maneuver," *Jerusalem Post* September 23, 1981.

34. Quoted by Sarah Honig. op. cit.

35. Donald Bremmer, "Begin Calls for Peace Talks to Proceed as Sadat Would Have Wished With All His Heart," *Los Angeles Times* October 7, 1981.

36. Ibid.

37. Ibid.

38. Trudy Rubin, "Israel Hopes Mubarak Will Keep Peace Process Rolling," *Christian Science Monitor* October 8, 1981.

39. Quoted by Donald Bremmer, op. cit.

40. "Excerpts From News Conference by Ford and Carter on the Future of Egypt," *New York Times* October 12, 1981.

41. Editorial, *Washington Post* October 12, 1981.

42. "Glenn Agrees on Role for PLO," *Los Angeles Times* October 13, 1981.

43. *Mideast Observer* October 15, 1981.

44. Interview, *Meet the Press* October 11, 1981.

CHAPTER 3: A CEASEFIRE IN LEBANON IS NOT ENOUGH

1. Bernard Gwertzman, "Begin Contends U.S. Policy Treats Israel Like A Vassal, Haig Retains Hope for Pact," *New York Times* December 21, 1981.

2. Bernard Gwertzman, "Haig Now Sees No Chance of Accord on Palestinian Autonomy Soon," *New York Times* January 30, 1982.

3. "Muffling the War Drums," editorial, *Jerusalem Post* February 2, 1982.

4. David L. Shipler, "Israel Is Said To Weigh An Invasion of Lebanon If PLO Raids Go On," *New York Times* February 10, 1982.

5. Wolf Blitzer, "U.S. Disputes Claim of Major PLO Arms Buildup," *Jerusalem Post* February 28, 1982.

6. Interview, *Meet the Press* March 25, 1982.

7. Ibid.

8. William Claiborne, "Israeli Opposes Lebanon Raid," *Washington Post* April 10, 1982.

9. Flora Lewis, "Arafat, Expecting Attack, Says He Won't Break Truce First," *New York Times* April 12, 1982.

10. Editorial, *New York Times* April 25, 1982.

11. Ibid.

12. "Beyond Sinai," editorial, *Washington Post* April 25, 1982.

13. Quoted by John M. Goshko, "Camp David Process Has Two More Goals," *Washington Post* April 26, 1982.

14. Quoted in "Eitan Confirms IDF Buildup in the North," *Jerusalem Post* May 16, 1982.

15. Ibid.

16. Walter S. Mossberg, "Israeli Defense Minister Denies Plans for Preemptive Strike on PLO in Lebanon," *Wall Street Journal* May 27, 1982.

CHAPTER 4: THE UNITED STATES IN LEBANON

1. "Looking for A Way Out," *Newsweek* July 19, 1982.

2. "President's Statement," *Department of State Bulletin* August 20, 1982.

3. "Time Is Running Out," *Time* July 26, 1982.

4. *Haaretz* July 1, 1982.

5. "Plan for the PLO Evacuation from West Beirut," August 20, 1982, *Department of State Bulletin* September 1982.

6. Milton Viorst, "America's Broken Pledge to the PLO," *Washington Post* December 19, 1982.

7. Yasser Arafat, interviewed by author, Amman, Jordan, December 2, 1982.

8. "U.S. Appeals for Calm in Lebanon, Is Silent About Israeli Troops," *Washington Post* September 16, 1982.

9. Ibid.

10. "Israeli Inquiry Into Beirut Massacres to Focus on 2 Key Questions," *New York Times* October 10, 1982.

11. Wolf Blitzer, "Officials Say U.S. Had Early Word of Massacres," *Jerusalem Post* January 31, 1983.

12. *Jerusalem Post* April 1, 1983.

13. "Shatila and Sabra," editorial, *Washington Post* September 20, 1982.

14. See U.N. Security Council Resolutions 508 and 509, June 1982.

15. "U.N. Lebanon Plan Is Vetoed By U.S.," *New York Times* June 27, 1982.

16. Ibid.

17. "Egypt and France Press Palestinian Rights at U.N.," *New York Times* July 28, 1982; also see "Security Council Opens Debate on Plan to Ease U.S.-PLO Talks," *Washington Post* July 30, 1982.

18. "U.N. Votes for Observers in Beirut," *New York Times* August 2, 1982.

19. Bernard Nossiter, "U.N. Council, Behind Closed Doors, Considers Next Move on Beirut," *New York Times* September 19, 1982.

20. George C. Wilson, and John M. Goshko, "U.S. Planning to Rebuild Armed Forces of Lebanon," *Washington Post* October 28, 1982.

21. Gerald F. Seib, "More Muscle: Role of U.S. in Mideast Strengthens in Wake of the War in Lebanon," *Wall Street Journal* November 5, 1982.

22. Ibid.

23. See David Ottaway, "Why Desperate Arabs Now Look to Washington," *Washington Post* September 26, 1982; also Leslie Gelb, "U.S. Assumes A Policeman's Lot in Mideast Peace Process," *New York Times* October 3, 1982.

24. "Gemayel Will Not Be Pressed to Punish Phalangists," *Guardian* November 6, 1982.

25. "Lebanon Quick March In," *The Economist* October 9, 1982.

26. Thomas L. Friedman, "Christians Won Vast New Power in Lebanon War," *New York Times* November 2, 1982.

27. Leslie Gelb, "U.S. Sees New Opportunities and Risks in Mideast After War in Lebanon," *New York Times* October 31, 1982.

28. William E. Farrell, "Lebanese Moslems Are Leery of Peace Talks and the Future," *New York Times* January 3, 1983.

29. Ibid.

30. James McCartney, "The Limited U.S. Mission in Lebanon is Deepening," *Philadelphia Inquirer* October 21, 1982.

31. David Ignatius and Yoran Kessel, "Israel, Lebanon Agree on Agenda for Negotiations," *Wall Street Journal* December 29, 1982.

32. See "Habib's Talks with Israelis at Standstill," *Los Angeles Times* December 29, 1982; also Bernard Gwertzman, "Israel Reported to Reject U.S. Plan Troop Pullout," *New York Times* March 2, 1982; also Bernard Gwertzman, "Israelis Reported to Balk at Plan for Withdrawal," *New York Times* March 25, 1983.

33. See "America Is Bracing for a Confrontation with Israel," *Wall Street Journal* January 27, 1983; also Leslie Gelb, "U.S. Quarrel with Israelis," *New York Times* February 11, 1983; also David Friedman, "Reagan Tells 150 Jewish Leaders that the U.S. Will Not Use Threat

of Sanctions Against Israel To Speed Up Israel-Lebanon Negotiations,'' *Jewish Telegraphic Agency* February 3, 1983.

34. Gelb, op. cit.

35. See Anthony Lewis, "Mr. Shultz's Move," *New York Times* March 20, 1982.

36. David Shipler, "As the Talks Stall, Israeli Doubts Deepen on the War," *New York Times* January 9, 1983.

37. Trudy Rubin, "Israelis Stuck in Lebanon Quagmire?" *Christian Science Monitor* January 12, 1983.

38. Ibid.

39. As examples of viewpoints advocating U.S. gains as a result of the war in Lebanon, see Elmo Zumwalt, Jr. "Israel and the U.S. Gained in Lebanon," op. ed. article, *New York Times* November 19, 1982; also, Robert Tucker, "Lebanon: the Case for the War," *Commentary* October 1982. For how these views were reflected in the Reagan administration, see Leslie Gelb, "U.S. Sees Opportunities and Risks in Mideast After War in Lebanon," *New York Times* October 31, 1982, and Gerald F. Seib, "More Muscle: Role of U.S. in Mideast Strengthens in Wake of the War in Lebanon," *Wall Street Journal* November 15, 1982.

40. Karen Elliott House, "Jordan's King Hussein Refuses to Join Reagan Talks," *Wall Street Journal* April 11, 1983 and "Hussein's Decision," *Wall Street Journal* April 15, 1983.

41. David Ignatius, "Beirut Attack Sparks Concern Over U.S. Role," *Wall Street Journal* April 19, 1983.

CHAPTER 5: THE AGREEMENT THAT DIDN'T WORK

1. "Mideast Attention Turns to Lebanon," *Wall Street Journal* April 12, 1983.

2. Trudy Rubin, "Shultz Priority: Break Deadlock in Lebanon," *Christian Science Monitor* April 25, 1983.

3. Thomas L. Friedman, "Syrian Army Said To Be Stronger Than Ever, Thanks to Soviet," *New York Times* March 21, 1983.

4. David Lamb, "Most Arab Nations Doubt Shultz Trip Will Lead to Mideast Peace," *Los Angeles Times* April 27, 1983.

5. Bernard Gwertzman, "Shultz Is Willing To Go to Damascus for Pullout Talks," *New York Times* May 1, 1983.

6. Mohammed Heydar, Director, External Affairs Department of the Baath Party, interviewed by author, Damascus, Syria, April 28, 1983.

7. Interviews by author with officials of Syrian Foreign Ministry in Damascus April 1983.

8. Itamar Rabinovich, "What Will Syria Do?" op. ed. article, *Los*

Angeles Times May 3, 1983.

9. Member of.Knessett Abba Eban, interviewed by author in Tel Aviv, Israel, May 19, 1983.

10. Oswald Johnston, "Sustained Effort by Shultz Led to Lebanon Pact," *Los Angeles Times* May 11, 1983.

11. David Shipler, "Israeli Furor Over Accord," *New York Times* May 10, 1983.

12. "Text of Agreement Between Israel and Lebanon on Troop Withdrawal," *New York Times* May 17, 1983.

13. Bernard Gwertzman, "U.S. and Israel Sign Agreement On Responding to Lebanon Raids," *New York Times* May 18, 1983.

14. "Lebanon Pact Near Completion Despite Tough Syrian Resistance," (Reuters) *Jordan Times* May 14, 1983.

15. David Shipler, "Israel Is Opposing U.S. Suggestion on Withdrawal," *New York Times* July 2, 1983.

16. Philip Taubman, "Shultz Says Syria Is Firmly Opposed to Troop Pullout," *New York Times* July 7, 1983.

17. Bernard Gwertzman, "U.S. Failure with Syrians," *New York Times* July 7, 1983.

18. William B. Quandt, "Reagan's Lebanon Policy: Trial and Error," *Middle East Journal* 38.2 (1984): 245-270.

19. See Abba Eban, "The Politics of Failure," *Jerusalem Post* May 13, 1983; also Sarah Honig, "Poll Launches Labor on New Wave of Buoyance," *Jerusalem Post* May 8, 1983.

20. "Two Hard Questions," editorial, *Washington Post* July 13, 1983.

21. Robin Wright, "One Year After Israeli Invasion, Lebanon Is Still Reeling," *Christian Science Monitor* June 6, 1983.

22. David Ignatius, "Caught in A Crossfire: Village Provides Test of Lebanon's Ability to Unite and Survive," *Wall Street Journal* July 5, 1983; also see David Ignatius, "How to Rebuild Lebanon," *Foreign Affairs* 3 (1983): 1140-1155.

23. *Washington Post* July 17, 1983.

24. Thomas L. Friedman, "Peacekeepers Become Another Warring Faction," *New York Times* October 23, 1983.

25. Anthony Lewis, "Why Are We In Lebanon?" *New York Times* September 15, 1983.

26. See Wolf Blitzer, "A Growing Sense of Despair," *Jerusalem Post* September 16, 1983.

27. President Ronald Reagan, "We Have Vital Interests in Lebanon," *Washington Post* October 25, 1983.

28. Wolf Blitzer, "Reagan Vows Revenge, But Won't Take Risks," *Jerusalem Post* October 25, 1983.

29. Bernard Gwertzman, "Lebanese Factions Provide Time for Pullout Plan," *International Herald Tribune* November 5, 1983.

30. Wolf Blitzer, "U.S. Opinion Split on Israel Role in Lebanon," *Jerusalem Post* October 26, 1983.

31. *New York Times,* November 14, 1983; *Washington Post,* November 18, 1973; and *Jerusalem Post,* November 20, 1983.

32. Steven R. Weisman, "Reagan Tries to Limit the Damage on Lebanon," *New York Times* January 1, 1984.

CHAPTER 6: THE REAGAN INITIATIVE: Arab and Israeli Responses

1. "Peace and Security in the Middle East," address before the Chicago Council on Foreign Relations, May 26, 1982, published in *Department of State Bulletin* July 1982.

2. Gerald F. Seib, "More Muscle: Role of U.S. in Mideast Strengthens in Wake of the War in Lebanon," *Wall Street Journal* November 5, 1982; also Leslie Gelb, "U.S. Sees Opportunities and Risks in Mideast After Lebanon War," *New York Times* October 31, 1982.

3. Leslie Gelb, "President's Mideast Plan," *New York Times* September 3, 1982.

4. Henry Tanner, "Jordan Welcomes the Reagan Plan," *New York Times* September 3, 1982.

5. Gelb, op. cit.

6. Tanner, op. cit.

7. Ibid.

8. David B. Ottaway, "PLO, Jordanian Officials: Plan Has Positive Points," *Washington Post* September 3, 1982.

9. Ibid.

10. "Arabs Offer to Recognize Israel in Return for a Palestinian State," *Jordan Times* September 11, 1982.

11. "The Surprising Spirit of Fez," *Newsweek* September 20, 1982.

12. Trudy Rubin, "Israel's Rejection of New U.S. Policy May Start Era of Diplomatic Conflict," *Christian Science Monitor* September 3, 1982.

13. Trudy Rubin, "Arafat and Hussein Work Out Joint Response to Reagan Plan," *Christian Science Monitor* October 18, 1982.

14. Mohammed Salmawi, correspondent for *El Ahram*, interviewed by author in Cairo, Egypt, October 20, 1982.

15. David L. Shipler, "Israel Rejects Reagan Plan for Palestinians' Self-Rule; Terms It Serious Danger," *New York Times* September 3, 1982.

16. "Peres on the Reagan Proposals; A Most Realistic Basis," op. ed. article, *Washington Post* September 14, 1982.

17. Member of Knesset Abba Eban, former foreign minister of Israel, interview by author in Jerusalem, December 28, 1982.

18. *Jerusalem Post* August 31, 1982.

19. "A Defiant No to Reagan," *Time* September 20, 1982.

20. Former President Jimmy Carter, interviewed in *New York Times* September 3, 1982.

21. Ibid.

22. Jimmy Carter, interviewed by Vincent Coppola, *Newsweek* September 13, 1982.

23. "An Old Pro's View," *Newsweek* September 13, 1982.

24. Wolf Blitzer, *Jerusalem Post* September 5, 1982.

25. "A Call to Moderates," editorial, *New York Times* September 3, 1982.

26. Editorial, *Washington Post* September 3, 1982.

27. "Reagan's 'Fresh Start,'" *Time* September 13, 1982.

28. Dusko Doder, "Moscow Assails Plan by Reagan for Mideast," *Washington Post Service* in *International Herald Tribune* September 8, 1982.

CHAPTER 7: WHY THE INITIATIVE FAILED

1. Flora Lewis, "Mideast Hopes," *New York Times* November 19, 1982.

2. Henry Tanner, "King Hussein Says Israel Blocks Peace," *New York Times* November 18, 1982.

3. James McCartney, "Hussein Gives U.S. 7 Demands on Talks," *Chicago Tribune* December 23, 1982.

4. James McManus, "Jordan Worried by Peace Logjam," *Guardian* November 18, 1982.

5. Loren Jenkins, "Jordan, PLO to Prepare Mideast Plan," *Washington Post* December 1, 1982.

6. "Jordanians Agree to Special Link with a Future Palestinian Entity," *New York Times* December 15, 1982.

7. McCartney, op. cit.

8. Ibid.

9. Bernard Gwertzman, "Hussein Tells U.S. He's Not Yet Ready for Mideast Talks," *New York Times* December 22, 1982.

10. "Talking About Peace," editorial, *Washington Post* December 22, 1982.

11. "Remarks by Reagan and Hussein After Talks," *New York Times* December 24, 1982.

12. James McCartney, "Pressure on Israel Offered to Hussein," *Philadelphia Inquirer* December 28, 1982.

13. Ibid.

14. Adnan Abu Odeh, Minister of Information of Jordan, interviewed by author in Amman, March 1983.

15. *Jewish Telegraphic Agency* November 12, 1982.

16. *Jerusalem Post* November 11, 1982.

17. David Landau, *Guardian* November 22, 1982.

18. Quoted by Norman Kempster, "U.S.-Israeli Relations Are At A Low Point," *Los Angeles Times* November 14, 1982.

19. Wolf Blitzer, "Arens: Never a U.S. Hint of Halting Economic Aid," *Jerusalem Post* November 14, 1982.

20. Ibid.

21. Max Frankel, "Looming Over the West Bank," *New York Times* November 15, 1982.

22. Max Frankel, "Help Us by Cutting Aid," *New York Times* November 16, 1982.

23. "Israeli Dispute Erupts Over Column in the Times," *New York Times* November 18, 1982.

24. Israel Gatt, interview by author in Tel Aviv, February 1983.

25. "The West Bank Struggle, in Lebanon," editorial, *New York Times* December 7, 1982.

26. Wolf Blitzer, "Aid to Israel a Metziah, Says Senator Boschwitz," *Jewish Week* December 10, 1982.

27. Joseph Churba, "Israel's Left vs. American Security Interests," letter to editor, *New York Times* November 21, 1982.

28. Wolf Blitzer, "U.S. Pressuring Israel on Pullout, Mideast Initiative," *Jewish Week* January 21, 1983.

29. David Friedman, "Reagan Tells 150 Jewish Leaders that the U.S. Will Not Use Threat of Sanctions Against Israel To Speed Up Israel-Lebanon Negotiations," *Jewish Telegraphic Agency* February 3, 1983.

30. Asher Maniv, "Blaming the U.S.," *Jerusalem Post* Febuary 3, 1983.

31. Loren Jenkins, "Meeting Endorses Arafat: PLO Chiefs Assail Reagan Plan," *Washington Post* November 27, 1982.

32. David Friedman, "State Department Contends the PLO's Central Council Did Not Reject Reagan's Peace Initiative," *Jewish Telegraphic Agency* November 30, 1982.

33. Ghassan Bishara, "Washington Debates PCC," *Jerusalem Palestinian Weekly* December 10, 1982.

34. Ibid.

35. Yasser Arafat, interview by author in Amman, December 2, 1982.

36. Nabil Shaath, interview by author in Amman, December 1, 1982.

37. David Bernstein, "Arafat: Mutual Recognition a Possibility," *Jerusalem Post* December 30, 1982.

38. David Ignatius and Tewfik Mishlawi, "Arafat Facing A Crucial PLO Meeting," *Wall Street Journal* February 9, 1983.

39. Thomas L. Friedman, "PLO Council Says Reagan's Proposal Is Not Acceptable: No Mandate for Jordan," *New York Times* February 22, 1983.

40. "PLO Sets Limit on Territory," *The Times* of London, February 17, 1983.

41. Trudy Rubin, "What Arafat Wants From Washington," *Christian Science Monitor* February 23, 1983.

CHAPTER 8: NEW OPPORTUNITIES

1. Karen Elliot House, "Precarious Nature of Peres's Israeli Coalition Makes It Difficult to Broaden Peace Efforts," *Wall Street Journal* November 26, 1984.

2. Quoted in "U.S. Urged to Push Israel Toward Peace," *Chicago Tribune* November 23, 1984.

3. "Jordan Defends Move to Resume Diplomatic Relations with Egypt," *Jordan Times* September 27, 1984.

4. "Jordan's Big Step for Arab Moderates," *Jordan Times* September 27, 1984.

5. Ibid.

6. "U.S. and Israel Welcome Jordan's Move Toward Egypt," *New York Times* September 27, 1984.

7. Judith Miller, "Syria Denounces Move by Jordan," *New York Times* September 27, 1984.

8. Ibid.

9. John Kifner, "Mubarak Begins Jordan Visit, His First to an Arab Capital," *New York Times* October 10, 1984.

10. "Mubarak Urges Reagan for (sic) Urgent Mideast Action," *Jordan Times* November 9, 1984.

11. "Baz Calls for a New American Initiative," *Jordan Times* November 9, 1984.

12. David Bernstein, "Arafat Beats Syria, But Bids for Accord," *Jerusalem Post* November 23, 1984.

13. Ibid.

14. Edward Walsh, "Hussein Urges PLO to Join Peace Effort,"

Washington Post November 23, 1984.

15. "PNC Resolutions Urge PLO Unity," *Al Fajr* English language edition, December 7, 1984.

16. Khaled al Hassan and Yasser Arafat, interviews by author in Amman, December 1984.

17. Trudy Rubin, "What Arafat Wants from Washington," *Christian Science Monitor* February 23, 1983.

CHAPTER 9: A NEW EFFORT FOR PEACE?

1. *Wall Street Journal* July 25, 1984.

2. Wolf Blitzer, "U.S. Planning to Resuscitate Reagan's 1982 Peace Plan," *Jerusalem Post* July 26, 1984.

3. Wolf Blitzer, "U.S. Official Calls for West Bank Withdrawal," *Jewish Week* August 17, 1984.

4. Ya'acov Friedler, "Now Is the Time for a Mideast Initiative," *Jerusalem Post* November 29, 1984.

5. David Bernstein, "Where the Peace Process Went Wrong," *Jerusalem Post* November 6, 1984.

6. David Friedman, "Reagan Optimistic That Moderate Arab States Are Moving Toward Negotiations with Israel," *Jewish Telegraphic Agency* November 29, 1984.

7. "Bringing Home the Troops," *Time* January 28, 1985.

8. Thomas L. Friedman, "Israel Announces Three Stage Plan to Leave Lebanon," *New York Times* January 15, 1985.

9. Hirsh Goodman, "Retreat from Lebanon," *Jerusalem Post* January 18, 1985.

10. Quoted by Thomas L. Friedman, "Living with a Dirty War," *New York Times Magazine* January 20, 1985.

11. Editorial, *New York Times* January 18, 1985.

12. "Bringing Home the Troops," *Time* January 28, 1985.

13. Wolf Blitzer, "Holding Off on Lebanon," *Jerusalem Post* January 4, 1985.

14. Ibid.

15. "Mubarak Congratulates Peres on Becoming Prime Minister," *Jewish Telegraphic Agency* September 19, 1984.

16. Mary Curtis, "'Cold Peace' Between Egypt, Israel Begins to Thaw," *Christian Science Monitor* November 13, 1984.

17. Wolf Blitzer, "Three Sided Diplomacy," *Jerusalem Post* November 23, 1984.

18. David Landau, "Peres Initiative Seen on Taba Issue," *Jerusalem Post* November 30, 1984.

19. "Are They for A Middle East Summit?" interviews with Peres

and Mubarak, *U.S. News and World Report* January 14, 1985.

20. "PLO Pact with Jordan," *New York Times*, February 24, 1985.

21. David Bernstein, "Arafat Seen Accepting Land for Peace Formula," *Jerusalem Post* February 17, 1985.

22. "King's Gambit," *Newsweek*, February 25, 1985.

23. "Hussein, Arafat Agree on Joint Platform," *Al Fajr*, English language edition, February 19, 1985.

24. "Eban, Narrow Opening," *Near East Report* March 4, 1985.

25. Wolf Blitzer, "Varied Reactions in U.S. to Hussein-PLO Accord," *Jerusalem Post* February 15, 1985.

26. Bernard Gwertzman, "U.S. To Ask Arabs to Clarify Hussein-Arafat Agreement," *New York Times* February 15, 1985.

27. Judith Miller, "Arafat Denounces U.S. Response to Jordan Accord As Shameful," *New York Times* March 3, 1985.

28. Jonathan C. Randal, "Jordanian-Palestinian Hopes Ebb As U.S., Israel React Coolly to Plan," *Washington Post* March 24, 1985.

29. Judith Miller, "Hussein Says U.S. Must Take A Role in Peace Process," *New York Times* March 17, 1985.

30. David Richardson, "30 West Bankers Tell Murphy That U.S. Should Talk to Arafat," *Jerusalem Post* April 17, 1985.

31. David B. Ottaway, "PLO Seeks Concessions from U.S.," *Washington Post* April 30, 1985.

32. Shlomo Lahat, mayor of Tel Aviv, interview by author March 14, 1985.

33. Meir Merhav, "A Consensus of Nonsense," *Jerusalem Post* March 10, 1985.

34. Bernard Gwertzman, "Israel Now Backs U.S.-Arab Meeting," *New York Times* May 12, 1985.

35. Christopher Dickey, "Arafat Moves Toward U.S. Demand," *Washington Post* May 15, 1985.

36. Bernard Gwertzman, "Joint Arab Team Expected To Meet U.S. About Mideast," *New York Times* May 30, 1985.

37. David B. Ottaway, "Shultz Sees Mideast Talks," *Washington Post* June 1, 1985.

38. Judith Miller, "PLO Said to Offer List of Palestinians for Talks with U.S.," *New York Times* July 14, 1985.

39. Yasser Arafat, interview by author in Amman, June 22, 1985.

40. Bernard Gwertzman, "Shultz Asks Israel to Back Talks with Jordan and Palestinians," *New York Times* June 3, 1985.

41. "U.S. Hopes Amman Meeting Will Loosen Mideast Logjam," *Boston Globe* July 17, 1985.

42. David B. Ottaway, "U.S. Says Israel Has No Veto Over Next Moves in Mideast," *Washington Post* July 19, 1985.

43. Barbara Rosewicz, "Peace Process in Middle East Hits New Snag," *Wall Street Journal* August 19, 1985.

44. John M. Goshko, "U.S. Eyes Talks Including Aide Regarded As Member of PLO," *Washington Post* September 6, 1985.

45. John M. Goshko, "U.S. Still Shuns PLO, Shultz Assures Israel," *Washington Post* September 7, 1985.

46. John M. Goshko, "All-Out Effort Required for Mideast Initiatives," *Washington Post* September 12, 1985.

47. Mary Curtis, "Jordan's Openness to Direct Peace Talks Stirs Debate in Israel," *Christian Science Monitor* September 28, 1985.

48. Michael J. Berlin, "Israel Asks U.N. Role in Talks with Jordan," *Washington Post* October 22, 1985.

49. Judith Miller, "Hussein Welcomes Spirit of Speech on Peace by Peres," *New York Times* October 24, 1985.

50. Michael Getler, "Jordan Lowers Hopes for U.S. Role in Mideast," *Washington Post* December 5, 1985.

51. Op. ed. article, *New York Times* April 7, 1985.

52. See advertisement in *New York Times* p. A 9, March 31, 1986.

ABOUT THE AUTHOR

Ronald Young served, along with his wife Carol Jensen, as Middle East representative for the American Friends Service Committee 1982-85. From a home base in Amman, Jordan, Ron and Carol travelled regularly to Israel, the West Bank and Gaza, Egypt and Syria, interviewing hundreds of Israelis and Arabs, including senior government officials in each country, and leaders in the PLO.

From 1972 to 1982 Ronald Young was the national secretary for the Peace Education Division of the AFSC and 1965-72 served as national director of youth work for the Fellowship of Reconciliation. Ron was coordinator of the March on Washington for Peace in Vietnam in November 1969. In the early 1960s he participated in the Student Interracial Ministry in Memphis and was active in the civil rights movement.

Ronald Young led interfaith study missions to the Middle East in 1985 and 1986 and currently is coordinating the development of a U.S.-based Interfaith Committee for Peace in the Middle East. He has lectured extensively on Middle East issues. Ron lives in New York with his wife, who attends Union Theological Seminary, and their two children, Jonah and Jamie.

Other Publications on the Middle East Available from the American Friends Service Committee

Reflections on the United States Policy in the Middle East, by Stuart Schaar, Professor of History, Brooklyn College
$1.50 each, 10 or more $1.25 1987

Questions and Answers about the Arab-Israeli-Palestinian Conflict
25 cents each, 100/$15, 1983

A Compassionate Peace: A Future for the Middle East
$7.95 each, 10 or more/$5.00 each, 1982

Questions and Answers on Lebanon
$1 each, 10 or more 75 cents, 1983

Lebanon: Toward Legal Order and Respect for Human Rights
$2 each, 10 or more/$1.50 each, 1984

Academic Freedom Under Israeli Military Occupation, by Adam Roberts, Boel Joergensen and Frank Newman;
$2 each, 1984

Middle East Mission: The Story of a Major Bid for Peace in the Time of Nasser and Ben-Gurion by Elmore Jackson;
$4 each, 1984

West Bank Data Project: A Survey of Israel's Policies, by Meron Benvenisti, $2 each, 1984

In Their Own Words (Human Rights Violations in the West Bank) by Law in the Service of Man
$2 each, 1983

Israeli Settlements on the West Bank and the Gaza Strip, Slideshow.
$50.

Field Diary (Israeli Occupation of West Bank) 16mm film, 90 minutes.
$100.00

Toward Understanding the Islamic Resurgence in the Middle East, by Ronald Young.
$2.00 each, 5 or more/$1.50, 1986

For more information contact: *Program Resources*, **American Friends Service Committee, 1501 Cherry Street, Philadelphia, PA 19102 (215) 241-7167.**